A VICIOUS LOVE S[T...]

A VICIOUS LOVE STORY

TEDDIE DAHLIN

A VICIOUS LOVE STORY

Copyright © 2012 Teddie Dahlin
All rights reserved
ISBN:
ISBN-978-0-9575170-0-4

A VICIOUS LOVE STORY

Second Edition

Published by
New Haven Publishing Ltd 2012

The rights of Teddie Dahlin as the Author of this work has been asserted in accordance with Copyrights, Designs and Patents Act 1988.

All rights reserved. No part of this book may be re-printed or reproduced or utilised in any form or by any electronic, mechanical or other means, now unknown or hereafter invented, including photocopying, and recording, or in any information storage or retrieval system, without the written permission of the Author and Publisher.

Cover design © Peter Cunliffe
pcunliffe@blueyonder.co.uk

A VICIOUS LOVE STORY

PROLOGUE

Teddie was 16 years old in 1977, when she was asked to be the translator for the Norway leg of The Sex Pistols Scandinavian tour. The book tells the inside story of the romance between Teddie and Sid Vicious. Instead of the self-destructive caricature of popular myth, Teddie reveals a troubled, vulnerable and generous young man. She gives a first-hand account of four young men at the eye of an international media storm, labouring under the sudden weight of expectation at the height of their fame. We are given a closer look into the dynamics between all the band members and their associates. The last chapters are written in part by Eileen Polk (ex girlfriend of DeeDee Ramone) and Peter Gravelle, who were in New York at the time of Sids death.

A VICIOUS LOVE STORY

DEDICATION

To the memory of John.

Sid Vicious

Writing these memories of Sid has been like living with his ghost. May we both now find peace.

A VICIOUS LOVE STORY

Table of Contents

Chapter 1   TEDDIE   **7**

Chapter 2   SUMMER 1977   **15**

Chapter 3   AND SO THEY CAME...   **33**

Chapter 4   DINNER AND A CONCERT   **78**

Chapter 5   THE HAWK CLUB AFTER-PARTY   **114**

Chapter 6   THE HOTEL AFTER-PARTY   **128**

Chapter 7   SEX AND DRUGS AND ROCK AND ROLL   **161**

Chapter 8   REVELATIONS   **174**

Chapter 9   FRIDAY THE DAY OFF   **196**

Chapter 10 THE LAST EVENING IN TRONDHEIM   **225**

Chapter 11 THE LAST GOODBYE   **260**

Chapter 12 DESPERATION   **269**

Chapter 13 NEW YORK   **292**

A VICIOUS LOVE STORY

CHAPTER 1 TEDDIE

It isn't easy being multicultural; you feel like you don't completely belong anywhere. It's like you are always the odd one out. You are the one who doesn't quite fit in. My family moved from Norway to a quiet Yorkshire village when I was four years old. My mother married an Englishman from Liverpool and they chose the village of Harworth to live in because it was close to some of his relatives.

The Village, as it is collectively called, is really two villages that grew together over time. Bircotes was a mining village, where most of the men made their living at the local colliery. Harworth was pretty much just a church, a pub and a post office to begin with. As it grew, it became connected to Bircotes, and I never really knew where Harworth ended and Bircotes began. People simply called them The Village.

I had only just turned 14 when my mother and stepfather decided it was the right time to move back to Norway. The job situation in the UK wasn't good in the early and mid-70s. Kids were leaving school to the bleak prospect of signing on the dole. Some were 'lucky' and managed to secure jobs at Bircotes Colliery or the Glass Bulbs Factory. Some went down the pit from the age of 15 or so, straight after leaving school.

The mid-70s was a time of great unrest in the UK. There were a lot of strikes and people were losing their jobs.

A VICIOUS LOVE STORY

There was a great deal of racial tension too. I never really considered that I was a foreigner most of the time.

I would sometimes get a comment from my friends, if I gave an opinion on politics, that it wasn't really any of my business since I wasn't English.

I remember well the year ABBA won the Eurovision Song Contest with *Waterloo*. Suddenly, a few of my friends were confusing me with being Swedish. When I told them it was a completely different country, though related, I was told it didn't really matter because we all look the same to them anyway. People were not being rude, although I know it might sound like it; it was just a matter of fact. I was 'that Norwegian lass' and it didn't really bother me. There were no other foreigners living in the village at the time, as far as I can remember, and with our long blonde hair and strange sounding names, my sister and I didn't blend in.

My mother and stepfather had spent some time separated, and when they got back together again at Christmas 1974, they wanted us to move straight away. My sister and I were told that the decision of where we would live would be ours. We could move to Norway, where my stepfather already lived, or we could move to one of the larger villages near Doncaster. The prospect of moving to another country was the most exciting option. We had been there for holidays, and longed for the snowy winters and better lifestyle.

So we moved to Norway in March 1975. My step-father had a large flat in the upmarket area of Singsaker in Trondheim. It is the third-largest city in the country and a 45-minute flight northwest of Oslo, the capital. Trondheim,

A VICIOUS LOVE STORY

which had a populace of 130,000 at the time, is situated where the Nidelven River meets Trondheims-fjord. It has sheltered conditions and a mild climate, compared to the northern regions. The river runs through the city, which has several bridges, of which Elgeseter is the largest and newest.

I was enrolled in the local school with pupils who were a year older than me; the reason being, I was later told, because I had started school very early in the UK. I didn't really get that. Surely it would have been better for me to go to school with pupils my own age, giving me a year more to get fluent? It felt really strange being in Norway. There were no school uniforms and the children called their teachers by their first names. They took packed sandwiches to school for lunch as no dinners were provided.

There wasn't a hockey field, tennis court, squash court or swimming pool like I was used to at the local comprehensive in Bircotes. PE was usually a case of running around in the school attic. I found getting a shower after gym class a dreadfully embarrassing experience. All of the girls would just strip off and get in. They seemed very comfortable with their bodies and I wasn't used to this. I would hide painfully inside my oversized towel and soon became and expert at getting my underwear on without showing an inch of my body. My boobs had ballooned the previous year and I was very self-conscious of them. They seemed to get in the way all the time.

Another thing I found out very quickly was that most, if not all, of the girls in my class had already had sex, or so they said. With hindsight it was probably not the case. They seemed to have a completely different outlook on things than I was used to, and I suddenly found that while I had been 'that Norwegian lass' in England, I was now very much 'that English girl' in Norway.

My first day at school was a disaster. I had been told to arrive half an hour after the other pupils. I was wearing platform shoes and a checked coat that wasn't warm enough for the arctic weather. My teacher, Inger, had told the class they were getting a new student and that she couldn't speak much Norwegian. That was an understatement as I could only say one word and that was goddag (hello). I was introduced to the class and given a place to sit. The classroom was shabby and I could see plaster falling off the walls.

Then Inger had a call of names. That is when things started going wrong for me. She called out the name Paul Bang and I thought that was the strangest name. How could you have a name like Bang? It is a common surname in Norway, but I found myself thinking crash, boom, bang! I thought it was a joke and I started to giggle. The next pupil was called Odd, and then came Randi. There was even a Birger (pronounced Burger) and a Bård (pronounced Bored). These are all common names in Norway, but to my ears they sounded so funny. I tried to suppress a chuckle, but you know how it is when you know you really shouldn't laugh and that makes it even harder not to?

Inger went on calling out the names of all the pupils. The girl sitting to my right noticed I was having trouble. She had dark hair and a huge ring on her finger. She wore a large woolly jumper that was all the rage in Trondheim at

A VICIOUS LOVE STORY

the time and had teamed it with Wellington boots that were turned down. It was a strange ensemble to my eyes, as wellies were only for children surely? But the thing that sent me in to a hysterical bout of the giggles was when Inger told me that what she was holding in her hand, a small plate, was called a fat (pronounced fart). I almost howled laughing and had to leave the room.

   I soon noticed the cultural differences between Scandinavia and England, and it took some time before I was comfortable with the way people acted around me. I was 15 or so when I was invited to a party at the home of a girl in my class. It was a 'no alcohol' party, and we basically just hung out and ate pizza, that we made together. As it got late the girl told us the sauna was ready. She'd turned it on earlier and it was now hot enough. Everyone just stripped off and went in naked. I was mortified and spent some time in the bathroom, debating with the dark-haired girl from my class, Ragnhild, as to whether I should get undressed like everyone else. She couldn't understand my problem.

   You can't wear anything in a sauna. Everyone sat there chatting and the boys were naked too. I put a towel around me that barely covered my bottom and it made them laugh that I was so shy. They explained to me that just because you were all naked in the sauna, it didn't mean you were up for grabs. The boys behaved respectfully and no one got up to anything. It was so different to what I was used to in England, but I found it strangely nice. It made us closer as friends, and I found I was accepted as a member of the class now. I wasn't 'that new girl from England any more.

A VICIOUS LOVE STORY

We soon settled in to life in Trondheim. My stepfather, Arthur, worked afternoons and evenings at the cinema as a film machinist, while my mother worked as a chef at a local restaurant. So my sister and I were pretty much left to our own devices in the evenings. Ragnhild and another girl called Hanne became my best friends. They had a lot of fun at my expense in those early days. They would teach me a Norwegian word and then tell me to ask a teacher what it meant. I learned mostly swear words and the teachers got used to it. If this had happened at my Comprehensive in England, we would have been in constant detention, but in Norway the teachers were very tolerant. I was soon fluent in Norwegian, swear words and all.

Ragnhild, Hanne and I started going to parties when I was 15, going on 16, and they were, of course, a year older. The discos in the city centre were pretty much out of bounds for us as they had minimum age limits of 18. Trondheim has a large music community, stretching from jazz to classical and rock. There were a lot of bands playing gigs at small towns scattered around the city, at venues without age limitations. We travelled out to these remote places to see bands we knew or thought would be good. We always took care of each other and made sure we all got back home safely, but we loved the parties and the music and most of all, to dance.

My situation in Trondheim was completely different to the one I'd had in the UK. We had been a one-parent family, growing up in a Yorkshire mining village. Now, in Norway, the situation had changed radically. Suddenly there was money to spare and we had a large apartment. My parents made good money and we found we could pretty much buy what we wanted and do what we wanted. My sister and I soon became a little blasé and spoilt, but we didn't think of ourselves that way at all. We had the teenage arrogance of most of our friends at the time. I tried to stay in contact with my old friends in the village, but after a few letters back and forth, this ebbed away, and I soon came to think of myself as mainly Norwegian, with a hint of English.

Norway didn't have many of the social problems that the UK was experiencing at the time. Life in England was hard for a lot of people. The whole of Norway had a smaller population than Manchester alone, and life was good for most people. There was a multitude of jobs available and a good social welfare system that took care of most problems effectively as they arose. It wasn't perfect, but it was certainly better than a lot of other places. I missed England; the people and their unique sense of humour, mostly. I felt that life was very good in Norway, but fashion-wise, fun-wise and music-wise, I was living in an arctic outpost that might as well have been Planet Blob.

We spoke mainly Norwegian at home, and English only if we didn't want people to understand what we were saying. My mother would mix the languages, sometimes with hilarious results. My friends got used to her not exactly knowing which one she was speaking. People were taught English as a second language at school, but the older generation hadn't been and therefore didn't understand much. There wasn't much English on TV either, and what was on was always subtitled. It was the same with films at the cinema. I missed my friends in England, but after those few letters back and forth, I didn't have any contact with them.

CHAPTER 2 SUMMER, 1977

The summer of 1977 looked to be uneventful from the onset. Little did I know that the events of that time would shake my whole existence to the very core and change me forever. I'd broken up with my first boyfriend that spring, after being in a relationship for the best part of eight months. When I say broken up, I mean he dumped me. I was heartbroken to begin with, but with the help of my best friends, Grethe and Marith, I was slowly starting to move on.

I'd turned 16 that January, and my family had moved to a larger flat, above one of the cinemas in a more central part of Trondheim. My first boyfriend had been a few years older than me and had a Harley Davidson motorbike that he spent all of the winter polishing, and we didn't really go out much. So, when I got dumped, my friends decided it was time I got out, to meet other people and have some fun. The sun was shining and life was, if not good, then definitely getting better.

We started hanging out at the Hawk Club, in the centre of town, the trendiest place for the over 18s. It was a disco, pizza restaurant and pool-table place on the second floor of an old, wooden building, above a shop that sold hunting gear, rifles and ammunition. I remember wondering what would happen if there was ever a fire. As far as I could see, there was only one way out and that was down a winding staircase right over the ammunition shop. Sometimes we got in, sometimes we didn't.

A VICIOUS LOVE STORY

Teddie at the disco

It all depended on what sort of a mood the bouncer was in that night. My friends and I would dance the night away to Leo Sayer, Hot Chocolate, Earth, Wind and Fire, and Boney M. Grethe and I thought Bryan Ferry was the best looking guy, with Rod Stewart a close runner-up.

Nothing was more important than shopping for new clothes and shoes, and going out at the weekend. When I say the weekend I really mean Friday and Sunday. Saturday was considered amateur night unless there was a band on at the club. Marith and I would hang out at her house, watching films and eating pizza on Saturday nights and we generally saved ourselves for a good night out on Sunday.

A VICIOUS LOVE STORY

There was a gang of us who used to hang out together in my room over the cinema before we went out. Of all my friends' houses, mine was the most central, being within walking distance of all the good clubs. We would listen to music while gossiping and putting on make-up. We were not allowed to drink in my room, but we would sneak a few beers in if my parents weren't at home. Many of the local musicians in Trondheim used to frequent the Hawk Club on Sundays.

Tore Lande (left) and Casino Steel

A VICIOUS LOVE STORY

They would be out playing gigs on the Friday and Saturday, so Sunday was usually their night off. We all knew each other and were a tight-knit group. We hung out at the same places, went to the same discos and knew the same people. Tore Lande was one of them.

He started his music career in a band, but soon got more involved with organising events and booking bands. I always liked Tore. He was tall, with long, blonde hair and had a neat beard. He was a few years older than me, and I always thought of him as being very mature and business-like, but also the sweetest guy you could ever hope to meet. He sometimes used the local cinema for smaller concerts and therefore knew my stepfather.

The Hawk Club on Sunday became important to some of the local musicians, as it was their place to hang out with friends and not have to deal with any groupies or fans. At one point someone, I believe it was Casino Steel (The Boys), made a guest list and it was left at the door. On Sunday nights you could only get in if you were on the list. But I think the list thing happened a little later than the year I am telling you about.

In July 1977 there was a lot of excitement in Trondheim. Tore Lande had managed to book the Sex Pistols for a concert. They would be the first big-name band to play little Trondheim. That month they had a hit in the UK Charts with the song *God Save the Queen*. It was the Queen's Silver Jubilee and the rumour was that they had been banned in the UK. The Sex Pistols were causing a stir in the establishment with their music and attitude. There also seemed to be a war between Punks and Teddy

A VICIOUS LOVE STORY

Boys. Most concert promoters, TV stations, radio shows and record stores banned the Sex Pistols, but *God Save the Queen* was still the UK's best selling single at the time.

The band was desperate to get out of the UK, so their manager, Malcolm McLaren, and Virgin Records quickly set up a tour of Scandinavia, where they would only play small venues and clubs. They were originally set to come in June, but due to the fact that John Lydon and Paul Cook were badly beaten up by Teddy Boys, the tour was postponed until July.

Roadent, the Clash roadie, was offered the chance to join the Sex Pistols for the Scandinavian tour.

ROADENT : I met Joe Strummer at the ICA gig in 1976. I didn't have anywhere to stay and he said I could stay in the Clash rehearsal rooms. I then said, "If I carry the boxes in, can I get into the gigs?" So I carried the equipment in and that's how it started, and went on from there. This was in Camden Town. The rehearsal rooms are still standing. It's part of Camden Market. At the time the market was much smaller and was just Dingwalls and fairly derelict. It was just small workshops. Bernie (Bernhard Rhodes, The Clash manager) had his Renault repair garage there. He hired the place.

A VICIOUS LOVE STORY

Facsimile Daily Mirror 1977

A VICIOUS LOVE STORY

Downstairs were The Clash rehearsal rooms and upstairs was an office. There was a desk and a sofa. We had one blanket and about six sheets. We stole electricity from next door, so we could have a little electric fire on and that's how we lived. We'd take it in turns on the sofa and take it in turns with the blanket.
I was working for The Clash, but then I was asked to go along and help out on the Sex Pistols' gigs as well. So I ended up working for both of them. This was handy because whenever they played the same bill, I could do them both. I could do The Clash and then The Pistols.

The Sex Pistols stayed in Sweden for the first week or so, playing small clubs around Stockholm and in smaller towns in the area, and in Copenhagen, Denmark. One person travelling with them for a short while was Peter 'Kodick' Gravelle. He was, at the time, a well-known punk photographer with inside access to the figureheads of the movement, as well as being a fashion and studio photographer.

A VICIOUS LOVE STORY

Peter Gravelle © Photo

PETER GRAVELLE: I was a working fashion photographer and advertising photographer in London. I was quite friendly with a girl called Judy Nylon. She went on to form a band called Snatch with my first wife at the time, Patti Palladin. Judy was from the States and I knew her from modelling. She was like a model/stylist and she was going out with a guy called Brian James who was the guitarist in The Damned. She asked me to take pictures of the band for free as they had no money. I agreed to take pictures as long as I got to do what I wanted, and we did the pies in the face photos.

A VICIOUS LOVE STORY

Basically, I did one photo session. Soon after that, about six months later, they got signed by Stiff Records. Andrew Jakeman, aka Jake Riviera at Stiff Records saw these pictures I'd taken and loved them and wanted them for the album front cover. So I went down and worked a deal with them, because again, they didn't have any money, blah, blah, blah, the usual story. There was also a poster and they did a songbook.

Barney Bubbles (Colin Fulcher – radical English graphic artist) had worked for Stiff Records during Glastonbury, and he came back in to the equation. I felt it was like getting the old guard back together and mixing it in with some new blood. Then I did a single cover for Nick Lowe at the time called Bowi, which was part of the deal and they had to pay for that photo session.

The title, Bowi was a play on words since David Bowie had just released an album called Low. And also at the time, I opened up a company with Barney Bubbles, which very few people know about, called Exquisite Covers.

The Damned album cover. Photo Peter Gravelle ©

As the punk thing advanced and every record lable was signing a token punk band or repackaging some of their older bands in a more modern up-to-date punk aesthetic, Barney and me would churn out the record covers. Basically they would be sending us a lot of material that they had. We would send back fluorescent blue and pink with black lettering all over it. They would love it. The worst job we could do, the better it was for them. That was a money-spinner for a while and it snowballed.

People were using different names at the time like Rat Scabies, etc, and someone asked me if I would like to use my name on the photos. At the time I had a number of fashion clients and I didn't know what they thought about that work, but more as a spoof I used Peter Kodick, which was a play on the word Kodak and dick, obviously. I had a couple of other names I used to use. As the years progressed it became more and more difficult to remember who people knew me as, Peter Kodick, Hugh Heffer was another one, or Peter Gravelle, so it got a bit crazy.

Anyway, The Damned wasn't the first punk picture that came out as I'd already done some single covers, but it was the first punk album and it got me a lot of exposure. I was working with Generation X and the Sex Pistols. I went to Scandinavia on the tour with them (Sex Pistols) and tried to get a lot of pictures of them. But Malcolm McLaren wasn't paying me. McLaren was too cheap to hire anybody.

What happened afterwards was like an explosion. Every major record company would sign a punk artist, just in case it wasn't a fluke. In the beginning hardly any of them had been in front of a camera before, let alone thought of record covers. And there was also a lot of bad press, mostly around the Pistols, spitting on photographers and stuff. Some of the old guard photographers, people like Gered Mankowitz, didn't want to know any of these people. So the record company had signed the band and then thought about who they should get to do the photographs? I know, lets get a punk photographer.

Ray Stevenson was a good photographer, but he was a 'snapper'; he was a very good snapper but he mostly did live gigs. He wasn't a record cover guy. Later on, there was Dennis Morris; he was the same. He did do a PIL first album cover. If you take a look at the original photos and how they came out on the album cover, well that's quite interesting. He, too, was not a professional studio photographer. My conflict became more of I wanted to do just the photographs. I didn't always come up with the ideas. That would be a collaborative effort, but I didn't really want to be stuck doing the graphics.

People more and more tended to want you to. I really should have used it as a springboard looking back, getting into doing videos and all sorts, but I was at the time, and probably still am in a way, a purist as regards photography and I can't change that. I can't be one of these universal people. So I enjoyed a period of about two years where I could just go to any record company and ask for whatever I wanted. It cost £2,000 back then for a photo session, so it was a fortune. And they would say yes, because they didn't really have an option.

A VICIOUS LOVE STORY

The Sex Pistols came to Oslo for a gig at the Penguin Club and the day after, on Thursday, July 21st, 1977, they drove a white van up to Trondheim for a gig at the Student Union. A few weeks earlier, tickets had completely sold out. I knew several people who were excited about getting a ticket, but my best friend Grethe and I had decided we would give it a miss. My other closest friend, Marith, was going, but only because a male friend had asked her out and he was taking her to the concert.

It wasn't really our type of music. We liked Donna Summer and David Bowie, Gloria Gaynor and Supertramp. We wore clothes that were considered modern in Trondheim, but probably not in England. Everything was very conservative and moderate. I had seen a few punks around Trondheim, but they didn't frequent the same clubs as us. I thought them wonderfully colourful and exotic.

The Sex Pistols were so extreme in their music and their opinions that, although I instantly understood where they were coming from and why they had become so popular in the UK, they were very alien to the average Norwegian. So, although I had heard of the Sex Pistols, as everyone had, I wasn't really interested and couldn't relate to their music or message. I didn't like the fact that they offended the Queen. I'd learned at school in England that she was the symbol of what made Great Britain great.

I thought the Sex Pistols' music was crap and that they represented everything I disliked about Great Britain: the 'I don't give a fuck' attitude; the 'no future for you' lyrics; the spitting and the swearing; and their total lack of respect for anything. They seemed threatening and dangerous, and definitely not worth the price of the ticket.

ROADENT: I've got a very hazy memory of it. I remember Daddy's Dancehall in Copenhagen and staying at The Plaza, which was a lovely little hotel. Famously, I remember coming down in the morning and there was a British businessman in reception saying, "I hear you have the Sex Pistols staying here. Do you not know what sort of things they say about our Queen?" The hotel answered that they had several bands staying with them and they were no problem, except for the Bay City Rollers. The businessman checked out because the hotel wouldn't throw us out.

I used to like the Bay City Rollers when I lived in England, but they weren't really that popular in Norway. I remember the scandal when they had been on tour and the band that looked like butter wouldn't melt in their mouths had trashed their rooms at the hotel in Copenhagen, and there was a huge fuss about it in the media. So there was a music scene in England that differed from what we were listening to in Scandinavia.

I was at the Centrum cinema one night a couple of weeks prior to the Sex Pistols concert, trying to beg some money from my stepfather, when Tore Lande came over to talk to us. After the usual chit-chat, he casually asked my stepfather whether he would be available to help out with the Pistols concert. Tore said he needed someone to be a link between the band and their roadies, and between the roadies and the technicians he was providing. It wasn't common for Norwegians to be fluent in English back in the 70s, and they certainly wouldn't understand the various English dialects, so Tore needed someone to translate.

"Nah, sorry," my stepfather said. "I don't moonlight."

"Are you mad?" I asked. "You should do it. Might be a laugh and you can take me along for moral support."

My stepfather laughed, not really taking Tore seriously, and then he said, "Well if you think it would be a laugh, then why don't you do it?"

"No," said Tore. "I really need an adult as these guys have a bad reputation and are known to be a bit hard to handle."

"Don't you worry about that," my stepfather said, smiling broadly. "She knows how to handle herself and she won't put up with any cheek from yobs, I can promise you that. She knows how to stick up for herself and she's got a good head on her shoulders."

I could see Tore thinking about it. He studied me for a few seconds, as if he was rolling the idea over in his mind. With hindsight, I think the fact that my stepfather turned him down only really left me as the obvious candidate anyway.

"Okay, Teddie, you're on, but it will be a long day and hard work. These guys are known to be opinionated and aggressive, so you need to prepare yourself for some scary people."

I got the impression he was trying to frighten me off, so I smiled and said, "I love opinionated, scary people," which made him smile.

"Right, read up on the band, so you know who's who and what's what, and we can get together to discuss terms closer to the concert," Tore added.

ROADENT: When we were at the Hotel Plaza in Copenhagen I was sharing with John (Lydon), which was odd. Anyway he got on the phone and said, "Send us up a case of your strongest lager." They said, "That's Elephant Beer" and he thought that was really funny. I said, "Get some for me" and John said, "Make that two cases." I remember we had fans camping outside the hotel, and as we got drunker we ended up giving the fans a few bottles of beer. Well, we threw them out of the window to them.

I wasn't really excited about the job. The thought of hanging out with a few punk rockers held no attraction for me. I thought, if I could do a good job with the Sex Pistols, Tore would want to use me on other concerts in the future, and I might be able to make a career out of it. I had no job that summer and was getting bored. I'd done a little modelling for a couple of local shops ahead of Norwegian National Day, on May 17, but after that it was quiet. Helping Tore with the concert was just something to do to get away from the boredom of living in a little town where everyone knew everyone else.

A VICIOUS LOVE STORY

PETER GRAVELLE: I didn't actually come up to Norway. I was only on the Stockholm part of the tour. We were playing pubs and it was ridiculous. They were tiny places. People knew the beer at the pub would be watered down or whatever, so people would be coming in absolutely loaded as they knew they wouldn't be getting much alcohol at the gig. Drunk driving must have been a problem in Sweden at the time. Everyone had long hair and had come to rock. I guess it was a good place for them (the Pistols) to warm up together. They didn't really care who would come. They did their 45 minutes or whatever and then it was on to the next one.

Tore told my stepfather he'd come and pick me up around midday on the day of the concert, and promised to have me back home straight afterwards. As it turned out, that was a promise he couldn't keep. But to be fair, I was on my way home several times that night.

A VICIOUS LOVE STORY

Sex Pistols in Sweden 1977. Photo by Peter Gravelle ©

CHAPTER 3 AND SO THEY CAME

I spent a great deal of time getting ready on Thursday, July 21st, 1977. I put a lot of thought into what I would wear. I wasn't a punk and I didn't want to come across as a wannabe rock chick either. I was 16 and a half, and I was going to help out as the translator. At first I decided to put my hair up in a bun and wear a skirt, like a secretary. I wanted to look like Tore's personal assistant, but I decided against it at the last minute, thinking I looked frumpy.

I wanted to be taken seriously, but vanity got the better of me. Although it was the middle of summer and sunny, it wasn't really hot, so I decided a thin, long-sleeved, checked shirt would be okay. My hair was just below shoulder length, with blonde streaks from the summer sun. I used to put camomile tea in it before I went out in the sun to make it blonder. My hair was parted in the middle, with feathered cuts at the sides, which was much the rage at the time.

Tore had told me I should read up on the Pistols, so I would know who was who, but I had decided against this. I didn't really care who was who. I wasn't a fan and I didn't like their music, and I certainly wasn't going to waste any time researching. After all, the sun was shining and I had a tan to work on. I had heard they were hell-raisers, and the only thing I had decided beforehand was that if anyone tried to spit on me, they would get slapped.

A VICIOUS LOVE STORY

ROADENT: I remember doing all the -köpings. We did every -köping under the sun. There was Linköping and Jönköping. And most of the clubs didn't have stages. They just had ropes around pillars. I remember Stockholm had a half-decent size venue, a hall at least. There was a bit of nonsense with the Swedish Teddy Boys, the Raggare, which was all just a bit of a laugh really.

Tore came to my parents' flat for coffee early midday. My stepfather had heard of the Sex Pistols and we had agreed not to tell my mother about their reputation in case she said I wasn't allowed to go. I could twist my stepfather around my little finger, but not my mother . She was thrilled when Tore arrived, and immediately got out the coffee and the cakes. Tore got talking to my parents, and my stepfather handed him free tickets to the cinema, and suddenly we found we had to rush. We had lost track of time and were going to be late.

TEDDIE'S MUM: He was always such a nice boy that Tore. No airs or graces about him. I had no qualms about letting him take Teddie to the concert. I knew he would look after her to the best of his ability. She didn't smoke or drink and had never been much of a worry to me. Teddie was hoping to get more work like this, so I knew she would behave professionally. I'd never heard of the band the Pistols. When I heard the name of the group I simply assumed they played Country and Western music.

A VICIOUS LOVE STORY

Teddie

Tore and I entered the Phoenix hotel, which is in the centre of Trondheim, through the main entrance. It is a

A VICIOUS LOVE STORY

large six-floor building, dating back to 1914, and built in the New Baroque style. In 1977 it was a sleazy and shabby place, facing the central market square. We'd seen a white van parked outside when we arrived and there were a lot of people in the small reception area. The hotel is known as the local knocking shop and not a place I had ever set foot in before.

As we walked in, I saw two journalists and a photographer lurking around John Lydon and Steve Jones, trying to get them to talk. They both looked sullen and uncooperative. Steve was wearing tight jeans, a shirt that had most of the buttons open, revealing his chest almost all the way down to his naval, and a large military-style, dog-tag necklace. He seemed very confidant and looked me over from the roots of my hair to my toes as we entered the hotel.

One guy was fast asleep on a red sofa by the reception desk. He had a black leather jacket on that looked like it was a size too small for him and new Levi's 501 jeans. I knew they were new because they were dark blue, so the colour hadn't bled out of them yet. His T-shirt had crept up to reveal a flat, hairy stomach and he was wearing a heavy padlock on a thick chain around his neck. His short, dark hair stood on end and looked strange to me since most guys wore their hair long at the time.

A VICIOUS LOVE STORY

Phoenix Hotel Trondheim. Photo JBD ©

Three guys were sitting on some chairs to the side of the reception desk, looking bored. One was thin with dark ginger hair. The other was taller and darker, and the last guy was very blonde. I wasn't sure if the blonde guy was with the band, as he looked Nordic. The first thing that struck me about these people was how different they looked to anyone else I knew. They all had short hair. John Lydon and the sleeping guy had theirs standing on end, which looked very strange and outlandish in my opinion. John's was dyed quite red, and it made him look scary and strangely insane. The guys looked me over, disinterestedly.

A VICIOUS LOVE STORY

The ginger guy stood up, pointed to his watch and sullenly said, "What time do you call this then?" It wasn't a question!

I realised they were part of the entourage, but I had no idea who they were. I tried to look calm and confident, and older than I was. I smiled at the ginger guy, but he didn't smile back. He seemed annoyed with us for being late and didn't seem interested in chit-chat. I don't think they'd waited for us more than 15 minutes at the most, so I found their behaviour a little strange, but I didn't say anything.

Tore had said "Hi" to them and was trying to negotiate with the reception on how many rooms they had actually booked; the receptionist had to get the manager to help out. So things were taking time and there was nothing for me to do.

The guy who was asleep had his black boots on the red sofa, but nobody seemed to notice or even care. Tore was finally making some headway with the rooms, and John Lydon and Steve Jones were hovering over him, like they both wanted to make sure the other didn't get a better room. The hotel wanted the band on the top floor, on their own, away from the other guests. Their hell-raising reputation obviously preceded them and the manager seemed wary of having them there at all.

I had been standing beside Tore the whole time, and now he turned to everyone and said loudly, "This is Teddie. She's my assistant, and if you need anything and I'm busy then you can talk to her. She is also bilingual, so

A VICIOUS LOVE STORY

she will help with translating with my crew, who are waiting for us at the Student Union."

I was pleased about being called his assistant. It made me feel important. I put on my brightest and most professional smile, and said, "Hi boys," but they totally ignored me. I blushed and felt stupid.

John Lydon looked at me as if I was a bad smell and then started a heated discussion with Steve Jones about who would get the suite. There was only one available on the top floor. No one was backing down, so I could see this was going to be a lengthy procedure. I'm pretty sure they argued continuously about it for the best part of 20 minutes. I felt like I was in the way, so I went over to the red sofa and sat by the sleeping guy's feet. I lit up a cigarette and waited for Tore to get everyone checked in, so we could go to the concert venue where Tore's roadies and technicians were waiting for us.

As I was watching John and Steve's argument continue, the guy on the sofa stirred a little. He had been lying on his back, snoring quietly. His black leather jacket was open and, as I mentioned before, his dark brown, spiky hair looked strange to me as boys I knew at the time had it much longer. His hands were dirty, and I could see nail polish that was chipped and partly scraped off.

John, Steve and Paul Cook went outside to get their pictures taken, and to be interviewed by a few local newspapers. Roadent and Boogie waited patiently on their chairs, looking a bit bored and tired.

A VICIOUS LOVE STORY

ROADENT: I got my name because someone said that when I was drunk I looked like a rat, so they called me Rodent. Then as I became a roadie it became Roadent the roadie. Just silliness really.

Meanwhile, I was left alone on the sofa with the sleeping guy. He lay still for a while, and then suddenly opened his eyes and looked straight at me without moving a limb. He didn't say anything to begin with, just stared, like he either suddenly didn't know where he was or was trying to work out who I was. I ignored him, but it made me smile that he was watching me, very intently. After what felt like five minutes, but probably wasn't that long, he smiled at me, warmly. I smiled back, but kept smoking, and tried to just look straight ahead and ignore him. He kept staring and I found myself smiling to myself, thinking him a little strange. He suddenly sat up and yawned.
"Can we share that?" he asked, pointing to my half-finished cigarette.
I handed him my cigarette and he thanked me, before taking a couple of drags and passing it back to me. I did the same and gave it to him again. I had heard about the Sex Pistols as a band, and Johnny Rotten being the vocalist and front man, but I had no idea who the sleeping chap was. To me, he was just one of the English guys and because he wasn't outside being interviewed, I instantly assumed he was a roadie. He could have been anyone. I had seen a picture of the Sex Pistols in a music magazine, but it was from the previous year, and featured Glen

A VICIOUS LOVE STORY

Matlock as bassist, although I didn't know it at the time. I just didn't recognise this guy from that photo.

I liked his smile and we started talking as if we'd known each other for a long time. You know how you sometimes meet someone you connect with straight away? We just clicked. It's the only way I can think of to describe it. We were instantly comfortable with each other and I felt like I'd known him for ages, even though we had only just met. I felt that I could trust him, and I think the feeling was mutual because we were totally open with each other from the very first second we talked. He spoke slowly in a quiet voice with a deep cockney accent. He also looked pale and tired.

"Damn, I'm shattered," he said, as he took a long drag on my cigarette and ran his hand through his hair, making it stand on end, unevenly.

"I spent the whole fucking night dozing in a chair in Oslo." He stretched his long legs out, readjusted himself and yawned. "I fell asleep." He laughed as if I hadn't realised this.

"Why didn't you go to bed?" I asked.

He smiled at me again, as if we had shared a private joke and said, "Steve brought a bird up to a party in my room and they took my bed."

I smiled back at him as he handed me my cigarette.

"So, why didn't you just ask Steve for the key to his room and go to sleep there?"

I took a couple of drags on what was left of the cigarette and then put it out in the ashtray on the table. I looked for another in the Marlboro packet in my bag, only to find it was empty.

"I dunno. Didn't think about that. I thought I'd sleep in the van on the way up, but I just couldn't get comfortable. I'm knackered. The hotel in Oslo was crap and this one looks like it is too. I've stayed in better fucking squats in London than this shit. Got any more fags?"

I shook my head, pointing to the empty Marlboro packet on the table. His voice was quiet and the sentences came out slowly. It somehow seemed that he was weighing his words when he talked to me. The sentences were packed with swear words, which I wasn't used to, but I wasn't offended. It just felt strangely honest. I told him about the argument between Steve and John as a way of making conversation, and he laughed.

"Yeah, those two disagree about a lot of stuff," he said disinterestedly, while looking into my eyes with amusement.

"So, are you staying here at the hotel or are you a fan come here to welcome us?" he asked.

"No, I'm not a fan, sorry. I work for Tore. I'll be helping with translating and stuff," I explained. He nodded and seemed pleased with my answer.

The rest of the band trooped back into the reception area, and John and Steve were still arguing about who got the suite. I went over to buy a packet of cigarettes and I could feel the guy's eyes burning on the back of my head. You know how you can feel someone staring at you without actually seeing them. I remember thinking how thankful I was that I hadn't worn the frumpy skirt and bun.

A VICIOUS LOVE STORY

It was finally decided that Sid and Paul would share a double room. They would have to share a double bed since no twin rooms were available. It didn't seem to bother anyone, as no one protested. Boogie, the English tour manager, and Roadent, the roadie, would also be sharing, but they needed a family size room with a sleeper sofa for some reason, which Tore arranged. Again, the only room available had a king size bed, but no one seemed to be bothered.

"Why do you need a bigger room?" John asked Roadent with a sneer.

"Debbie and Tracey are coming, and we said they could share with us," Roadent answered. Boogie nodded in agreement.

John seemed satisfied with this answer, but he still wasn't giving up the fight for the suite and turned back to Steve again. Steve didn't look at all pleased that the girls who Roadent mentioned were coming. He shrugged his shoulders in annoyance at Roadent and Boogie, before turning his attention back to the suite fight.

I don't think Tuna, the Swedish tour manager, was at the hotel while this was taking place as I have little memory of him being there at all. However, I believe he was the only person who could have driven the van. I remember he later told me he had friends in Trondheim and he might have stayed with them. Tuna had big lips and a wide mouth. He liked the sound of his own voice and would blabber on for ages, hogging the conversation, usually about stuff that we didn't give a rat's arse about.

A VICIOUS LOVE STORY

The boys simply referred to him as Bollocks-chops behind his back.

I stood beside Tore, John and Steve while I paid for my cigarettes, and I was getting a little fed up of the argument.

"Oh for God's sake, can you two agree on this or we'll be here all day. It's childish. Toss a coin or something, and be done with it," I said, a little coldly.

I noticed Roadent and Boogie sit up, and suddenly pay attention to what I'd said. They were smiling at me and nodding to each other. I think John and Steve were surprised at first that I actually dared talk to them at all, and they seemed a little taken back by my rather rude tone. They looked at each other, unsure how to interpret what I'd said, and then at Tore, not knowing what to do. Tore backed me up by not saying anything at all and just shrugging his shoulders. I think he was as sick of their feud as I was, but was too polite to actually say what we had both been thinking. I was impatient to get to the Student Union and get stuck in with the rigging.

Steve looked at me intently, as if surprised at first, and then he smiled warmly. "She's got a point," he said. "Okay, just to end this, you get the suite now and I get my own double on condition I get a suite when we get back to Sweden."

They both agreed.

"Thank you. Now that wasn't so hard, was it?" I said, taking my cigarettes back to the red sofa. I offered one to the guy who had been sleeping and was now laughing at what had just taken place.

"What?" I asked, referring to his broad smile.

A VICIOUS LOVE STORY

"Nothing," he said, shaking his head and smiling.

"Jesus wept," I giggled..

He thanked me and took a cigarette, as did I. He quickly pulled a lighter from the pocket of his leather jacket when he saw me rummaging in my handbag, looking for matches. He stared at me again when he offered me a light and I found his attention a little too intense because he wasn't actually looking at where he was putting the flame; it was as if he was using it as a means to examine my face in more detail. The way he was waving the lighter around, I remember thinking I had to be careful my nostrils didn't catch fire!

I remember liking him from the second he opened his mouth. He just seemed very easy going and nice. He was different to anyone I had met before and I found him very attractive. His good looks were striking. He kept staring at me when he thought I wasn't looking, and I liked it. I noticed he had moved closer to me when I sat down.

"I can't believe how shit this town is," he said, as we sat smoking together.

"It's okay. What's shit about it? You've only just arrived, so save your judgment until you've actually seen some of it," I answered, but I was smiling at him.

"Steady on, Ali, I was only saying it looks fucking boring," he said jovially, referring to me as the famous boxer. "All the houses I've seen so far only have two stories and everything is spaced out. Oh, and it's tiny. I can't imagine this place rocking on a Saturday night."

"Yeah, it's small, but it's okay. We have been known to rock from time to time. I can see it's nothing compared to some places in England though."

He nodded. "So I get to spend some time with you today. Lucky me," he said, and we both laughed.

"I'd save your opinion on that too for later," I giggled. "You might find me hideous at the end of tonight."

"Strangely, I don't think that's going to happen, but I'm going to have to be careful since you sting like a bee," he said, referring to a popular song about Muhammad Ali. The lyrics say 'he floats like a butterfly and stings like a bee' – I think he was referring to the comments I'd made to John and Steve.

"Nah, you'll be all right," I replied. "I promise not to thump you too hard if you annoy me!"

We laughed again.

One of the journalists came back to the lobby, sat down beside us, and started asking the guy a lot of questions. The journalists English wasn't good, so I helped out a little by translating, but the guy on the sofa was not fully awake yet. He repeatedly got mixed up, and kept giving the wrong answers to the questions, confusing some words with hilarious results.

The journalist obviously didn't understand his cockney accent and the two of us kept giggling at the misunderstandings. The guy kept asking the journalist to repeat the questions, which only led to more confusion. We would giggle hysterically, and the guy kept leaning closer to me when he laughed. He ran his fingers through his hair, making it stand on end again when he saw the photographer move closer to us.

"Is my hair okay?" he asked me.

"No, come here."

The guy leaned closer to me while I pulled my fingers through his fringe and made it stand up more evenly. He kept looking at me as I did this, and I thought it strange that although his hair could stand on end, it was soft and not stiff. The journalist later wrote in his article that Sid Vicious was unconscious in the hotel lobby when they arrived and that when he came to, he was too drugged up and his speech too incoherent to make any sense. Of course, I had no idea it was Sid Vicious I had been talking to at the time.

As soon as all the rooms were sorted out and the interviews finished, the boys made their way towards the elevator with their luggage. I noticed the guy with whom I'd been chatting earlier, talking intently with John. They both turned and looked at me, and then had their heads together again as they entered the elevator. I had a feeling I was the topic of conversation, and I hoped John wasn't saying anything nasty about me to the guy, since I had been so rude towards him regarding the suite argument.

Tore and I drove over to the Student Union in his car. I think it was a tiny, puke-green Mini 1000. The boys were getting themselves settled in at the hotel and were going to join us a short while later. Tore's roadies and technicians were already there, waiting for us. Inside the large hall, where the concert was to take place, the atmosphere was dark and dismal, compared to the sunny day outside. The

A VICIOUS LOVE STORY

room was circular, with the stage at one end and a large area in front of it for standing only, and seats in a semicircle led upwards, ending in a balcony at the top. There was a small bar to one side.

There had been a lot of activity going on all day. Technicians and roadies had been hard at work, getting the electrical cables into place, and the warm-up band, Fatah Morgana, had brought their instruments along. It didn't take very long before the white van pulled up outside and parked on the pavement, just by the main entrance. I was standing next to one of the Norwegian roadies, a huge Pistols fan, when they arrived. As the Sex Pistols entered the main arena of the Student Union, he got very excited, and started jumping up and down, shouting giddily, "The Pistols are here! The Sex Pistols are here! They are here!"

I rolled my eyes at what I thought was pathetic behaviour, and suddenly saw that the guy who had been sleeping at the hotel was standing there, laughing at me. I blushed and hoped he didn't think I was as giddy as the silly roadie. As soon as they arrived, John Rotten looked around and was not pleased. He had been told they would be playing a small club and this venue could easily house a thousand people. He seemed to be in a constant state of displeasure with everything; the corners of his mouth were always pointing downwards. John reminded me of a Monty Python sketch I'd seen on TV, with Queen Victoria saying, "We are not amused."

Tore and I welcomed them as they entered the main hall.

A VICIOUS LOVE STORY

"We were told we would be playing a small club," John said sourly to Tore. "This is not a small club."

"It is a small club," Tore answered vaguely, shrugging.

"It's a fucking concert hall! How many people does this place take?"

"I don't know – maybe a thousand or so."

"Fucking hell! And how many tickets have you sold?" John asked, shaking his head.

"I don't know – maybe a thousand or so," Tore repeated, and I found myself laughing at his joke.

"It's sold out then?" John asked, to no one in particular, but he did smile and I could see he was actually pleased.

"You are very popular here in Trondheim. So, yeah, it's sold out," Tore replied, and began to show them around the stage area.

Roadent was very professional and well organised in a no-nonsense kind of way. I could see him checking where everything was, looking for places to put equipment and searching for electrical sockets.

"Right, young lady," Roadent said to me, "time to do some work."

Roadent seemed to know what he was doing and how he wanted things done, and he soon started organising the Norwegian roadies, with me translating. He walked quickly in front of me, towards the entrance of the building where the van was parked, shouting instructions, which I then translated to the Norwegian roadies walking behind me. The van was filled to the hilt with instruments, speakers and wires. Roadent opened up the back for the roadies, and he and I climbed in the front. He pointed out to the roadies which things he wanted moving and told me to translate.

I think I might have been a little overzealous at my job because one of the Norwegian roadies said I didn't have to translate every single word he said, just when they didn't understand. Roadent got them to carry the stuff from the back of the van into the hall and on to the stage. He told the roadies to empty all of the stuff from the back of the van, except for the large crate as it contained things that Tore was providing already. The box was large and heavy, and made of plywood with thick, heavy metal corners. Inside were cables and gadgets.

"Okay, bring in everything except that box," he said to the roadies who had climbed into the van from the rear.

The crate he was pointing to was filled to the hilt with equipment, and we both agreed it would be unnecessary to carry it out of the van. We left the roadies to do their work and re-entered the Student Union.

Roadent would call out to me at intervals, "Teddie, tell the yokels to handle those speakers carefully," and "Ted, will you get over here – this chap doesn't understand a word of fucking English, for God's sake." He was sharp-witted and very intelligent, and could be very hard on people he felt weren't doing the job properly. He wasn't a person you wanted to get on the wrong side of. Most of the Norwegian roadies were in awe of him as he was, to some of them, almost as famous as the band itself. Others thought him an arrogant oink, but they never dared say so to his face.

A VICIOUS LOVE STORY

Roadent suddenly let out an annoyed shout when he saw one of the Norwegian roadies hoist on to the stage the heavy box he had told them to leave in the van. The roadie was sweating and swearing, and having trouble carrying it on his own.

"Teddie, where the fuck are you?" he shouted. "This idiot has removed the box I explicitly told him to leave in the fucking van."

I was standing to the right of the stage, trying to help Boogie with a large, heavy bail of electrical cable. Boogie was tall, dark and very handsome, with Italian looks. He was quieter than Roadent and spoke softly, and I couldn't really make out a dialect. He was also very calm and didn't get easily irritated or excited, in stark contrast to Roadent. I liked Boogie, even though it did take him some time before he bothered to talk to me, and then it was only when he needed help. He wasn't much for chit-chat, but when he said something you knew you had to listen. We had just been duct taping some cables to the stage floor. It's amazing how much duct tape you need for a gig.

I could see that Roadent was getting really angry because his face was turning red. I thought his reaction a little over the top since he could just tell the roadie to take the box back to the van. I didn't understand why he got so angry, but that was just the way he was that day. I'm guessing they were all very tired after partying late the night before and having an early start that morning for the long drive from Oslo to Trondheim.

A VICIOUS LOVE STORY

"I said bring everything in except that box, you fucking moron. It isn't rocket science!" he said angrily to the blushing roadie.

Even though the guy didn't understand everything Roadent said, I could see he knew he was in trouble. He looked at me sheepishly and said in Norwegian, "He definitely told me to bring in the excerceptor."

I started laughing out loud. I had tears running down my face as I explained to Roadent and Boogie that the roadie had misunderstood the word 'except', and thought Roadent had called the box the 'excerceptor'.

Roadent, Boogie and I were giggling hysterically when John, Paul and Sid came over to hear what it was all about. We were laughing so hard that we could hardly get the words out. I had only got halfway through the story when I had another fit of the giggles, and Sid poked me in the ribs and laughingly said to get to the punchline. When I finally did, John broke out into a wail of laughter and I had to leave the stage when Tore called to me, wanting to know what on earth was going on.

The roadie felt really silly as he struggled to carry the heavy box back to the van while we all laughed so hard I didn't think we would ever stop. John had been very reserved so far, and Boogie had been quiet and hardly talked to me. But, from that moment on, the Sex Pistols started to relax a little. Roadent would make crude remarks about the local roadies, whom he called the "yokel roadies", and the sound technicians. He really had me in stitches and his remarks were always spot on. Of course, the Norwegian roadies didn't understand our sense of humour and thought we were stupid, giggling away at them.

After a while I could see they didn't need me, so I walked over to where Tore was sitting. "God, I'm bored," I said. "Do you think it would be okay if I cry off and go home for a while? I'm hungry."

"That's probably not a good idea because I need you, but just not right now at this moment. We are taking everyone out to dinner when we are done here," Tore answered.

Sid came over to us and started talking to Tore. I didn't interrupt, but when he was finished, I said, "I could just meet you all at the restaurant." I spoke in English so as not to be rude to Sid.

"I hope you're not thinking of leaving," Sid said, smiling at me.

"I was actually. Just for a little while to get something to eat. I'm starving. I haven't eaten since breakfast," I replied. "That consisted of a slice of toast at 8am. That's over eight hours ago," I added, looking at my watch and seeing it was 4.30pm.

"Yeah, I'm starving too. Take me with you," Sid said, laughing. "I could murder a greasy burger and chips."

"Ha! If you come home with me, all that's on offer is a ham sandwich and a glass of milk," I joked, laughing back.

"No, I'm sorry, but you can't leave. You won't be able to get back in on your own," Tore answered, dismissively. "Besides, I need you to be here, Ted. Can't you just have a

A VICIOUS LOVE STORY

coke for now? There's a whole crate of coke in the room backstage. Bring one for me too."

"Where exactly is it? I was backstage a few minutes ago and I didn't see any," I said.

"It's not there any more," Sid explained. "It's on the stage. We got thirsty. Come on and I'll get you one," he added, sweetly.

I walked over to the stage with him and he handed me two bottles of coke, which he'd opened. I found myself looking into this face with its twinkling eyes and such a nice smile, and decided I might just stay a little longer after all. Tore was watching us, and I think he could see what was happening, but he didn't comment, and I didn't say anything more about leaving. Sid had to go on to the stage for a while, so I went to sit down.

There were several people sitting in the rows of seats, looking on as the roadies and the band got things rigged up. The warm-up band, Fatah Morgana, had arrived earlier and were sitting a bit further up in the pews, looking on, and they didn't seem at all impressed by how the English band was getting organised. Actually, I thought they were making a point of being detached and unimpressed, which I thought a little silly.

I didn't know anyone well enough to talk to them. There was one local musician sitting there who I found particularly arrogant, so I sat a little to the side on my own. This guy pretended to be my mate, but had earlier made a stupid comment about me to a mutual friend. I played the acoustic guitar pretty decently, but he had commented that it would be better for Teddie to grow

A VICIOUS LOVE STORY

longer nails and act more feminine, and leave such things as playing guitars to the guys, who were far better suited for it. That infuriated me, particularly since he had never heard me play and obviously just assumed I was crap.

Another mutual friend, Earl, who was a skilled bass player, had suggested I let him teach me to play bass just to piss this guy off, to which I agreed. So, every Sunday at 2pm, Earl came over to my house and I secretly got a lesson before I went off to the Hawk Club. Unfortunately, I didn't master it very well, and Earl and I just ended up hanging out, chatting about music and books. I think the fact that my mother always invited him to have Sunday dinner with us was the main attraction for him.

I was getting bored again and there didn't seem to be anything for me to do. We had been in the Student Union for quite a while, and I watched as people came and went on stage. I watched Sid put a white bass on, plug it in and test the sound. He looked up from what he was doing and our eyes met briefly, and I felt myself blush. I don't normally blush and it was annoying as I felt my cheeks heat up. I was trying to act cool, like I didn't really care that he kept staring at me, and my blushing all the time made this unconvincing.

Sid was very attractive. I felt my heart miss a beat when he smiled at me. He had taken off his leather jacket and he was now wearing a singlet T-shirt. He was sinewy and muscular, tall and very good-looking. He wasn't the sort of guy I would normally find myself attracted to. Not that I'd had much experience with boys as boyfriends. I seemed to have a lot of male friends, but wasn't

A VICIOUS LOVE STORY

romantically involved with any of them. There was something about Sid that just clicked with me. I definitely liked him.

Sid jumped down from the stage and made his way towards where I was sitting. Several people called out to him, saying he could sit with them. One even made room for him by asking someone else to move, but he just ignored them. He practically had to climb over them to get to where I was sitting.

When the arrogant musician saw that he was making his way towards me, he made a rude comment in Norwegian, "Oh, right, I see. He's checking out the local babes." Some people laughed. It made me angry and I made a mental note that I would tell him off later.

Sid sat down beside me and I said, "Wow, aren't you Mr Popular," indicating the people wanting him to sit with them.

He seemed surprised by my comment at first, but then he smiled and said, "Yes, well, I don't bother much about that." Then he held out his hand for me to shake, saying, "Hi, I'm John, but you can call me Sid."

It made me laugh. "Hi, I'm Teddie. So how is Sid short for John then?"

I knew Bill was the common nickname for William, and I assumed this was a shorter version of John gone wrong, like he was making a joke.

"It's not short for John. It's just what they call me. So how come you've ended up here in this shit hole?" he asked.

A VICIOUS LOVE STORY

"Hey, Trondheim's all right. It's nice here," I answered indignantly, but smiling widely.

"No, I mean it must be very different after living in England. John told me you are half English. I can understand someone moving to Oslo, but this place... well."

"No, John's wrong. I'm 100% Norwegian. I lived in a tiny village in Yorkshire for a few years, so Trondheim is a metropolis in comparison. I do feel a bit cut off from civilisation from time to time though."

I had the bottle of coke in my hand and I took a sip, before handing it to him so we could share it, and he accepted appreciatively.

"Don't you get bored? I would be bored out of my skull if I had to live here. What do people do here for fun?" he asked.

"Yes, I do get bored sometimes, but then we get some interesting visitors from England to brighten up my life and it makes it bearable for a while until they leave again," I joked, and he laughed.

"So are you a roadie?" I asked, changing the subject.

"No, I'm the bass player," he answered, smiling at my mistake.

"I'm sorry. I know who John is, but I'm not really into punk music," I said, sheepishly.

Funnily enough, I felt a little disappointed that he was in the band. He didn't seem to mind that I had no idea who he was. We'd handed the coke bottle back and forth between us, and then Sid offered me the last sip of coke, which I declined. He emptied it and put the bottle on the floor by his feet. He pulled a packet of Wrigley's Spearmint Gum from his pocket and offered me one, which I accepted.

"Hey, thanks. I haven't had one of these for ages."

"I've only been in the band a little while," he said. "I was in The Flowers of Romance with Keith Levene, Palmolive and Viv Albertine earlier, but they never got any gigs and I got bored."

The name of the band made me laugh out loud. "That has got to be the most stupid name for a band I have ever heard," I said. "Did you play punk music or was it something girlier, with sugar and spice and all things nice; oh, and flowers." I giggled. "I'm betting money on it being the girl, Palmolive, who came up with that name."

"Hey, don't knock it. It's a perfectly decent name for a band, I think. But, yeah, girls thought of it first. We were quite good. Doesn't matter what we called ourselves," he said, laughing with me.

"When the chance to be in the Sex Pistols presented itself, I had to grab it," Sid told me. "I don't know how long I'll be allowed to play with them, but I've made myself available for as long as they want me. So I'm playing on a trial basis really. My band mates in The Flowers of Romance were not pleased with the deal as they've finally gotten some gigs lined up. I thought it was too little too late. Keith kept saying he'd get us some gigs, but he never did. We'd only been rehearsing and I got sick of it. It got fucking boring. We'd been rehearsing in The Clash's rehearsal rooms and never got out of there," he explained.

A VICIOUS LOVE STORY

"So are they a bit peeved you left?" I asked, just making conversation and not really interested in the band he was talking about.

"Yeah, Keith was, but Viv understood I had to do this. If you are mates, you want the best for them, don't you? Viv knows I didn't leave to split the band up.

He seemed quite shy around me, and I instinctively thought Viv was a man since this person was obviously close to Sid. He didn't seem like the type of guy who would be comfortable with close female friends since he seemed a little awkward around me. Of course, Viv Albertine is very much a girl and was a close friend of Sid's.

"I wrote a song, *Belsen Was a Gas*, and let them use it as a form of compensation for leaving them on short notice."

I was a little shocked by the title, and he added, "It's irony. Not meant as anything else. I hate people who don't get that. If they don't like the 'shocking' title, then don't listen to the fucking music. I make music for me, and I don't care if people like it or not. Why do people always have to have an opinion? Don't listen if you are put off by the title."

I knew he didn't mean me, personally, but I thought I'd put him straight and said, "Hey, don't get your knickers in a twist about it. I was just saying it might offend the people out there who had lost family in Belsen. I think your irony, as you put it, would be lost on them. But then again, they're probably not the people who would listen to it anyway."

A VICIOUS LOVE STORY

VIV ALBERTINE: I wasn't in the Flowers of Romance any more by the time Sid went on the Scandinavian tour.

He seemed to like the fact that I stuck up for my views and didn't just pay him lip service. I caught him staring at me when I talked and I tossed my hair back as it was making me a little nervous. Although Sid was obviously a working class guy from a poor background, he was very intelligent. He had a lot of opinions and seemed to think things through. When I asked him a question, he would answer in a calm and easygoing way, but at the same time I knew he was taking me seriously. He wasn't messing around and making the mistake of thinking I was an airhead.

ROADENT: We hung out in squats. The Flowers of Romance were allowed to rehearse in The Clash's rehearsal rooms by Camden Market. A few of us would gather to do drugs when we could get some. Once, a chap came into the rehearsal room with an unmarked bag of pills. I carefully took one, but Sid took a whole handful and swallowed the lot, smiled, and said, "What's this then?", while we looked on in shock.

We couldn't stop talking. He told me he knew Casino Steel of London-based punk band The Boys, and asked me if I knew him since Casino was Norwegian and from Trondheim. I said no, as I'd never heard of him.

A VICIOUS LOVE STORY

"He's in a band in London and writes about the London music scene for the local newspaper here, I think," said Sid.

"Yes, well, I don't pay much attention to that sort of stuff, myself. Now, if he was writing about make-up, I might know who he is," I answered as a joke, and he laughed.

CASINO STEEL: I moved to London because I was bored with the Norwegian music scene. I wanted to be on the same soil as my idols, The Rolling Stones and The Beatles. I sold newspapers at Paddington Station for three years whilst I pursued my dream of playing in a band and making new music. I joined Honest John Plain, Matt Dangerfield, Kid Reid and Jack Black in the punk band The Boys in 1976, and I was also writing a weekly column for the Norwegian newspaper *Adresseavisen* **about the music scene in London.**

By the autumn of 1976, I had written passionately about the changes taking place in the music that was popular in the UK, and featured bands such as The Ramones, The Clash, The Damned and The Runaways. I got to know Lemmy (Killminster, frontman for Motorhead) in 74-75, I reckon. Lemmy used to hang out at the St Moritz Bar, which was straight across the road from the Marquee Club. Lemmy was always on the pinball machine. That place was open after the Marquee Club closed and we used to go there. It's just a bar really.

A VICIOUS LOVE STORY

I got to know Sid in 75-76. He used to hang around the Sex Pistols. He was a member of the Bromley Contingent. We were up in Maida Vale in north London. The Pistols, Siouxsie and the Banshees, and Generation X were down in south London. Up in Maida Vale were The Boys, The Clash, The Damned and a few others. Sid Vicious moved up to Maida Vale, and we all basically just hung out at the same bar and the same basement studio, which was in Warrington Crescent. It was a four-track studio, owned by our lead guitarist. We would all hang around there and we would do demos.

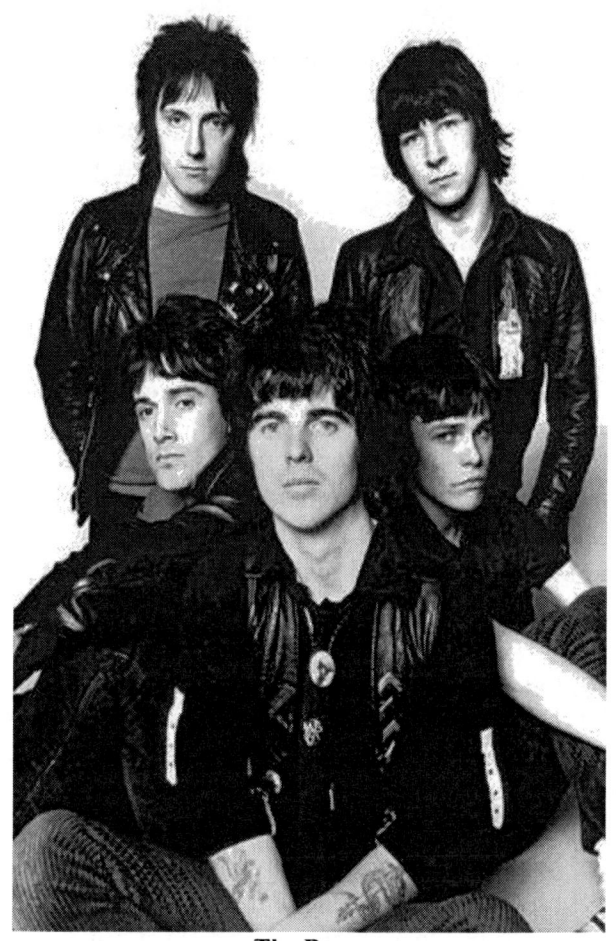

The Boys.

"Casino is a mate of mine. I would have thought you'd have heard about him since he's supposed to be famous here."

A VICIOUS LOVE STORY

"No, never heard of him, but then I'm not really paying attention to the music scene here and I'm not impressed with fame either. Honestly, some people get so arrogant. Just because they've been on TV or in the newspaper, it's like they're so far up their own arses they are practically inside out," I said, eyeing the arrogant musician sitting a little further along the row of seats.

Sid laughed at my expression, turned to look in the same direction, and smiled knowingly when he noticed it was the guy who had been so eager for Sid to sit with him.

"Yeah, I know what you mean. There are so many arrogant people in this business, it's incredible. Lots of backstabbing and manipulation going on. A while ago I was asked to try out for another band, The Damned. I bet you haven't heard of them either?" he asked, laughing when I shook my head. "I really like them. They were looking for a vocal/frontman and Rat Scabies said I could audition, and they'd let me know the time and place later. They sent a message with a mate and he never told me, bastard. I met him the same day and he didn't say a word," he said, sounding irritated. "I really wanted that job. I wanted it more than being in the Sex Pistols at the time."

"That's a shame," I answered. "Perhaps he just forgot."

"No, he didn't forget. He didn't want me to get the job. I thought he was a good mate and it turned out he was a better mate to David Vanian than me. That's who got the job. Later, I heard they gave the job to David because I never turned up for the audition. I didn't fucking know about it," he said sourly.

A VICIOUS LOVE STORY

"Well, I'm glad you didn't get the job, and that you're in the Pistols and not the Damned, or I wouldn't have met you," I said, smiling.

"Thanks, so am I now." He smiled back at me and nudged my shoulder.

"I suppose you will have to get used to people trying to use you, and things like that happening, now that you are in the Pistols," I said. "There's a lot at stake, I'm guessing, and people want to get ahead and don't care who they step on to get there."

"Yeah, you're right and I really hate the sort of person who wants to be friends with someone just because they're famous, makes me puke. In London there are people who wouldn't even look at me earlier who now want to be my best friend. They want to buy me a beer and talk, and I fucking hate them. Why didn't they buy me a beer last year when I was nobody?" He almost spat out the words.

"Because they didn't know who you were then," I suggested. "The fact that you're in a successful band and getting a lot of attention makes them pay attention. Maybe they just like what you are doing and want to be nice? It's not always sucking up, you know."

"I know who's sucking up and who's a mate. I'm not talking to some poncey prat just because he or she wants to say they're friends with us. You know, Teddie, I don't cooperate. I don't do what is expected of me. None of us do. That's why we are who we are. We do what we want. We can't be bothered with stuff we don't want. If people like our music and what we are about, that's great. If they don't then they can fuck off. I'm not making music for people to like. I do what I like," he answered.

He went into a long monologue about being pissed off with society, and people who came out of school, got jobs and did whatever they could to fit in. Sid hated the bowler-hat wearing, English-gent type that he so often saw prancing around London, swinging his umbrella. He referred to them as "people who fell into line".

He suddenly realised I'd gone quiet. He leaned in close and asked, "Am I boring you?"

Sid's face was just inches from mine and I could feel his warm breath, smelling of spearmint, on my face. It was a nice feeling, being this close. It felt comfortable, but at the same time there was a tension between us.

"No, it makes a lot of sense, even though I don't completely share your views on everything. Some people have to get up every day to earn a crust. It's probably not what they want to be doing. I'm sure they'd prefer to be sitting outside in the sunshine instead of going down the pit. Some of my friend's fathers go for days on end, without seeing the sun at all, because they have the day shift down the pit. It's dark when they go to work early in the morning, dark when they're down the pit covered in coal dust, and it's dark when they go home to their families. They have no choice. They have to feed their families. Ideals are a great thing in theory, but sometimes life just isn't like that."

I was so engaged by what I was saying that, to begin with, I didn't see how widely he was grinning. "What?

A VICIOUS LOVE STORY

Why are you looking at me like that? I'm not stupid, you know."

He laughed. "No, I didn't say you were. I am starving. When is Tore taking us to dinner?"

"I have no idea. I think that chewing gum has actually made me even more hungry." I looked at my watch.

Sid put his hand under my mouth, indicating that I should spit the gum into his hand. I thought it was funny, and that I'd totally gross him out if I actually did do that, so I expected him to move it away. As I spat the gum into his hand, he looked me in the eye, like he knew what I was thinking. I saw a glint of wicked humour in the corner of his eye as he put the gum straight into his mouth and started chewing it happily. I was so surprised that I started laughing and so did he.

"Eeeegh!" I said.

"What? It's no worse than kissing. Seriously, I need a large burger with chips, or a curry with chips, or just chips. Can't you just tell Tore we are going out to find some food? We should just take the keys with us. Won't be a problem to get back in," he said, getting up from the seat.

We walked down to where Tore was sitting, and Sid went over to the stage with our empty coke bottle and got his jacket. I saw John, Steve, Paul, Boogie and Roadent talk to Sid, and give him money. He came back to where I was standing next to Tore. I thought there was a bigger chance of Tore letting me have the keys to the Student Union for a while if Sid asked. The boys had given him money to buy some food for them too, so Tore reluctantly gave me 100 kroner and the keys, and I was told to return as soon as possible.

"I'll come with you, Sid. You might need help carrying the food back," Roadent offered.

"No thanks. Ted and I will manage," he answered, and pushed me hastily ahead of him out of the room, which made me laugh.

"Don't you like Roadent much?" I asked Sid, as we opened the door and walked out into the afternoon sunshine. It was around 5pm and the sun was still shining, but it wasn't warm.

"He's okay. We spend so much time together on tour. I just want to be on my own with you for a while," he said, and I blushed again.

I handed Sid the keys to the door since my jeans were too tight to get them into my pocket. Sid put them into the pocket of his leather jacket and I laughed when he struggled to get his hand in there. We walked together along Elgeseter Street in the sunny afternoon, looking for a kiosk that sold hot dogs or a burger place. The small kiosk across the street was closed, so we walked towards the general hospital while we talked about this and that. I was sure the cafeteria at the hospital would be open at least.

Sid asked me about myself, showing a great deal of interest in why I had left England and what my life was like now that I lived in Trondheim. He got my weird sense of humour and we found we laughed at the same things. He would push me when I said something funny, and when I pushed him back he'd grab me from behind and grab my throat like he wanted to throttle me, and it made me giggle.

We entered the hospital just as they pulled the metal blinds down in the little shop in the lobby. The lady behind the counter said she had no food to offer, but we could buy chocolates or sweets if we liked. Sid and I looked at the counter, but neither of us wanted anything sweet, so we thanked her but declined. Sid joked that we could take the elevator up to the wards and steal some food as the patients were being served their dinner, which made me laugh. We started to make our way back towards the Student Union, taking a different route and still not finding anywhere that sold food, although the area consists mainly of flats and small houses.

"Take me home with you, Ted, or I'll die of hunger at this rate," said Sid. "Is it far?"

"No, just across the bridge," I answered and he nodded.

We had decided to go back to my flat and eat, but we had to pass the Student Union to get there. Just as we got closer, and while we were laughing and playing around, I noticed the front door open and Tore poked his head out. As soon as he saw us, he waved us over.

"Shit, that's put a spanner in the works," Sid said under his breath and sighed.

"I told you, you wouldn't find a place that's open around here. You'd have to go over the bridge and into town. Besides it's the wrong time of day," Tore called out to us.

"We are going back to Ted's."

A VICIOUS LOVE STORY

"Can't you wait just a little bit longer?" asked Tore. "We are ready to do the sound check. If we get that out of the way then we can go straight to the restaurant."

We nodded reluctantly, and went with Tore back inside the Student Union. It was such a dark contrast to the balmy, sunny afternoon outside, and I was disappointed that I wouldn't be spending more time with Sid alone.

"Oh well, you can take me home with you another time," he said, with his hand around my shoulder.

"What makes you think I'll want to?" I asked, laughing.

Sid removed his hand and looked embarrassed, so I nudged him playfully. We walked together towards the main hall, only to be met by disappointed grunts from the others when they saw we'd returned empty handed.

"We thought you two had eloped," Roadent shouted from the stage.

"We almost did," Sid answered, cheekily. "Ted was taking me back to her place to feed me, but we got caught before we managed to cross the bridge."

"I would have brought you all something from home," I said, feeling guilty that we had planned to take off.

"We can all go back to Ted's," Steve suggested.

"Yeah, let's all go back to Teddies house, and say hello to her mummy and daddy, and get her to cook for us," John said, laughing. "You can do the washing up, Roadent."

We sat down on the first row of seats with Tore and a couple of the sound technicians. I remember thinking that going back to my flat for food wasn't such a bad idea. I was pretty sure my mother would whip something up for

A VICIOUS LOVE STORY

us all. She was an excellent cook and loved it when my friends visited. No one left there hungry. Then I remembered that she was going to be working at the restaurant tonight and wouldn't be at home.

"It was a nice walk and you're good company, and it was good to get some fresh air, even though we didn't find any food," Sid said quietly to me.

"I don't normally get to walk around when we are away playing gigs, so it was great to have a little look around the area. And I still think this town is shite and boring!" he added, laughing.

I knew he was just teasing me, so I thumped him playfully in the arm and he made a big show of how much it hurt. It was time to do the sound check and he got up to leave. "Right," he said, "work to do. I won't be a minute. Don't go anywhere. I'll be right back. I like talking to you."

He left me sitting there, watching him walk back to the stage. I really liked him, but at the same time I didn't have any idea whether or not he liked me back, beyond the point of us getting on simply to break up the tedium. I wasn't really confident about my looks and he was four years older than me. Now that I look back, I think I must have been blind not to pick up on the flirting.

I think, in truth, I did realise he was flirting and that he seemed to like me, but what I didn't know was whether it meant anything. I thought he would just move on to the next girl that caught his fancy when we went somewhere later, so I tried to be a little careful not to put too much into it. The sound check was a dreadfully noisy business.

A VICIOUS LOVE STORY

Tore shouted to Paul that he couldn't hear the drums properly.

"I can't hit them too hard 'cos they keep moving," Paul answered from the stage, where he was seated behind his drum kit.

"You play like a fucking old woman anyway, so they won't notice the difference," Roadent commented from the side of the stage.

"They will notice when my drums start falling off the fucking stage into the mosh pit, followed by me and my sticks," Paul shouted back.

As Paul's drums kept moving around on stage, Boogie and Roadent decided they needed to secure them. The only thing we had was duct tape and they spent several minutes taping the drums to the stage floor. This caused a problem for the warm-up band as there was no room for Fatah Morgana's kit. Paul suggested that Vidar, the drummer, could use his drums, but he would have to use his own drumsticks as Paul was keeping a close eye on his. He'd lost a pair at the Oslo gig, so he wasn't lending his to anyone just before a concert.

A VICIOUS LOVE STORY

Photo Arne S Nielsen

A VICIOUS LOVE STORY

When they were done taping, Tore sent me to the top of the hall to check that the sound was good all the way up. That was a redundant exercise if ever there was one, since I couldn't tell a good sound from a bad one. In my opinion, the Sex Pistols weren't all that good, but I went to the top anyway. The Pistols played the beginning of the song *17* and when they stopped, Tore shouted, "Is the sound okay where you are, Teddie?"

I decided that diplomacy was my best bet and answered, "I can hear the sound, but whether it's good or not, I have no flaming idea. It's loud though."

Tore looked exasperated and sent one of the Norwegian sound technicians up to where I was sitting. He was a mate of mine and was laughing at me as he said, "Apart from flirting with Sid Vicious, Teddie, you are a total waste of space."

"I'm not flirting. We talked; he's nice, that's that."

"Yeah right, but he seems to have taken a shine to you. If you're not interested then you need to make that clear. He's been asking everyone here about you; who you are, if you are Tore's wife or if they know if you have a boy friend," said the technician with a chuckle.

"Why on earth would he think I'm married?" I asked the technician, and we both laughed.

Most people in Norway at the time didn't get married, but simply chose to live together. It was generally thought uncool to be married and very few young people would seriously consider it, even if they had children. It was certainly not something you would do in your teens and I knew I didn't look much older than I was. I could pass for

A VICIOUS LOVE STORY

18 at a stretch of the imagination and Tore was almost 10 years my senior. It made me reflect once again on how different the Norwegian and English cultures were.

I sat down on a chair in the highest place in the hall. It was dark, as the lights didn't reach all the way up. I could see the stage clearly and I watched as Sid put his bass down. I could see him looking around the concert hall as if he was searching for someone. I decided to just wait and see what he did next. I sat there quietly, thinking that this was a good way to test if the sound technician was right. I moved around a little, tossing my hair and hoping the movement caught his attention. I watched as Sid looked around the room again and then he suddenly saw me, and his face broke into a wide smile. He made his way to the top where I was sitting alone and sat down next to me.

"Why are you sitting up here? I was afraid you'd left," he said, a little breathless after the climb.

My heart missed a beat, and I fiddled with my hair again in the way I had started doing whenever I got nervous. You know, the way you do when you want to attract someone's attention and at the same time you don't know what to do with your hands. I had a fringe that kept flopping forward into my face and I found it good to hide behind.

We stayed up there in the dark, talking, while the rest of the band and crew were getting their belongings together. All the instruments except the drums were locked in a little room backstage. Sid's bass was on top of one of the large speakers, and we watched as Roadent picked it up and unplugged it. He looked around and suddenly saw us. He didn't say anything, but shook his head and took Sid's bass into the backstage room.

"So, how are you liking Norway so far?" I asked, as a way to make conversation because I didn't know what else to say.

"I like it a lot – even better now," he said.

Smiling at me, he pushed me gently on my shoulder closest to him. I looked at him with surprise, as if not understanding what he meant when I did really, but I didn't want him to think me easy to flirt with. I wanted him to work harder at it if he wanted my attention.

Sid suddenly seemed uncertain. "Sorry, joke!" he said, laughing awkwardly. "I spent over a week in Sweden playing small clubs and it was a nightmare. Seriously, I am so happy to be in Norway. I have to go back and do a few more gigs there next week. Then I have to go back to the UK for a day as I've got a court case coming up."

"Oh," I said, a little shocked "What did you do?"

"Nothing. People always assume I'm guilty of something!" He laughed. "I was at a concert at the 100 Club in London, and someone accused me of throwing a glass that smashed and took someone's eye out. It was serious and the girl was blinded. It was touch and go whether I could come on this tour since I have to go to court personally. But they've arranged for me to go back for a day," Sid explained.

I didn't know anyone who had been in trouble with the police and I assumed from the fact that it had become an actual court case that it was serious.

A VICIOUS LOVE STORY

"For the record, it wasn't me who threw the glass, I don't know who threw it," he said, seeing how shocked I was. "But it's easy to blame me because I do sometimes do some crazy stuff. It gets fucking annoying."

"Won't that get in the way of you playing in the band?" I asked. "You did say you were on a trial basis. I mean, if you get thrown into jail."

"Nah, it's going to be fine. There was this journalist that sat next to me that's going to witness for me, so it's all a waste of time really. It's money and time consuming, and I'm innocent, but that's the English law for you. I feel really sorry for the girl, but it wasn't me, and I am not going to take the blame for something someone else did." He sounded quite sad.

I started thinking how different his life was to mine. Squats and gigs, fights, and spitting and swearing. Just then, in the dark, at the top of the Student Union hall, I wondered whether I ought to like Sid Vicious as much as I seemed to.

CHAPTER 4 DINNER AND A CONCERT

We left the Student Union when everything was in place and ready for the evening's concert. It was getting close to 6.30pm and I was very happy to be finished. Tore said he had arranged for us to have dinner at the restaurant at the Phoenix hotel. I drove back with him in his car, and the band drove in the white van with Bollocks-chops at the wheel.

It was quiet in the car for a while and I could see the white van behind us, and then Tore said, "I can see you are getting on well with the boys. They aren't as bad as I'd expected." He was smiling, like it was a joke.

I felt myself blush again and it was starting to annoy me. "Yeah they're great. They're very nice actually. John's a bit scary, but they seem very, erm, very nice."

We were nearing the hotel when Tore said, "You know, Teddie, what you do is your business. I'm not going to talk to your dad about stuff. But I think maybe you should keep a distance to these guys and to Sid in particular. I don't want to see you get hurt."

That was a very sweet thing to say, but it fell on deaf ears. I knew I could trust Tore with my life and nothing shocked him. He'd probably seen it all before. But I was in way too deep already to be able to walk away now. Sid intrigued me, but I couldn't understand his obvious interest in me, which everyone had picked up on except me to begin with. I decided I shouldn't expect too much and that Sid was used to having girls fall all over him. I was convinced he wouldn't be interested in me when there were other girls around, so I told Tore I was being careful and that he didn't need to worry about me.

The Swedish tour manager, Bollocks-chops, didn't come with us to the restaurant. He seemed to come and go when he was needed to drive the van, and he said he would meet us later. Tore was to phone him to let him know when we were on the move again.

A long table had been reserved for us to one side of the hotel restaurant, in front of the windows. It was covered in a crisp white tablecloth, and they had set out plates and wine glasses, with white napkins at the side by the cutlery. It looked very nice and quite posh, and I was sure the boys would have preferred to eat at a local burger joint than this place.

There were several people in the restaurant when we arrived and it suddenly went quiet. All eyes were on us and I found it rather unnerving, so I decided to sit with my back to the rest of the room. Tore positioned himself at the head of the table and John sat at the other end. Roadent sat to Tore's right and Steve to his left. Tore wanted me somewhere in the middle, so I sat down between Roadent and Boogie. Roadent was such a funny person. He would soon have me in fits of laughter and I felt comfortable with him.

Sid wasn't at the restaurant to begin with and I would never have dared sit next to him anyway. He made me nervous and I was afraid I would embarrass myself by

A VICIOUS LOVE STORY

spilling my coke or choking on a chip or something. I felt safer with Roadent. Sid came to the table a few minutes later than everyone else and John had saved him a seat to his right.

I picked up on some tension between the boys. My impression was that the band was split into two camps: John and Sid on one side with Boogie as an ally, and Steve and Paul on the other with Roadent as an ally. They all got on well enough, but there seemed to be some one-upmanship between John and Steve. I got the impression that Steve wasn't pleased about John being the front figure who got most of the attention. They seemed to compete and argue over the smallest issue. John wasn't really close to Steve, and seemed to take great pleasure in taking control during interviews, and making himself the bandleader and spokesman. I noticed that while Steve was happy to sit anywhere at the table for dinner, John was calculating who would sit where, as if it was a question of military rank.

Sid arrived and saw there was only one seat left, on John's right. He looked around the table as if searching for a better option, but sat down when he saw there wasn't one. As he sat, he and John started talking intently and quietly. At intervals they would look up in my direction. I tried to listen in, but Roadent was also talking to me, so I had difficulty hearing what they said.

"Yeah, she's alright, go for it," John said quietly to Sid.

"I can't get near her," I heard Sid whisper back.

I got the impression that Sid was asking for John's advice and somehow it had something to do with me, but I

A VICIOUS LOVE STORY

wasn't sure. I'd translated the menu and everyone had eagerly ordered what they wanted. When our meals arrived, we started eating and drinking Coke. The food wasn't very fancy and, if I remember correctly, most of us just ordered sausage and chips, which was served with peas. It was all a little dry, tasteless and burnt, and we used a lot of ketchup to put some flavour into it. By now I was so hungry that even flambéed napkin would have gone down well. It had been a long day and we were famished.

    I listened to the different conversations taking place at either end of the table and at one point Sid tried to talk to me, but it was difficult since he was sitting too far away, and John and Boogie were talking too. I had to shrug, indicating I couldn't hear him properly. Roadent then asked me something about the food and, turning my attention to him, I saw that John and Sid had their heads together again.

    Suddenly John spoke loudly, addressing everyone, "Why is Roadent sitting on Tore's right?"

    We all went quiet and looked up in surprise.

    "Surely Sid should have that place? He is a member of the band, after all," he said.

    It surprised me. I thought John was joking, so I smiled at him. We were halfway through our meal and I thought it a little odd that John should start talking about seating arrangements now. Roadent wasn't paying much attention to John and had been talking to Tore, but now he looked up as well and went quiet.

A VICIOUS LOVE STORY

We were even more surprised when Sid got up from where he was sitting, walked around the table and said, "Move Roadent! Swap places with me."

I could see Roadent getting angry. He was halfway through his meal and at first he thought Sid was kidding, but he said it again, that he should move. Roadent got up, taking his plate with him, and walked over to where Sid had been sitting and said, "Yes, fuck off, why don't you, Roadent," to himself, which made us all laugh.

"So are you happy with me sitting on your right, John, or would you prefer me to take my plate into the kitchen and eat with the rest of the servants?" Roadent added jovially, but he was pretty red in the face and I could see his smile didn't reach his eyes.

He carried his plate to where Sid had been sitting and Sid was handed his own plate, via me, over the table. A few of his chips fell off, and Roadent simply picked them up with his fingers and threw them back on the plate. I placed Sid's plate in front of him. I knew he'd seen that Roadent had touched his food, but he didn't seem to care and soon got stuck in happily.

I could see how angry Roadent was. I smiled reassuringly to him and rolled my eyes in support. I couldn't understand what had just happened. I wasn't sure whether this was John's way of belittling him for some reason or whether it was Sid's way of getting to sit next to me.

It was all very strange because when Sid did sit down, it was like he didn't want to talk to me after all; like he felt he'd made too much of a fuss about swapping places and now he didn't know what to say. He spoke to Tore at length and I sat in silence, listening. I wasn't sure whether he was shy or if I had misunderstood the signals he was sending.

When Tore left the table to make a phone call to the Student Union to get an update on the situation there, Sid finally turned to me and made polite conversation. He was sweet and attentive, and once again we seemed to get on really well.

As Tore returned, I started talking to Steve about Norwegian food, which he wasn't enjoying much, and John agreed that they were looking forward to a decent pint and some proper chips when they got back to England the following week. They told me they thought the beer in Norway tasted a lot better than the Swedish beer, even though we were all drinking coke. I'm guessing with a good amount of certainty that they had sampled copious amounts of Norwegian beer the previous night in Oslo.

"We made the mistake of buying beer at a shop for the party after our first gig in Stockholm. We got several crates of it and were so disappointed to find that there was only about 0.1% alcohol in it," Steve said, and we all laughed.

"I'm sure you are not the only person to have made that mistake before," Tore said, laughing.

"Yeah, that did put a damper on the whole after-party," John said.

"So what did you do?" I asked.

"What could we fucking do? We tried to drink as much as we could, as quickly as we could, but that only meant pissing it out just as fast. We ended up going to bed early," he replied.

"We didn't know that you had to get normal beer at an off licence. What's that all about?" Steve added, indignantly.

"And what is it with Scandinavians and chips? I mean, how hard can it be to fry a chip?" asked John. He picked up a thin, dry French fry from his plate that he had been struggling to get his fork into. Holding it up in two fingers, he examined it closely. "You take a potato, you cut it up, and you fry it in a chip pan. This is a fucking cremated matchstick!"

"My mother is a chef and I know they don't actually fry chips at the restaurants here, but heat them in the oven. Frying is not considered a good way to heat food at restaurants and you'll find that small burger joints will deep fry just about everything they sell, so I think they do it as a contrast to that," I answered, laughing.

"And what the fuck is this?" John asked, holding up a long, thin sausage vertically between forefinger and thumb so that it drooped. It was covered in red skin and popularly known as a Danish wiener in Norway.

"I cannot eat anything wearing a condom," he said, pointing at the sausage's red, rubbery covering.

This comment sent me into a fit of giggles that I didn't think I would survive. I had to dry my eyes with my napkin as the tears of laughter ran down my face.

Sid turned towards me and put his arm around me. "I'm sorry, Ted, I don't usually have this effect on girls," he said, which only made me laugh even harder.

A VICIOUS LOVE STORY

"The only thing that's remotely good about Scandinavian food is sandwiches. They can't even make a decent breakfast here. I mean, seriously, some of the scrambled eggs here are so springy, if I dropped it on the floor I swear it would bounce right back up again. I bet you are going to tell me they make them in the oven too," John said, and laughed when I nodded. He seemed to like the fact he had an appreciative audience as I was having trouble breathing through my fit of giggles.

"I go to the breakfast buffet warily these days because I never know what's there. Gone are the days when I would carefully try something new without asking exactly what it was first. There will be raw fish in mustard, reindeer burger or filet of whale with creamed possum or something, and a tube of disgusting fish paste they try to pass off as caviar," he said seriously, making me laugh even more.

"I have actually tasted caviar and I don't know what the fuss is about – horrible, salty bubbles. That orange stuff in a tube tasted disgusting, and nothing like caviar. Not that I like caviar either," John added.

Everyone was laughing while they ate, and I think John was the only person who didn't finish everything. We were all famished beyond bothering about what exactly it was we had on our plates.

"Why is the cheese brown here, Ted? I find that very worrying," said John seriously, with a straight face.

"It's made from goat's milk," I answered, giggling. I could see how Norwegian food would be strange and horrible to someone from England. We don't eat possum, by the way!

"Yesterday, I was eating some salami that didn't taste too bad and I asked the waitress what it was, and she said 'horse'. I almost puked. Later, I tried something I thought was fish and nearly threw up when they told me it was fish sperm, or balls or something. I'll be thin and scrawny, and suffering from malnutrition when I get back to my dear wife in London. And I swear she'll think I'm lying when I tell her about all the crap you people have been trying to force me to eat," he said, laughing.

I found it strange that John Lydon talked about a wife. He couldn't have been more than 20 or 21 years old, but he seemed so mature and very bright. He would sometimes lean back and just observe the conversations around him, and then jump in and make an absolutely brilliant comment. I felt John was a man who controlled his environment whereas Sid would act impulsively, but he wasn't any the less intelligent, just different. Sid was less manipulative and more real in my opinion. But that could also be because he let me get really close to him while John kept his distance. I could see that John behaved much as an older brother to Sid. There was a deep bond between them.

Sid started talking to me again about his life back in London, and about his friendship with John being the reason he was invited to join the Sex Pistols in the first place. He was nice and I think a little shy. Even though we had already spent hours together, it was like he didn't really know how to act around me. I sensed he was trying

A VICIOUS LOVE STORY

to see if I was being polite or whether I actually liked him. Sid wasn't pushy or crude, just sweet and funny. We got on really well and he was very attentive towards me, but I put that down to me being the only other English-speaking girl there – the only girl there at all. It seemed to me that he would do things to get close to me, and then pull back to see my reaction. Sid would be very sweet and then suddenly serious. It confused me. I didn't understand his behaviour and decided to do nothing in case I was misunderstanding the situation. I didn't want to presume too much and make a total arse of myself in front of everybody.

There was a couple in their 40s sitting at a table close to us who seemed to be listening in on what we were talking about. The man was getting very drunk and was red in the face. They had finished their meal and were sharing what was left of a bottle of red wine. I could see they didn't like the fact that we were there. They would comment loudly to each other at intervals on what we were talking about and what we were eating. It was loud enough for the whole restaurant to hear. The man made crude remarks about us that made the other guests laugh, and I found myself getting annoyed at their rudeness. I didn't say anything. I could see Tore was aware of them too, as he looked at me with raised eyebrows after some of their comments.

Suddenly, Sid let out a really loud burp. We'd been laughing at what John and Steve had been saying, and I think this was Sid's contribution to the conversation. He

A VICIOUS LOVE STORY

was just trying to be funny. Everyone, except Tore and I, laughed. I was shocked and embarrassed.

"Charming!" I said, indicating the exact opposite.

"Sorry, but we have to do this sort of stuff sometimes. It's expected and it does make good headlines," Sid replied.

"I find it disgusting, embarrassing and childish. Would you please not do that when I'm around?" I answered, angrily.

This only made Sid laugh. "It's what we do, who we are. People expect us to be shocking and outrageous. And, to be fair, I did let you finish your meal first," he added.

I don't know if he expected me to thank him for that. It seemed like this was just what the rude couple were waiting for. The husband made another loud remark that some people acted like animals and really shouldn't be let out of their cages. John asked me what they had said. I thought it was funny so I translated it, which made him laugh.

Steve grabbed some cold, congealed chips from his plate and threw them at the couple. Unfortunately, some of them were covered in ketchup and the couple quickly got up to leave, while Sid and John also started throwing food at them. The man stopped at the head of our table and spent a few minutes telling Tore what he thought of us. Tore tried to plead that they were the ones who had started the whole business with their crude remarks.

I could see Tore was just as embarrassed as I was, yet he had no option but to defend the band. We laughed and jeered as the couple stormed off to talk to the hotel manager. It didn't take long before the manager came over and had a quiet word with Tore, who offered to pay for the couple's meal. The manager said it had already been taken care of, and politely asked us to leave, but first could we please come to the kitchen and say hello to the staff, as the chef was a huge fan.

I had noticed a young man in a chef's uniform standing to one side of the restaurant. He had watched us intently all through the meal and his staring had made me uneasy since John was criticising the food. It felt like he was studying our every move and listening intently to everything we said.

We were taken down a dingy hallway and into a large kitchen, where the staff were thrilled to have their idols visit them. John was in a much better mood now and the boys signed autographs. John swiped the chef's hat from his head, and cheekily pranced around and juggled some pans, trying to make us all laugh. The chef was thrilled that John had his hat on and let him have it if he signed his other spare one.

Then it was time to leave. Tore said he and I would go in his car, ahead of the van, and get the back entrance of the Student Union secured, ready for the band to just run in. We had been told there was a crowd of fans gathering there. John was still wearing the chef's hat as we left the hotel lobby.

When we got outside, Sid suddenly said to John, "I'll go in the car with her." He pointed at me.

Sid and John were walking behind me, and I don't think I was supposed to hear it. I turned around and smiled

A VICIOUS LOVE STORY

at Sid, and he seemed slightly embarrassed. I was pleased he wanted to go with me in the car, but I didn't quite know why. I could see John was as surprised as I was, but he said it was okay. He and Sid would go in the car with Tore and I. Then Steve said he, too, should go in the car – why should he go in the van? We finally decided that everyone would drive in Tore's car!

Tore's car was tiny. I remember John got in the front seat and Sid, Steve and I got into the back. Sid put his arm on the back of the seat behind my head and I thought, yikes. I was squashed in tightly between Sid and Steve, which was very uncomfortable, and there was absolutely no room for Paul. I offered to go in the van with Roadent and Boogie, but Sid quickly protested. Bollocks-chops had arrived a little earlier while we had been in the kitchen and would drive the van to the Student Union.

"Roadent and I will squeeze ourselves into the van then," Boogie said. They both thought it was hysterically funny that they would drive in an empty van while we'd all be squashed like sardines in Tore's little car.

"Ted, you're the smallest, sit on someone's knee," Tore said.

Sid smiled at me and I had a feeling he wanted me to choose him. Sid had been running hot and cold on me all day. One minute he would be all over me and flirting, and the next he would pull back, act like he didn't really give a toss, and try to look bored. I was unsure whether he was just shy or if he was like this with everyone. I knew I wouldn't get the answer to that question until there were

A VICIOUS LOVE STORY

more girls around. So I decided to test the situation and see what he did when I chose someone else instead of him.

"Steve, would you like me on your knee?" I asked in a flirty way.

"Yes, darling, I can't say no to that," he answered, laughing.

Steve got a tight grip around my waist and hoisted me up on to his lap. He pulled my arm around his neck and tickled me, and we giggled. Sid didn't say anything, but I noticed that for most of the ride he was looking intently out of the window, away from us. Steve was a good-looking guy and he flirted with me. He said I smelled nice and put his nose closer to my chest.

As I was sitting on his knee with my chest at eye level, there wasn't much I could do about it, so I just laughed, but I was prepared to tell him off should he try to get any closer. He was flirting, but it wasn't working since there was absolutely no chemistry between us, so it was more just a little fun. Luckily, it was a short drive. We parked, unnoticed by the group of fans gathering by the back door.

"Teddie, you get out and make a knock in this rhythm on the back door. That's the signal to open the door. When it's open, you stand there and hold it, keeping the fans out and thus letting the boys run in," Tore explained, knocking on the dashboard.

Now I'm not a big girl, and his faith in me being able to stop stampeding fans was truly misplaced. I had to climb over Sid to get to the door and ended up sitting on his lap for a few seconds, making sure it was a tad longer than really necessary. I had to wriggle to get out and we laughed. "Are you enjoying this?" I asked, to which he whispered in my ear, "Mmm...."

So, off I ran. The crowd of fans at the back entrance hadn't yet noticed the band all squeezed inside Tore's little car. I think it was the last place they were expecting their heroes to be. They had gathered, 20 men abreast and 15 deep, outside the back entrance. There were steps leading up to the door and there was no way I could get close enough to knock. The fans wouldn't let me get near the door, no matter how hard I pushed.

I turned around and looked at Tore and John, sitting in the car. Tore waved me on, indicating I should try harder to get to the door, but I shrugged my shoulders and raised both my hands, palms up, indicating that I was at a loose end. I could see they were all laughing at me in the car, obviously finding it hilarious that we couldn't get into the venue. I tried once more and pushed past a couple of guys, but they soon pushed me to the back of the crowd again.

A VICIOUS LOVE STORY

> TORE LANDE PRESENTERER:
>
> **SEX PISTOLS**
>
> Nr. 1568
>
> Studentersamfundet - Trondheim
> Torsdag 21. juli kl. 20.00

    The fans, mainly young boys, wouldn't let me get closer, and there was a lot of pushing and poking going on. I decided there was just one option left for me and that was to somehow get them to realise I had business at the door, that I was serious and they had to let me through.

    "Get out of my fucking way. I am going in there, you morons!" I shouted loudly, in English.

    That made a few of them laugh, since they obviously knew who I was and that I was fluent in Norwegian.

    One guy looked at me in surprise, and I said to him, "I really do have to get to the door. I'm going in. I work there and if they don't let me closer to the door, there won't be a fucking concert."

A VICIOUS LOVE STORY

I didn't normally swear, but I found it strangely liberating after listening to the boys' tirades all day. The guy seemed to believe me and started pushing people away so that I could get closer to the door. He shouted to others in the crowd that I was serious. When I had two people in between the door and me, I managed to push my arm past them so that I could make the knock, but I was too far away to do it loud enough for the guy on the inside to hear!

Then, for some reason, it seemed like the people closest to the door started believing me too, and I was pushed and poked, finally getting close enough to knock harder and louder. Some of the fans started banging the same rhyme too, and finally the door swung open inwards, and I stood face to face with a huge bouncer.

"Fuck off!" he said angrily, and almost shut the door in my face.

"No, stop!" I cried. "Tore sent me. We're here!" I tried not to mention the band by name as I was afraid the fans would mug Tore's car if they knew they were inside.

I was still getting pushed into the door, but managed to point in the direction of the car. Tore had gotten out and was waving at the bouncer, who then pulled me towards him so that I stood on the inside of the door, facing the fans.

Tore and the band had been watching me from the car. When the door opened, they welled out and made a run for the entrance, pushing their way through the shocked fans. I shouted to the crowd to move and let them pass. I think I came across as a little sergeant major, but they finally took

A VICIOUS LOVE STORY

me seriously when they saw Tore bringing up the rear. The Sex Pistols ran into the Student Union with John still wearing the silly chef's hat, while the fans cried for them to stop and sign autographs.

Some of the fans tried to push past me and go in after the band. One guy pushed harder than the rest, managed to get my arm away from the door, and ran into the hall. This made the rest of the fans shove even harder. The bouncer instinctively ran after the fan, which left me at the door on my own. They kept pushing, but I don't think they were giving it their best shot, as I would never have been able to hold them off.

The bouncer came back after a few seconds. He had given up pursuing the fan and could see that I couldn't be left on my own for long. I wanted to close the door, but Tore had to lock his car doors and was taking his time. I shouted to him that I couldn't hold them for much longer and he only just made it inside before we quickly shut the door. The warm-up band had already been on stage for a while and everything was ready for the concert.

Vidar Kvenild, the drummer of Fatah Morgana, had used Paul's drums. He was a really nice guy and seemed to get on well with Paul, as they sat chatting backstage. The drum kit was still firmly taped to the floor! Paul was the nicest person. He would talk to everyone and there was none of that pop star attitude about him at all. I remember thinking that none of the guys were very diva-like; just nice, normal and down to earth. They were also very professional.

A VICIOUS LOVE STORY

I also reflected on how both Boogie and Roadent were included in everything. I had expected a group of stuck-up pop stars with diva behaviour and disgusting manners, and the sex, drugs and rock-and-roll image they seemed to portray. What I saw, once I got to know them a little, were intelligent, well-mannered boys who were very funny. The rude behaviour was more of a show they put on to get PR and media attention. I personally labelled it 'Pistols mode' when one of them did something politically incorrect. Usually it was Sid, cheered on by John.

Tore and I walked together down the narrow hallway and up a winding staircase leading from the back door to the backstage room, which wasn't very big. A few chairs stood against one wall and above them was a shelf running the length of the room. Someone had left some electrical equipment cluttering up a corner, and there was another door leading off to a little room where the instruments were stored, which was locked.

The band and roadies were there already, and I was amazed to see Sid standing in front of a large mirror, jumping up and down, and practising his moves. He stopped as soon as he saw us and seemed embarrassed. We just laughed. Fatah Morgana were also there too, as they had a short break before the next part of their gig.

The concert started late. There was a roar of cheering when the Sex Pistols came on stage. Sid wore his leather jacket, but soon found it to be too hot. He removed it and gave it to Roadent, who was standing to one side of the stage, by the door to the backstage room where I was.

A VICIOUS LOVE STORY

"Give that to Teddie and tell her to look after it," he said, and Roadent threw it to me. I smiled at Sid from where I was standing, backstage left. I gave him a thumbs-up and he smiled, sent one back and winked at me.

Then a fuse blew, so there was no sound! While Roadent was working frantically to repair the fuse, Sid simply lay down on the stage with his bass on his stomach, looking like he was having a nap. I remember wondering why he didn't just come off stage, instead of just laying there, but I soon realised it was the place they loved to be. John had entered the stage still wearing the chef's hat. Steve was wearing an orange boiler suit and had taped silver duct tape to the seat of them, hoping to start a trend. He had tied four knots in the corners of a handkerchief and was wearing it as a cap on his head. It was reminiscent of the style worn by old English men on the beaches of Brighton to protect their bald heads from getting sunburnt.

A VICIOUS LOVE STORY

Photo Truls Berge ©

A VICIOUS LOVE STORY

Photo Håkon Finne/foto.samfundet.no

A VICIOUS LOVE STORY

Photo Truls Berge ©

A VICIOUS LOVE STORY

Photo Håkon Finne/foto.samfundet.no

A VICIOUS LOVE STORY

Photo Arne S Nielsen ©

A VICIOUS LOVE STORY

Photo Arne S Nielsen ©

A VICIOUS LOVE STORY

Steve had told me during dinner that the safety pin thing was a mistake. A shirt had torn just before a gig and someone had pinned it together, but the pins ended up showing and it became a trend. So Steve duct taped the rear of his boiler suit and kept turning around on stage to see if it caught on. I remember saying that maybe he needed a larger and more international venue to make any impact on trends.

The fuse was soon fixed, and the Sex Pistols started playing again. It was getting very hot and the lights on stage made it even hotter for the band. Soon Sid removed his T-shirt and again threw it to Roadent and merely pointed towards me, so the roadie flung it to me. Again, Sid and I smiled at each other, and I was thrilled he chose to send his clothes to me. But, I soon got bored of waiting and looking at my watch, wondering what time it would end. It was hot back there and even hotter for the band on stage.

I was bored out of my brains, so, carrying Sid's jacket, I left the T-shirt on a chair and went out into the audience to see if I could find anyone I knew. I didn't dare leave the jacket for someone to steal. I could see Sid looking at me from the stage, and if he was surprised I'd taken his jacket with me, he didn't show it. I remember saying "Hi" to Angus, a local biker and chef. He was wearing his biker jacket and very dirty jeans.

"My jeans are so dirty, I have a clean pair underneath," he said as I passed him.

A VICIOUS LOVE STORY

There was a lot of spitting going on, so I kept far away from that. The crowd had started to chant, "Spit, spit, spit!"

John and Sid spat into the audience. What they hadn't anticipated was that the audience would spit back. Some very young and elated boys pressed closer to the stage, and kept spitting at the band. I thought it was disgusting. When John and Sid spat into the audience again, Angus put his biker helmet on, which made John laugh. John had to stop the music and appeal to the audience to stop spitting or else they would leave the stage.

When the concert was over, the Pistols trooped into the little room backstage. They'd all been tense and nervous prior to the gig, and now that it was over they seemed elated, almost. John had cheered up during dinner and now Steve seemed in a very good mood too, jumping around the room with his guitar, doing split jumps and laughing.

"God, that was fun! They kept fucking spitting at us. It was hilarious!" Steve said.

I found it strange that he seemed to like the spitting. Sid had been the last one to come off stage, and he was still wearing his white bass guitar. It was like he was on a mission and decided to simply go for it. I was standing there waiting for him, holding his jacket.

Sid walked straight over, put his arms around me and kissed me, as if it was the most natural thing in the world. He was topless and sweaty. His bass guitar got in the way and he pushed it over to his side. This was not a peck on the lips, but a long, drawn-out kiss that seemed to last for several minutes. It caught me by surprise. Even though we'd been flirting all day, we hadn't actually hooked up. I think I'd been expecting it, but since he seemed quite shy, I thought he would have a more subtle approach and maybe wait until we were alone at least. But it was nice and after a while I pulled away.

"You must know by now that I really like you?" he said.

"Yeah, I have picked up on that. I really like you too, but I don't want to get any spit on me," I answered.

He said it was okay because he'd wiped it off, but I wasn't reassured. We stood together, talking quietly, while the rest of the band chatted and joked around us.

"Something happened when I woke up at the hotel earlier and saw you there. It was like something went 'bang'," he said quietly.

"Yeah, that was probably the sound of you snoring," I joked.

"No, I mean it, Teddie. I've been trying all day to figure out how to make you see how much I like you. When did you notice?" he asked.

I thought to myself how young and immature he seemed, even though he was a lot older than me. Nobody had told me they "liked me" since I was in junior school. It was something you said in the playground. His awkwardness was such a contrast to the confident bass player that I'd watched on stage a few minutes earlier. He was like a puppy in need of a cuddle and reassurance that I liked him.

"Well, you've been very attentive all day, and you keep staring at me when you think I don't notice," I said half-jokingly, "but I think I realised it seeing your reaction when I sat on Steve's knee in the car."

"What reaction? I wasn't bothered about you choosing to sit on Steve's knee instead of mine. Didn't mind at all," he replied, unconvincingly.

"Was that why you spent the whole journey looking in the opposite direction, out of the window?" I asked, teasingly.

"I was looking at the view," he said and laughed.

"Yeah, but there was a view both ways!" I laughed.

"Okay, I admit it, I did mind. I didn't think I would, but yeah, I didn't like it at all. I would have preferred you to choose my knee, because I definitely would have kissed you then, and I wouldn't be so fucking awkward now. Steve is a ladies' man and I didn't want to lose you to him."

"I'm not some prize that you can hand back and forth, Sid. It's not like I belong to who gets to kiss me first." I was thinking he meant that I would have been an easy victim for any man's charms.

"That's not what I mean. It's just that Steve tends to get all the girls he wants. They hang around him like flies, and I was afraid if he started flirting with you then you wouldn't like me as much. Anyway, this is not coming out the way I'd planned," he said, laughing again.

"Steve's not my type, so that would never happen," I answered, and gave him a hug, followed by another kiss, just to make the point that I really liked him. Besides, I found kissing him to be soft and sensual, and very nice.

A VICIOUS LOVE STORY

"Where's my T-shirt, Ted?" Sid asked, looking around the room and not seeing it.

We had a look around, but it was gone. I'd seen a few people backstage, coming and going, and I suddenly feared it had been stolen. It was my fault. Tore said it was time to go, but Sid refused to leave without his T-shirt.

"I can't leave without that T-shirt. We have to find it," Sid said. "I got a stack of them from Malcolm's shop and we are supposed to wear them as much as possible. He won't like it if I lose it."

"What do you mean?" I asked, nervously.

"Our manager's wife has a shop and they gave us these T-shirts to wear. I have to wear them for shows and when we get photographed. That way they'll sell more T-shirts and they definitely won't be pleased if I've lost one."

As he spoke he was laughing, and he held me close while we searched the room. I thought he would be annoyed with me, but he simply gave me a hug, and said it was no big deal and he had more of them at the hotel. Luckily, Tore, being the tallest, found it on the top shelf behind the door. Someone had probably moved it in order to use the chair I'd put it on. I was so relieved,

"Okay, now let's get drunk. Where are you taking us?" John asked Tore, who replied that he'd arranged for them to go to the Hawk Club.

"We're going to a club. You have to come," Sid said.

I didn't have time to answer before Tore boomed, "No way! She's too young for the club and I promised her parents I'd take her home straight after the concert. You do know she's only 16?" Tore added to Sid.

A VICIOUS LOVE STORY

I think he was trying to tell Sid that he should back off because of my tender age, but Sid knew how old I was and he didn't seem to care. He was standing behind me with his arms around my shoulders. To my surprise, they all protested.

"Oh come on, Tore, let Teddie come to the party with us. She deserves to. After all, she's had to put up with us all day and it'll make Sid very happy. He's been slobbering over her all day. You don't want to make Sid unhappy, do you?" Steve asked.

Slobbering over me? Why hadn't I noticed that? I knew I really liked him more than I should, but I was surprised at how other people seemed to see and understand things better than I did. I could see Tore was considering the comment intently.

"Yeah, let her come. She's useful and can translate when Steve wants to pick up birds," John said, laughing.

"I don't need her to translate. Girls find me irresistible in any language!" Steve laughed.

"Shut up, Steve! You're supposed to be pleading my case," I said, which everyone found funny.

"Right, okay then, if they let you into the club, you can stay. Otherwise, you walk home from there. I'm leaving the car so I won't be able to drive you anywhere," Tore said, laughing.

"I've been to this club before. The bouncer at the weekend is my aunt's neighbour. I don't think he works there on weekdays though, so I might not be allowed in," I told Sid.

A VICIOUS LOVE STORY

"No problem, Ted. If you don't get in then I'm not going in either. We'll go back to the hotel and relax there instead. We're having a party at the hotel later anyway, so no big deal," Sid reassured me.

I was thrilled that Sid would not go into the club if I couldn't. With hindsight, I wish I hadn't been let in.

Paul had a tight grip on his drumsticks when he entered the room backstage, with Roadent right behind him. "Oi, give me the sticks!" said Roadent, whereby Paul automatically handed them over.

Bollocks-chops entered the area backstage, and he and Tore started planning how we would get out of the Student Union without getting mugged. A large crowd of fans had gathered at both exits, eagerly awaiting a glimpse of their idols.

"I think we should send Ted out to make a path through the fans so that we can run into the van. She did it so well when we arrived," John said, laughing.

"Yeah, she's like a one-man little army," Steve added.

"Hey, leave her alone," Paul said. "She did okay, eventually."

They were making fun of me, but we all laughed, and I knew it was meant light-heartedly. Tore organised a few big roadies to get the van parked as near to the front entrance as possible. Bollocks-chops was ready with the engine running and the doors open.

Just as we were leaving, Paul reminded Roadent that he must make sure he kept his drumsticks safe. He couldn't understand why he kept losing them. It made me smile, as

A VICIOUS LOVE STORY

I had just seen Roadent flogging them to a fan a couple of minutes earlier.

ROADENT: I had to make money somehow !

Roadent and Boogie got the guitars loaded into the van, and on a signal the rest of us made a dash for it, helped by the roadies who kept the fans out of the way. The fans at the back exit came running to the front when they spotted the van, and it was quite a large crowd by the time we made our dash.

Bollocks-chops drove and Tore sat in the front, giving him directions for the shortest route to the hotel. I sat next to Sid, who had his arm wrapped around my shoulder. It felt like the first meeting with the band at the hotel had happened weeks ago. It had been a long day and I was tired. I put my head on Sid's chest inside his leather jacket, and he hugged me tightly and kissed the top of my head. The van was old, and the seats were springy and lumpy. I could easily understand why Sid had trouble sleeping in there on the long drive from Oslo earlier that morning.

We could see people waving to us as we drove over Elgeseter Bridge. As we crossed it, some fans called out to us waving, and we waved back. Some started running after the van, but soon gave up. Others shouted to us, asking where we were going. We drove to the Phoenix hotel. Bollocks-chops parked the van and we all got out.

A VICIOUS LOVE STORY

"Right, I'll see you all later," Boogie said, starting to make his way up the stairs towards the entrance to the hotel.

"No, wait Boogie!" I called to him. "Where are you going?"

"I can't be arsed with a club. I'll see you all when you get back," he answered, but hesitated slightly.

"Please come with us," I tried again "We'll have some fun. If you don't come, I'm going to miss you."

Boogie smiled at me, but turned and kept walking towards the hotel door. He waved to me as he went inside. I didn't understand why he didn't want to come with us. I released the grip Sid had around my shoulders and made my way to the back of the van where Roadent and Bollocks-chops was collecting some fan material.

"Roadent, Boogie won't come with us to the club. Has someone upset him?" I asked.

He just shook his head, like it was no surprise to him at all that Boogie preferred his own company to ours. "No, he does that sometimes. He can't be bothered."

Roadent locked the back of the van and threw the keys over my head to Bollocks-chops, who stood behind me.

"We are coming back here anyway, so you'll see him later," he said.

"That's not my point. I don't want him to feel left out. I want him to come with us," I answered, not really understanding why Boogie hadn't felt like hanging out.

"Well, you can't force him if he doesn't feel like it," Bollocks-chops said.

A VICIOUS LOVE STORY

It was only a short walk to the club and no one minded. There weren't many people on the streets and nobody bothered us. Sid had his arm around my shoulder and his leather jacket felt soft against my face. His long legs took one step while mine took two. Everyone seemed happy and excited about going out to wind down.

CHAPTER 5 THE HAWK CLUB AFTER-PARTY

We all trooped up a winding staircase to the second-floor entrance of the Hawk Club disco. Inside the door was a small reception area where two bouncers sat, with a wardrobe behind them. I recognised Wally, the head bouncer. Tore went in first and cleared it with him that everything was okay for us to come in. I could see Wally raise his eyebrows when he saw me, and he said something to Tore about me. Tore had a quiet word in his ear, and I was relieved when they nodded in agreement. I have no idea what was said. That was the sign that I was okay to come in.

A door led from the reception into the club. Inside, the bar was the first thing you saw, stretching along the far wall. There was an area with a pool table to the right and the disco was to the left. They had a VIP area chained off to the side of the dance floor for us. The tables were basically wooden booths. They had made a large, rather scruffy sign on a piece of cardboard, stating that the area was off limits for guests, but there was a man and two girls sitting at the booth closest to the window. They had ignored the sign and simply taken a table.

People stared at us as we stood by the bar, waiting for Wally and Tore to get the people to move out of the VIP area. Sid had his arm around my shoulders, and I could see a few people looking at us and pointing. I didn't really

A VICIOUS LOVE STORY

care. Tore was annoyed that the man and two girls had ignored the heavy chains separating the tables from the rest of the room. They reluctantly got up and scurried out of the VIP area, and we all trooped in.

I sat with Sid, Steve, John and Roadent at the table nearest the chains. Tore ordered a beer for each of us and the staff served us at the table, so that we didn't have to leave the VIP area and go over to the bar like everyone else. The guy who had to move to make room for us was very drunk and not a happy bunny. It was only a few minutes before he came back. He made a great show of stepping over the chains separating us from the rest of the disco, and said in a loud and drunken voice in Norwegian: "I think your music is crap!"

John asked me to translate straight away. I tried to be diplomatic as I didn't want to piss anyone off, and I thought the man was more than a little pathetic. He spoke in a dialect that wasn't native of Trondheim and was probably from one of the small villages around the town. He was wearing jeans and had a packet of tobacco in the breast pocket of his white shirt.

"The idiot is telling us he's not a fan. He seems a little upset that he was asked to leave," I said.

I could tell they knew I wasn't telling the whole truth when the silly little man started prancing around on the dance floor by our table, shouting in Norwegian, "I think your music is crap. It's rubbish! It's shite!"

He kept shouting to us as he marched back and forth on the empty dance floor.

A VICIOUS LOVE STORY

"Sod off and leave us alone!" I said to him in Norwegian, finding him rather irritating.

The man was quite drunk and would not go away. I could see John just found it amusing, but Sid was starting to get annoyed. He took his music very seriously and didn't suffer fools lightly.

The little man seemed to suddenly realise I was translating and said, "Tell them what I think of their crap music. Go on, translate to English!"

We just laughed at him, which seemed to make him even crazier. When he saw we were ignoring him, he pulled down his trousers and mooned at us while shouting in Norwegian, "This is what I think about your crap music, arseholes!"

I could feel Sid tense up beside me. He got mad. I put my hand on his arm and said, "He's just a stupid little peasant who is too drunk to know what he's doing. Not worth getting pissed off at even. I'll get Wally to sort him out."

"What the fuck is he saying, Ted?" John asked, laughing at the man standing there waving his bare bottom towards us and pointing at his own anus.

"I wouldn't have thought that needed translating, John," I answered, giggling.

Although John and Steve had been laughing at him earlier, the mooning made them suddenly take notice. They wanted to know exactly what he had said as he'd obviously made a crude remark about them. I couldn't keep making excuses for the silly man any more, so I told

A VICIOUS LOVE STORY

them. John and Steve didn't seem to take him seriously at all.

John, who was wearing a short jacket and had his hair standing on end, got up from his seat and walked slowly towards the man, shouting, "Take your ugly fucking arse out of my face and fuck off before I kick your ugly fucking teeth in!"

John is scary when he shouts at you, and the guy shuffled off, hitching his trousers up over his naked bottom, while the rest of the club laughed at him and cheered. John turned towards the other guests and made a dramatic bow, as if he had just finished a big performance, and the people clapped and cheered him.

Tore had been watching and he got up from where he was sitting, a couple of tables away, and came over to me. "What on earth is going on?" he asked in Norwegian.

"Nothing any more, I have the situation under control," I lied.

I could see he wasn't totally convinced, but went back to where he had been sitting, talking to Paul Cook, Bollocks-chops and a couple of journalists.

Everyone seemed happy. The club was filling up and the news was obviously spreading around Trondheim that the Sex Pistols were partying at the Hawk Club. It was noisy and smoky, and we had to shout at each other to be heard above the sound of the music blasting out in the disco.

Teddie (second left) with Steve Jones and Roadent at Hawk Club after party. Photo Arne S Nielsen

A VICIOUS LOVE STORY

The journalist and a photographer asked Tore if the boys would let him take some pictures before we all got too drunk, himself included. Bollocks-chops had brought some PR material with him so the photographer took a picture of Steve showing me some cards and I pretended to be a fan. We got it out of the way and Tore had a word with the media people to leave us alone after that.

A lot of people wanted autographs. They shouted to John and Sid from the chain boundary that they didn't dare cross. People in Trondheim had never before had a visit from such a famous band and seemed a little in awe, but they were very respectful. When the boys didn't acknowledge their shouts, they started calling to me instead.

Trondheim wasn't a big town and I knew many of them, so it would have been rude to ignore them. I went over to the chains and took the pieces of paper from the people who wanted autographs and the guys signed them in turn. A few minutes later, there were calls from more people who had learned the Sex Pistols were signing autographs and also wanted one, but the boys were getting bored and really just wanted to be left alone.

Bollocks-chops, Sid and Paul Cook with Teddie and Steve Jones
Photographer Arne S Nielsen.

A VICIOUS LOVE STORY

Although people had gathered in the main disco and were staring over to where we were sitting, no one ventured over the chains again. Tore ordered beers for us all, and we chatted and laughed at the evening's events. Steve kept looking at all the pretty girls on the other side of the chains and I could see that one in particular had caught his eye. When it was time for the next round of beers, I asked if we couldn't just get rid of the chains, and relax and have a good time with the people in the club. Everyone agreed, and John got up from where he was sitting and removed the chains, leaving them in a coil on the floor to one side of the dance floor.

The lights were dimmed and the disco started, and we had a good chuckle at the people who didn't see the chains on the floor in the dark and kept stumbling over them. Nobody bothered us. People were respectful and nice, and I think the guys had a good time for the short time they were in the club.

ROADENT : I remember little of the Scandinavian tour. For years I had forgotten it completely, until when being interviewed and denying ever having been to Sweden with the Pistols, I was shown the photographs. Since then recollection has come slowly. I must have been in some sort of coma to have suffered such amnesia. I do remember the fight in Trondheim, or at least that there was a fight in Trondheim.

Sid didn't mention the guy who mooned at us again. But I could see he was somewhat distracted and kept

A VICIOUS LOVE STORY

glancing around the room like he was searching for someone. I tried to see what he was looking at, but there were simply too many people around. The disco was on and the music was loud, and we settled in for an evening of fun.

Steve was the first to trot off to the bar to check out the local talent under the pretence of buying a beer. He was such a good-looking guy that it didn't take more than a few seconds before the girls were hanging around him, flirting. He simply oozed confidence. I could see what Sid meant about girls being attracted to him like flies.

My friend, Nina, is absolutely beautiful and it didn't take long for Steve to strike up a conversation with her. I remember smiling at that because his efforts would be redundant with her. She was very much in love with her boyfriend and didn't play around.

"That's a nice beer mat," John said, looking at the dirty, stained mats on the table. "I sometimes take one or two with me when I'm in Europe. I have a relative that collects them."

"Those are horrible," I replied. "Let me get some new ones from the bar, just a sec."

I made my way over to the bar, where Nina, Marith, Eva, Wenche and a few other girlfriends of mine were standing.

"Hi Teddie, what are the band like?" Marith asked me.

"They're really nice and hysterically funny. I don't know if I've got any mascara left, I've laughed so hard today," I answered cheerfully. "We've been hanging out with them all day, and Tore and I have had a great time."

A VICIOUS LOVE STORY

"Looks like you are getting on really well with that tall, punk guy," Nina teased, and she gave me a hug when she saw me blush. I never used to do that and I couldn't understand why it kept happening. I found it extremely annoying.

"Yes, I like him, he's nice. We get on really well. We just clicked straight away. God, it's hot in here," I answered, and we all laughed.

"He seems to like you too. He keeps looking at you." Nina laughed. "Look, he's doing it again now!"

I turned and looked in the direction of our table. There were too many people going back and forth for me to see if Sid was in fact looking for me or not. I wasn't really all that confidant and I thought that if he was looking in our direction, it was more likely at Nina than me.

"Steve has asked us all to come to a party later tonight at the Phoenix hotel. Don't know about that though," Nina added.

"Oh, please come. I've been the only girl all day and I miss you. They are not at all like their reputation. They are just really nice. Okay, so sometimes they do stuff that none of us ever would, but they have told me it's just for the media so they have something to write about. Please come, it will be great to have you there," I said, thrilled they were even considering it.

Out of all the people there, Marith and Nina were probably the two whom I was closest to, and we used to hang out together all the time, so for them to come was for me really great. The other girls were not close friends of mine; some I hardly knew at all, but Trondheim being a small town, we all knew of each other at least.

A pretty, blonde girl called Anne joined us. She had been standing at the bar, trying to flirt with Steve, but not having much luck. Turning around, she asked, "Who's that guy that's sitting next to you, Teddie?" She indicated Sid.

"He's the bass player," I answered absentmindedly, and I could see her looking towards our table and at Sid with interest.

I made my way back and gave John the clean beer mats. Paul had joined us and took Steve's place. Bollocks-chops had been sitting on the armrest of the bench beside Sid. He talked to us a little and then made his way towards the bar to get another beer. The disco had started and the room was dark with flashing lights. The loud music made it difficult to talk and we had to shout into each other's ears to be heard.

Sid still seemed distracted from time to time and a bit moody, and I found myself wondering what was going on in his head. He would be taking part in the conversation one minute and then looking around the room, like he was searching for someone. He suddenly excused himself and said he had to go to the men's room. We'd only been in the Hawk Club for a short while because the boys had only had one or two beers tops, and I had managed two sips.

A VICIOUS LOVE STORY

John Lydon Photo Arne S Nielsen

A VICIOUS LOVE STORY

Sid had been away from the table for only a few minutes when John suddenly jumped up mid-sentence, and ran towards the bar by the entrance to the club, closely followed by Roadent. My eyes followed them and to my horror I saw Sid standing there, bleeding heavily from his nose and his lip was split. John was by his side in an instant. I could see him quickly sum up the situation and he flew at Wally, the bouncer, who was clearly angry, red in the face and had bruised knuckles.

Bollocks-chops had been with Steve at the bar, chatting up some local girls, but I saw him react as soon as he saw John literally fly towards Sid. He got hold of John and tackled him to the floor to stop him hitting the bouncer. He held him until he calmed down. I ran over too. I got Sid some paper napkins from the barmaid. Some of his blood had dripped on to his beloved T-shirt.

"I thought he was going to fucking kill me," Sid said to me. He smiled sheepishly as he took the napkins, but was distracted by Anne helping him to hold his head backwards to try to stop the nosebleed.

I backed off towards Wally. "What the hell happened?" I asked him, angrily.

Wally told me Sid had followed the guy that mooned at us into the toilet, and that he had gone in after them to see what was going on and there was a fight.

A few more people were gathering around Sid, showing concern. Some of the girls were more concerned than others. I stood a little to the side, and Sid looked at me and tried to smile, but he was holding the napkin towards his face to stop any more blood dropping on to his T-shirt. I smiled back carefully, but I didn't want to push past the people around him, so I just left him to it.

I half expected him to make his way from the crowd towards me, but Anne was suddenly there in front of me and started talking to him. Wally was extremely angry and said Sid had to leave. The rest of us could stay, but Sid was barred. That was the second time we had been thrown out of a place that day.

It was decided that if Sid had to leave, we would all leave. Steve persuaded some of the local girls to come with us for a party at the hotel and we marched off. We walked as a group and I could see one of the girls from the Hawk Club eyeing up Sid, but he didn't seem to notice. His nose was still bleeding and he was sore, and his lip was beginning to swell where it had split. He didn't hold on to me as he had done earlier, but we all walked together, talking about what had happened and asking Sid questions.

I fell towards the back of the group, and walked with my friend Marith and another girl. I felt a little left out and it was as if Sid had totally forgotten about me. He was lapping up the attention and everyone wanted to talk to him, so I left him to it. At one point, Sid seemed to notice I wasn't at his side and he turned to look for me. I smiled at him, but didn't go to him. Steve was keeping close to Nina. The girls had been a bit sceptical to begin with, but everyone seemed to be chatting and getting on really well now.

CHAPTER 6 THE HOTEL AFTER-PARTY

We met some journalists in the hotel lobby as we entered. We ignored them, walked straight past and made our way up to the top floor where the band had their rooms. We had one guard by the elevator next to the stairs at the end of the long corridor, and one guard by the stairs on the floor below to stop people coming up to us. The walls were painted white, and the carpet was so old and worn it was hard to define what colour it was. There was a small loo beside the lift.

The boys had the top floor to themselves. The first room, as you left the elevator to the right, belonged to Roadent and Boogie, and it was straight across the corridor from Steve's. Sid and Paul had their own room a little further down the hall on the left, and furthest down to the right was John's suite. There were several more rooms on this floor, but they were locked and empty.

I was standing in the corridor with my friends Marith and Nina, and didn't know where to go to begin with as all the doors were closed. I hadn't spoken to Sid since the fight and I was unsure how to behave towards him. We had walked to the hotel as a group. Several girls had been making a point of talking to Sid and asking him if he was okay after the fight. He was the famous pop star with all the girls hanging around him and I suddenly felt very shy.

A VICIOUS LOVE STORY

Sid smiled at me from where he was standing a little further down the hall, over the head of a girl making polite conversation. I smiled back, but made no move to join him. Marith and Nina were telling me a funny story, so I just stayed to listen and tried to look busy. Marith told me she had been to the concert with a mutual friend who'd asked her out, but she decided to just leave him at the Hawk Club to come to the after-party at the hotel.

"Oh, my God, he's going to be upset," I said, laughing.

"Nah, not my problem, I had to be here to support you. We couldn't leave you alone here with all these guys. God knows what could happen," Marith said, also laughing.

"I doubt I'm in any danger," I answered, but I did get that it was meant as a joke. "Just nice to have more people around, but I've had such a blast today. I can't remember laughing so much in a long time."

"I thought you had hooked up with Sid," Nina said, looking from me to him.

"Yes, I had, but he seems a little busy at the moment." I glanced at him, talking to a few of the girls from the Hawk Club.

"Why don't you just go and grab him? He keeps staring at you, Ted, with this look like a puppy who's lost his bone. He's probably wondering what he's done wrong, poor thing." Nina laughed.

"Nah, he knows where I am if he wants to talk to me. If not, then sod it! I don't care either way," I lied, trying to act tough and cool, when in fact I was getting a little worried.

A VICIOUS LOVE STORY

I sneaked a glance at Sid talking to Anne, the girl from the Hawk Club, who was standing very close to him, and saying something into his ear as if she was sharing a secret. He seemed a little tense around her.

Tore entered the corridor from the elevator. "Hey guys!" he said, loudly, getting everyone's attention. "Can you come back with me to the lobby as there are some journalists that would like a quick interview if that's okay?"

Tore was holding the elevator door open and looking around. As John, Steve and Paul trooped passed him into the elevator, he said, "Teddie, mingle!"

As Sid passed me, he touched my shoulder lightly. His lip was a little swollen, and he had a red mark on his cheekbone and nose. I made a point of smiling to him warmly.

"Relax and get me a beer from Roadent, Teddie. They are in there," he said, pointing to the door of a room behind us. "I won't be long."

I nodded.

"You have got to come and meet Roadent and Boogie," I said to Marith and Nina. "You are going to love them."

I turned my back to Sid as he entered the elevator with the rest of the band and Tore.

Roadent and Boogie had a family size room. Entering, I saw a large double bed to my right and a sofa to my left. There was another sofa against the far wall. The room had two windows, with a view to the street below, and it was full of crate upon crate of beer. They had made a makeshift bar from the grotty table, and Roadent was resident barman for the night.

I could see two English girls sitting on the windowsill. This surprised me, as I hadn't seen them before. One was short and chubby, with short hair, and she wore a cap and a tartan jacket. The other girl was taller and slimmer, with brown, shoulder-length hair. They were ordinary looking, not the extreme punk-with-safety-pins type of girls. I don't remember their names exactly, but I'm pretty sure it was Debbie and Tracey. And, with hindsight, who else could they have been really?

ROADENT: The only two English girls I remember hanging around a lot were Debbie (Juvenile, nee Wilson, 2011 RIP) and Tracy O'Keefe, both employees of McLaren in his Kings Road clothing boutique, Seditionaries – though I don't know if they came over to Scandinavia. Debbie has disappeared. She was into some high-class prostitution last I heard, though that might be a myth. Tracey died in the early 80s (1978 RIP).

I hadn't seen these girls at the concert, so I walked over and said, "Hi, I'm Teddie. I don't think we've met. I'm the Norwegian promoter's assistant and translator. And you are?"

I sounded pretty self-important and pompous, and they smiled slyly to each other.

The taller girl, Tracy, said, "Hi, and we are the groupies."

A VICIOUS LOVE STORY

I was shocked, but with hindsight I'm guessing this was their intention and they hoped they would get rid of me quickly. Nina and Marith backed away towards the sofa, and sat down to talk to Bollocks-chops about the concert. I got the impression that the English girls were friends with Roadent and Boogie mostly. What they didn't anticipate was that I found the concept of them fascinating. I'd never knowingly met a groupie before.

Some mates of mine who played in bands would call certain girls groupies. Usually, they were just desperate girls who thought they were in love with some guy in a band. They would hang out at gigs, hoping to hook up with them and become the next girlfriend. It rarely worked, of course. I knew groupies to be quite different. They slept with as many famous band members as possible. It was simply a game where the goal was to bed as many as they could, and there were seldom any feelings involved.

The girls on the windowsill probably expected me to be put off by their comment. They were definitely not expecting it when I sat down to ask them some questions. Well, I had to make the most of it. It was probably going to be the only time I would have a groupie available for questioning.

ROADENT: No, I don't think it was Debbie or Tracey – they were friends of us all – must have been as they said, just some groupies. Not even real groupies; the only real groupie we ever had (unfortunately) was Nancy.

A VICIOUS LOVE STORY

Roadent was dishing out beers and organising the crates, etc. There was one bottle of spirit at the bar. I can't remember whether it was whiskey or brandy, but it was reserved for John. The room was quite big. The beer crates were placed alongside the wall in a tall tower and there were more under the table that formed the makeshift bar. Boogie sat to one side, on the sofa with his feet on the table. Roadent was telling Boogie and the girls about Sid getting beaten up, and they discussed what might have taken place in the men's room at the Hawk Club. I told them briefly what had happened and they laughed.

"That stupid guy that mooned us was a right tosser," Roadent said. "Seems like he got what was coming to him really."

"That is so typical of Sid. He'll get so pissed off. He'll bide his time and then he'll get his own back. Pity the bouncer got involved," said Boogie.

"I'm really annoyed with Wally. I'm not completely sure what went down in the men's room, but what could Sid possibly have done that made Wally take the idiot's side in the fight? I'm guessing Sid was beating the crap out of the tosser, and Wally simply got hold of the one that was nearest to him to get them to stop fighting," I said. "I couldn't believe how much Sid was bleeding. Scared me."

"So you're the groupies?" I asked, turning my attention to the girls who had been listening to us in silence. "I'm sorry, but I've never met anyone who calls herself a groupie before. Do the boys fund you to get to the gigs?"

It made them laugh.

A VICIOUS LOVE STORY

Roadent handed me two lukewarm beers for Sid and myself. He had opened them and I eagerly took a long sip. He gave one to Nina, who accepted, and offered one to Marith, who refused since she was driving. There were a lot of people in the room and several more standing in groups in the corridor.

"No," explained Tracey. "We work in England and all our extra cash is spent on following the band. We see it as a hobby. Some people collect stamps and we follow the Sex Pistols."

"Okay, strange hobby, but who am I to judge?" I smiled. "I presume you got a lift with them in the van from Oslo. I didn't see you earlier. Did you enjoy the concert?" I asked politely.

They seemed to find my questions tedious and annoying, but I kept smiling.

Roadent put his arm around my shoulder and said, "She's all right really, just a little nosey. She's led such a sheltered life she has to find excitement through the lives of others."

He gave me a hug and the girls seemed to relax a little. This was such a typical 'Roadent comment' that it made me laugh.

Compared to these people, my life had certainly been uneventful. After I'd gotten Roadent's stamp of approval, the girls seemed to warm to me a little.

"We got a boat to Oslo and the train to Trondheim. We were late getting in. The train didn't get here in time for the concert, so we just came here and waited for everyone," Debbie explained.

A VICIOUS LOVE STORY

"The boat takes ages. You must have a very nice boss, giving you time off from work in the middle of the week like this," I said, smiling at the girls, and hoping they would open up a little more and relax.

They looked at each other like they were trying to decide whether or not to tell me about their lives back in London.

"Yeah, we have a very understanding boss. She's a member of the manager's family, so she lets us take time off to see the Pistols play," Tracey said.

"I don't get it. Do you work for the band?" I was confused now and regretting not doing a little background reading, like Tore had asked me to.

"We work for Malcolm McLaren's wife. He's their manager and his wife has a shop on the Kings Road in London," Tracey said clearly and slowly, as if she was talking to a person of limited intelligence.

Now at the time I didn't know of Malcolm McLaren or Vivienne Westwood. I do know now that they were never married, but this is just the way they talked about them; as a married couple.

There was a call for me from the door. Sid, Steve and Paul had returned from the interview in the lobby. I think they were finding the same questions a little tedious. John, however, seemed to thrive on the attention and stayed behind, talking to them and getting his picture taken.

"Bring me that beer, Ted, and come and look at John's suite. He has a lounge," Sid called to me from the doorway, and he walked further down the corridor, not waiting to hear my answer.

A VICIOUS LOVE STORY

Steve went straight over to Nina to pick up from where he had left off flirting. I noticed Tracey shift a little uneasily, but she stayed where she was on the windowsill with Debbie. They looked at me for a little while, as if considering whether I could be trusted, and then Tracey asked, "Teddie, who's that girl talking to Steve?"

"She's called Nina and is one of my best friends," I answered, a little absentmindedly. "Why do you ask?"

"No reason. So she's Steve's squeeze for tonight then?" Debbie added, laughing, as if it was a joke, but I was starting to get a vibe that there was some other reason behind their questions.

"No, I don't think Steve will have any luck there. Nina has a boyfriend and they are very much in love. It's serious and she would never betray him, so if Steve is flirting I can guarantee you she is only talking to him to be polite."

The two girls both nodded and seemed pleased with my answer. They seemed relieved when I got up to leave. I looked back one last time as I exited the room and they had their heads together, talking intently, glancing in my direction as I left. There was definitely something fishy about those two groupies.

As I entered the corridor I found myself with a problem. Anne had clearly taken a shine to Sid and she wasn't taking no for an answer. Of course, many girls at the party were trying to flirt, but they soon gave up when Sid was polite and moved on to talk briefly to the next person, as he slowly made his way down the corridor and into John's suite, with me behind him.

A VICIOUS LOVE STORY

Anne was really aggressive and doing some heavy flirting. She followed him down the corridor and interrupted his conversations with other people, and I could see he was getting a little stressed by her. She wanted to examine his sore nose and split lip, and kept pushing up against him. She even touched his sore lip and I saw Sid step back from her, but she wouldn't leave him alone.

MARITH (close friend to Teddie): What I remember best from that after-party was Anne trying her hardest to get with Sid Vicious and him doing his best to get away from her. She wouldn't leave him alone and followed him wherever he went. She wasn't going to give up without a fight. And she simply ignored the fact that he wasn't interested. He looked like he was scared stiff of her.

Anne was a couple of years older than me, and I had always thought her very pretty. She was a regular at the Hawk Club and popular with the boys. I knew she had a boyfriend, whom she had left at the club when they wouldn't allow any Norwegian guys to come back to the hotel, except Tore. I was surprised her boyfriend had let her go.

Sid was sitting in the only chair in John's suite. I handed him his beer and went to sit on the sofa with John, who had just returned from the lobby, and Anne. She wore a white boiler suit, with a broad belt tied tightly around her small waist. She had opened up the zip at the front and, although we didn't have push-up bras back then in the late 70s, she had her boobs right up and on display, so she looked like she was trying to smuggle two bald guys into the party. Her boobs weren't that big, but they were up there, almost under her chin.

We were in the sitting room of the suite, and it was small and dingy, with a wall-to-wall carpet marked by time and cigarette burns. The sofa stood towards the far wall and there were two windows, which opened on to the market square below. In front of the window there was a huge TV on a small table.

Roadent entered the room carrying a cassette player. He plugged it in and put it on a shelf over the sofa. He took a worn cassette from his trouser pocket, put it into the player and turned it on. I was astonished to hear ABBA blast out loudly. *SOS* filled the room and no one said anything, apart from singing along happily.

ROADENT: I used to play ABBA before the Pistols took to the stage. It used to annoy all the little Scandinavian punks so.

First I thought it was a joke and that John would grab the cassette and throw it at Roadent, but he didn't. Everyone seemed to love it and they sang along at the top of their voices. They only had one cassette, *ABBA Greatest Hits*, and they played it over and over.

"Sid and I used to do some busking in London before we started the band, and we would play ABBA," John said. "Sid would play the tambourine and people would come over to us and offer to pay if we shut up."

That made me laugh, and Sid confirmed it. "We had to make money somehow. We were living in a squat and had no money for food. One guy gave us a fiver to shut up," he said.

Anne was staring intently at Sid. She made comments in broken English about how she thought he looked so good in his 501s.

Sid just said, "Thanks", and continued talking about life back in England.

"A whole fiver?" I asked, laughing.

"Yeah, we could live for days on a fiver, couldn't we, John?"

John nodded and I suddenly realised they were actually being serious.

"I love ABBA," he said. "I went to a concert with them earlier this year in London. I went with Casino Steel and Lemmy. He's in Motorhead."

I shook my head again, as I didn't know Casino and I had never heard of Motorhead.

"Ted, you really should get out more," Sid laughed."She has no fucking idea, John."

"Yeah, you've been in Norway for too long," John added, laughing.

Sid did not motion for me to sit with him, nor did he treat me any differently to the other people in the room apart from giving me a warm smile from time to time, as if we shared a secret. I could see Anne pick up on the connection between Sid and I, and I could tell she didn't

A VICIOUS LOVE STORY

like it. She would hog the conversation and try to exclude me. I caught myself wondering whether Sid could see how insecure this made me feel. I wanted him to do something so that Anne would realise he wasn't available and give up. I couldn't make up my mind whether he had no grasp of the situation, whether he was testing me to see how I would react, or if he just found Anne's attention nice.

I decided the best thing to do was simply let nature take its course. If Sid wanted to be with Anne, or anyone else for that matter, then nothing I could do was going to change that. I must admit it did look as if he was simply being polite to her. He answered her questions and he moved away when she got too close, but he wasn't paying me a lot of attention either.

I decided to remove myself from the situation and let them get on with it. It would be easier for Sid to do whatever he wanted if I wasn't there. We hadn't promised each other anything and I felt he was free to hook up with someone else if he preferred. I got up from the sofa without saying anything. I stroked his face carefully as I passed him, and he smiled up at me, and then I left the room and went to look for Roadent.

There were quite a few people in Roadent and Boogie's room by now. I sat down on the sofa next to Roadent and sighed. His sense of humour was wasted on me now. Debbie was still there and much more willing to chat, now that she'd had a little beer or two. There was no sign of Tracey. When I asked about her, I was told she'd "gone out". I instantly knew I was being lied to about something, but I didn't really care. I made conversation with Debbie and found she was actually a really sweet girl when she let her guard down.

I'd been in the room for a few minutes when I saw Sid in the corridor. He glanced into the room, but didn't enter, and then went back to John's suite, which I found odd. I waited for 10 minutes and decided I'd given Anne enough time to make her move. I sneaked out into the corridor and peeked carefully through the door to the suite. My plan was to leave if Anne had succeeded in her blatant pursuit of Sid.

PETER GRAVELLE: I can't remember the first time I met Sid. It might have been 'out' in London. In the beginning there were these bars and clubs that people went to. There was The 100 Club; The Nashville was another place in West Kensington. It was a big pub that had a stage and they put bands on. I think I saw The Damned down there first of all. Basically, there were places that people played around the giggy circuit. But there was no real meeting place.

I think the only real meeting place was when The Roxy opened in Covent Garden. It opened in two phases. The first phase was for about three months only. That's when Andrew Czezowski and Barry Jones were involved. They got fed up because it was basically owned by a band of East End gangsters. It had been a gay bar before that and they took it over for certain nights. Then I think these people saw that the revenues had shot up and that there was something in this. When Barry and Andrew left, they found somebody

A VICIOUS LOVE STORY

else to take it over and run the place. But by then it had become the punk scene's place to be. I'd say it only lasted about three to six months. I'm not sure about the time span on that. But six months at the very most that club ran for.

It was a place to go every night. And if you look at the club listings you will find Siouxsie and The Banshees, followed by Generation X, followed by Chelsea, followed by Eater. All these bands went on to have success and do well. Then The Heartbreakers came over and they would have this regular weekend residency there. The Clash played there a couple of times. The Sex Pistols never played because the Pistols weren't allowed to play in England, which has all been proved to be false anyway. But they would hang out there all the time. Barry Jones' flat in Maida Vale is where I think I met Sid and got to talk to him the first time.

Sid and Anne were sitting next to each other on the sofa, but it didn't look like he was letting her get any closer. He looked bored. John was sitting in the chair with his back towards the door. Sid saw me straight away. I thought I hadn't given it enough time, and was just about to go back to the other room when he signalled for me to come over and sit on the armrest of the sofa beside him. Anne was still trying to flirt, but she certainly wasn't succeeding.

"Where have you been?" he asked as I sat down, and he sounded annoyed.

A VICIOUS LOVE STORY

"Here and there," I answered, casually, feeling just as angry. I was peeved with him for not taking control of the situation. "I was talking to the groupie in Boogie's room. Have you seen them?"

He looked surprised and started to say something, but then just nodded. "You've been gone ages. I thought you'd left," he said, without looking at me.

"It's only been ten minutes, Sid. Anyway, I wouldn't leave without telling you first."

Suddenly, Sid seemed to have had enough of Anne's constant flirting. He asked her politely to move over, which she completely ignored, pretending not to understand what he said. When I translated, she simply shrugged her shoulders, but didn't move an inch. Sid asked again, and again she refused to move, so he pushed her gently. She misunderstood the gesture and pushed him back, giggling. So he asked her one more time and said he was serious. She moved about five inches and laughed when he moved in the same direction. So, when he then pushed her all the way to the other end of the sofa, she willingly let it happen.

However her smile froze when Sid pulled me down from the armrest beside him and put his arm around me, said, "That's better," and gave me a long kiss.

I could feel his sore lips on mine and he flinched. "We don't have to kiss if it hurts," I said quietly, whereby he pulled me closer and said, "Shut up."

We kissed again, and this time I didn't think he was going to stop. If you are reading this and wondering what it was like kissing Sid, the answer is that he had very soft

A VICIOUS LOVE STORY

lips and it was very nice. Finally, Anne seemed to get the message and got up.

"Thank fuck for that," Sid said, laughing as she walked out of the door. I'm pretty sure she heard his remark.

"I thought she was going to eat me alive. Why didn't you do something? Why did you just fuck off and leave me here?" He sounded annoyed.

"I wasn't sure whether you wanted me to do anything. I was waiting for you to make it clear you weren't interested. When you didn't, I thought I'd leave you to it. You could just have left her and come to find me," I answered.

"I did, but you looked busy, talking to those guys, and I was trying to be polite. I was wondering why you didn't come over to the chair and sit with me. I was waiting for ages for you to join me, and I couldn't understand why you just left. I thought maybe you'd changed your mind about me after the fight," he said.

"What guys? I was talking to everyone, but Debbie mainly. I didn't change my mind, and I was worried about you when I saw how badly you were bleeding."

"I didn't think you gave a toss," he added.

"There were so many people who were concerned about you. I couldn't get close enough to tell you I cared. There are so many pretty girls here and they all seem to like you, so I thought I'd just take myself out of the equation and leave you to do what you want," I explained.

"And I was worried you didn't like me any more and that I'd misunderstood you when we hooked up earlier. I thought you didn't want to be with me after the fight. I felt stupid, Ted."

"You are not stupid, far from it, but you need to keep me a little closer because I don't always understand what it is you want."

"I thought I made it very clear what I want," said Sid. "You've got absolutely nothing to worry about with those girls. I'm not interested. They don't know me. They just want to fuck someone in the band. It's pointless."

We sat together on the sofa in John's suite, talking and laughing. Sid was very attentive and kept close. Even if I went off to talk to some of the girls I knew, he would come and get me after a few minutes.

EILEEN POLK (DeeDee Ramone's ex girlfriend, and friend to Sid and Nancy in New York) : I spent enough time with Sid to know that when people were bothering him, or girls were trying to come on to him to put a notch in their belt, Sid would be standoffish. You probably did the one thing that sparked his interest, by ignoring him a bit. John Lydon was like that too; he'd rather talk to the punk fans or street people, or hit on some chick who didn't even know who he was, than be with a groupie.

It was getting late. Steve joined us in John's suite. My beautiful friend, Nina, who he'd been pursuing, told him she was flattered, but not interested and she'd left. Steve sat down beside Sid and me on the sofa. I sat in the middle, between them, and Sid had his arm around me.

A VICIOUS LOVE STORY

John was standing by the door, talking to a group, but most of the people were in Roadent and Boogie's room where the beer was.

"So, do you ever get back to England?" Sid asked.

"Yeah, occasionally, I've been back once since we moved here. I miss England, so definitely thinking of visiting soon," I answered, vaguely.

"So let's say, if you came to London, where would you go?" Sid asked.

"I don't know. I've never been to London before. A West End hotel, I imagine. Isn't that where people stay? Why do you ask?"

Sid kissed me again and then said, "Because I would be very glad to see you if you came, so if you come, would you like to look me up?"

"Of course you can show me London. I would love that," I answered happily. I remember thinking it would never happen as trips to England usually meant being in Yorkshire with my family.

"You could stay with me if you like," Sid said. "I want to see you again."

Much as I would have loved to visit Sid in London, I seriously doubted my parents would ever let me stay with a punk rocker. I wasn't taking him seriously and just thought it was the usual polite remarks to look him up should I be in the same city.

"I have another week on tour and then I go back to London. So any time after next week would be a good time for you to come," he added.

A VICIOUS LOVE STORY

"Oh," I answered in surprise. "You really want me to come? Seriously?"

"I wouldn't be asking you if I didn't want you to come. What would be the point of that?" he asked, and chuckled. "I want to see you again. I want you to come and see me in London. You can stay with me and we'll have some fun. I think it would be good for you to get out of this place. It's a dump."

We both laughed.

"Sid, can you get me a packet of fags from my room and pick up some beers from Roadent on the way back?" Steve suddenly asked.

Sid and John's eyes met in a flash across the room, and I could feel the tension building.

"Go and get your fags yourself, Steve," Sid answered.

"Seriously, mate, I'm knackered and my back's hurting," Steve pleaded.

I decided to intervene and asked, "What did your last slave die of, Steve? I'll do it, just tell me where they are."

It was meant as a joke, but no one seemed to think it was funny. There was a battle of wills going on about issues I was completely unaware of. John didn't say anything, yet I could see he was no longer listening to anything but the conversation between Sid and Steve.

"No, Ted. It's not that I don't trust you, but my fags are in a bag and you wouldn't know where to look," Steve answered, politely.

He asked Sid again, "Go on mate, please. I really need some fags. Take a packet for yourself as well. You know where they are – in the blue bag.

A VICIOUS LOVE STORY

Sid thought about it for a few seconds and slowly rose from the sofa, putting his almost empty beer bottle on to the table. "Okay, Steve. I need to go to the toilet anyway," he said, making his way towards the door and out into the corridor.

I was surprised when I saw Steve then take a packet of cigarettes out of his breast pocket. He looked inside and showed them to me, and there were quite a few left. He smiled slyly at me, but I was a bit dim and didn't get it to begin with. He threw the packet on to the table beside his beer, along with a lighter.

Sid had only just left when Steve moved closer to me. He took a long sip from his beer bottle and placed it back on the table. Then he put his arm on the back of the sofa behind me, and suddenly leaned in and planted a kiss on my lips. He pushed his wet tongue into my mouth and moved it around. It was cold and tasted of beer. It took me completely by surprise, so I let it happen for a couple of seconds to be polite before I pulled back.

"Can you please not do that, Steve?" I said.

I tried to move away from him, but Steve kept coming closer. I leaned back so that he wouldn't be able to kiss me again. I was worried what Sid would do if he saw it; I didn't want to risk getting in trouble with him for something I didn't do willingly. I could see John was watching us intently, but he didn't say anything.

"You are really nice," I said, "but I'm sort of spoken for. But, hey, you know this already."

John walked over to where we were sitting to turn the cassette over for what must have been the hundredth time.

A VICIOUS LOVE STORY

It was quiet in the suite and only John, Steve and I were there; the group of people having left at the same time as Sid.

"So you prefer Sid then? I heard him asking you to stay with him in London. I'd be careful there if I were you," Steve said, indignantly. "Sid's girlfriend won't like you messing around with her boyfriend, and you should keep well away from her as she is a junkie and a total nutcase."

This was the first time I'd heard anything about a girlfriend. My heart sank. Of course, when I found someone I really liked he had to have a girlfriend. But, I definitely didn't get the impression that Sid was after a one-night stand. He didn't seem to be messing around either, quite the opposite in fact. He had made a great effort to get to know me. I didn't see the point of him doing that if he just wanted a quick shag. There were plenty of other girls at the party who would happily oblige. I was confused.

"Tell her, John," Steve shouted above the sound of ABBA. "Isn't it true, Sid has a girlfriend? I was just telling Teddie not to get too involved with Sid, as she's an evil, crazy person."

John looked at me like he didn't know what was going on, when in fact I knew he'd been listening to everything. "Yeah, Sid's girlfriend's called Nancy. She's a total maniac. Keep well away from her," he answered.

NEON LEON (Friend to Sid and Nancy in New York) : I knew Nancy (Spungen) from Philadelphia. She was one of my girlfriend, Honi O Rourke's best

friends. There were these girls that you would call the super groupies of Philadelphia. Nancy and Honi and Tori Hamilton. These girls knew Rod Stewart and the Faces. They knew Aerosmith and they knew The New York Dolls. They knew everybody. The scene in Philadelpia wasn't punk. It was more like Rolling Stones kind of music. Nancy wasn't living at the Chelsea Hotel at first in New York. She was living on 23rd street. She said once that she was going to go and marry Johnny Thunders or Jerry Nolan and going to England. We thought that was great. She left and we didn't hear from her.

We would always buy Melody Maker and the English rock papers and we saw her in one with Sid. We thought it was cool. She didn't get Johnny Thunders and her second choice was Jerry Nolan.

Everybody thinks she went to England to hook up with Jerry Nolan. No, she didn't. She was in love with Johnny Thunders. She was really, really into him.

She would bribe people with guitars and stuff to talk to her. She was lonely, actually. She was very clever and very manipulative, but in the beginning it wasn't in a bad way. London really fucked her up. She got in to the hard drug thing heavily. When she left for England she looked good and healthy and quite glamorous and if she wanted something she knew how to get it.

A VICIOUS LOVE STORY

Neon Leon Photo Aigars Lapsa ©

It was at this point that Sid re-entered the room. No one spoke and, apart from ABBA, everything went quiet. I could see Sid pick up on the fact that the atmosphere had changed while he had been gone. He looked at us all and asked, "What?"

"Go on, Teddie, ask him," Steve said, smugly.

"Ask me what?" Sid replied.

A VICIOUS LOVE STORY

"Who's Nancy?" I asked, getting a little annoyed.

Sid's face turned pink and I saw him send a hateful look in Steve's direction.

"She's my missus, my girlfriend," he answered jovially.

I had half-expected him to deny everything and that comment simply pissed me off. I had spent the best part of the day flirting with Sid and he'd made an awful lot of effort to get close to me. I suddenly thought that all this time he'd just been leading me on, and I couldn't work out why.

What was the point of it all? He hadn't pestered me for sex, or been anything other than sweet and attentive, and I was sure he was falling for me in the same way I was falling for him, so I didn't understand. Why make such a big effort to get me to come to London when he was already seeing someone? Had he planned to see me in secret or was he just full of bollocks? I didn't get it. I was confused again and pretty angry.

"So what do you think you are doing with me then, peeling potatoes? " I asked angrily.

Everyone laughed at my comment, even Sid. He threw Steve's cigarettes on the table in front of him and placed new beers for each of us on the table. He squeezed down on to the sofa, pushing roughly in between Steve and I, like he felt he needed to place himself between us.

Sid suddenly understood what had happened. "Fuck you," he said in Steve's direction.

He turned his back towards Steve, and then took my hand and kissed it. I reluctantly let him, but I was fuming inside. I felt so silly. I knew I shouldn't have let Sid get so close to me. I knew it was stupid to fall in love with someone I knew so little about, that it could never come to anything. But I had fallen in love the way only a teenager can, totally and completely, and it was too late to change that, girlfriend or no girlfriend. I had been so sure Sid felt the same way, but there was no way I was going to let him kiss me again if he had a girlfriend. I wasn't a one-night stand for anyone and it infuriated me that he obviously thought I was.

"It's not that kind of a relationship. It's not exclusive. We can see other people if we want to," he explained.

"Well good for you, but that's not an option with me, "I said, indignantly. "I don't share. If it's a casual shag you're after, then you chose the wrong girl. I could never have an open relationship and I can't be here with you if you already have a girlfriend."

I started to get up, but Sid held me back, pulling me down on to the sofa again. John and Steve sat quietly drinking their beers, and listening to us. I could hear the anger in Sid's voice when he talked about his girlfriend.

"Don't go. Let me explain. We haven't been seeing each other for long. She treats me like crap. I am seriously thinking about what to do. Just before we came on tour, we had a big fight. I'd been out one night and when I got home in the morning she was still in bed, and there was a guy in the bathroom. She said he'd only come to use the bath, but I knew she was lying and that he'd stayed the night. He was so fucking smug. She has no respect for me at all. She fucked him in my bed, for God's sake. She didn't even have the decency to take him somewhere else." He was clearly agitated.

"I don't give a rat's arse who she fucks – just don't bring the sods back to the place I have to sleep. It's my fucking place, not hers."

Sid told me he hated this particular guy, and Nancy knew it. They'd had a fight earlier, before he met her, and he thought she found some weird satisfaction in sleeping with this guy in Sid's bed.

"I couldn't live like that. Where's the loyalty? When you're with someone in a relationship you are meant to be a team, and support each other and love each other. When you love someone you don't want to be with anyone else. I could never have an open relationship and I can't be with you if you are already with someone," I said sadly, and got up from where I was sitting.

Sid tried to hold me back again by grabbing my arm tightly, but I shrugged his hand off roughly. I could see Steve and John watching us. I grabbed my beer bottle and left the room, fuming like an Aberdeen Angus.

"Nice one, Steve. Now go after her, Sid," I heard John say as I left the room.

I felt so stupid. Why had I let him get so close to me? I went to Boogie and Roadent's room, where there were a lot of people, including Tore.

"Hey you," Tore called to me. "About time you went home, it's getting late."

I told him I would go as soon as I finished my beer. I sat down between Paul and Boogie on the sofa. Paul was a really nice, decent guy. We talked about life in England and what he'd been doing before they went on tour.

It only took a couple of minutes or so before Sid also entered the room. He lingered in the doorway first, as if assessing the situation, and then he sat down on the other sofa to my right. I could see a couple of the local girls looking at him with interest. He didn't look at me, but busied himself in conversation with a few of the girls.

Paul seemed surprised and asked, "Hey what's happened with you and Sid? I thought you two were getting on really well?"

"Yes we were, but he failed to mention his girlfriend. Steve just told me," I answered quietly, giving him a short account of what had gone down a few minutes earlier in John's suite. Both Paul and Boogie laughed.

I could see Sid looking at Paul and me when he didn't think we were looking. I hated the whole situation. I was so angry. They would be leaving the next day, so I decided I would finish my beer and leave. Boogie was sitting on the other side of me and had been listening to what we were talking about.

"Ah, yes, Nancy, but I don't think that's a proper relationship, as such," Boogie said, quietly. "I think it's more a case of convenient shagging when they both feel like it."

"Well, I got the impression they are living together in some sort of squat," I answered, quietly.

Boogie thought about it for a moment and Roadent leaned in to listen to our conversation. Boogie quickly filled Roadent in on what had I told them happened in

A VICIOUS LOVE STORY

John's suite earlier, and he laughed too. I wasn't sure if Sid getting caught out by not telling me about Nancy or Steve coming on to me was the amusing point of the story. With hindsight, it was probably the latter.

"He's not squatting any more. If he's living with her, it must have happened recently, because he certainly wasn't a couple of weeks ago. I helped him move and it was just him, not her. It's probably more a question of her staying over, if you get my drift. She's a total nutcase and I can't for the life of me see the attraction. Dreadful person. I have to say, keeping well away from her is a good plan, Teddie," Roadent added.

PETER GRAVELLE: We all basically lived in Maida Vale. Sid didn't live in Maida Vale, but he did soon after joining the Sex Pistols. Maida Vale used to be known as the place to keep all the prostitutes for the West End. It was still a nice area, but there were a lot of empty houses so people squatted. There was a mixture of people there, which was quite good. And because of where Maida Vale was situated, it was just one short bus ride and you were at Marble Arch. So a lot of people lived there. Sid had moved into an apartment, not very far from us.

So basically, after the club ended, everyone used to end up back in Barry Jones' (guitarist for The London Cowboys and Johnny Thunders, and co-owner of The Roxy club in Covent Garden) house. He had a bigger apartment than the rest of us. He was in the basement, so we could play music loud and do whatever kids get

A VICIOUS LOVE STORY

up to. So that's where we used to hang out mostly. Sid then moved down the road. Malcolm McLaren got him a mews place in Pindock Mews, and I lived in Elgin Mews, which was nearer the Tube station. Five minutes walking, ten at the very most, and you were at another mate's house.

The four of us had our heads together. I was drinking more quickly now and decided it didn't really matter what sort of relationship Sid was having. As long as there was a relationship, I wasn't interested. I glanced over to the other side of the room, where Sid was sitting. One of the girls was talking to him intently, but I could see him keeping his eyes on us. When he caught me looking, he smiled.

I quickly turned away and started talking to Boogie about beer brands in Norway. I told him every area had its own brewery, like the UK. The maternity hospital in Trondheim was actually named after the local brewery, EC Dahl. I don't think Boogie or Paul thought my topic of conversation very fascinating, but they listened politely and asked questions.

Boogie, Paul, Roadent and I probably looked like we were conspiring, and Sid suddenly got up from where he had been sitting. The girl he had been talking to seemed surprised as she was stopped mid-sentence. I heard him apologise before he crossed the room.

Sid put his hand on my shoulder and said, "We need to talk."

A VICIOUS LOVE STORY

"No point," I answered, "there's nothing more to say. I'm pissed off with you and you probably don't want to listen to the abuse I want to throw at you. I'm going home soon."

He looked sad, and Boogie said, "Oh come on, Ted, listening to him won't do you any harm."

I sighed, but got up, and we both left the room together. There was no one standing in the corridor, so I stopped there. I didn't say anything, just waited for him to speak. He put his hand on my shoulder, and when I didn't remove it he put both of his arms around my neck and placed his forehead against mine. We stood like this for a few seconds before he pulled away, so that I could see his face.

"It's a crap relationship. I have been thinking seriously about what I want to do. We fight all the time and it's tiring, and I don't want to do it any more. I really don't want to argue with you about her and I don't want you to leave, and I can't stand it when you are cold towards me."

I stood there quietly for a minute or so, thinking about what he'd just said. I didn't feel there was much point to all this anyway. He was leaving the next day and I'd probably never see him again. He sighed and kissed me. The door to Boogie and Roadent's room opened a little and closed again quickly. I managed to catch a glimpse of the two girls Sid had been talking to earlier. I pulled away.

"I don't understand why you would be so eager for me to come to see you in London when you already have a girlfriend," I said, irritably. "Had you planned on hiding me from her? Maybe meet up with me in some sleazy

A VICIOUS LOVE STORY

hotel? Can't you see what you are making this into? What you are making me into by doing this?"

He stood quietly, holding on to me, and kissing the top of my head and face as I spoke.

"Yes, and I'm sorry. I hadn't planned on meeting anyone. We had the huge argument before I left and I decided I just needed some space to think. I hadn't really thought about her at all when we were in Sweden, and then I met you and I got a bit carried away. I wouldn't have asked you to come to London if I didn't mean it and I wouldn't hide you. She wouldn't give a shit if she saw us together. It's none of her fucking business anyway. I meant it when I said you can stay with me. I want you to come. I'm serious. I want to see you again," he said, quietly.

"Okay, so let's say I come over to London to see you, I won't come unless you are free to see me. I don't share. How would it work?" I asked, trying to be practical.

"I don't know yet," he said." She couldn't care less if I saw you."

"I'm guessing she would care if she thought it was more than a fling. But you need to free yourself, so you can see me, Sid. I won't come if you have a girlfriend, you can't have it both ways. Get rid of her."

"I know. I will," he answered, and seemed a lot happier.

He smiled and hugged me. We went back to Boogie and Roadent's room, where the two girls once again made room for Sid on the sofa. He was holding my hand. He thanked the girls for moving over, sat down and pulled me down on his knee. I caught Tore giving me a disdainful look, which I chose to ignore. Boogie smiled at me and I winked back. The two girls were really nice and if they were in any way disappointed that Sid obviously wasn't interested or available, they didn't show it.

CHAPTER 7 SEX AND DRUGS, AND ROCK AND ROLL

After a while, Sid and I decided to look for John, so we went back to his suite further down the corridor. There were a few people in there, sat in groups, talking. I think the main reason most people wanted to be in Roadent and Boogie's room, apart from all the booze obviously, was to get away from the dreadful ABBA cassette, which was replayed constantly and at full volume. The song *I Do, I Do, I Do* was blasting loudly. Funny, but I actually liked ABBA until that night.

Sid and I were back on track, talking, laughing and kissing on the sofa. We were totally wrapped up in each other and I was beginning to worry about where this was leading. I was falling for him hard, and I shouldn't as they would leave the following day. But just then all I wanted to think about was the present, not the future.

"So how soon can you get to London, do you think?" he asked me again.

"Ah, I really don't know," I answered, realising now how serious he was about it. "I can try to get over as soon as I work out what I'm going to tell my parents. I doubt they will agree to me coming to visit you, so I need to work out a plausible story to get them to agree to me going."

"Yeah, I keep forgetting that you are so young," he said, with a chuckle. "But promise me you'll come."

"I promise," I nodded, in agreement.

At some point later, Tracey appeared. She stood in the doorway of the suite, but didn't come in. She kind of hovered there, trying to get Sid's attention. Then she waved at him, indicating she wanted to talk to him.

He didn't get up, but just said, "Not now, come back later."

She seemed wary of entering the room. I got the impression she was wary of John somehow, but I couldn't put my finger on it. It was like she wasn't allowed in and waited at the door instead. She went away, but it wasn't long before she came back with the same question. "Sid, can you come?"

He would say, "No go away, come back later."

I found myself wishing she would sod off and never some back. I wondered what she wanted, this self-confessed groupie who seemed to have urgent business with Sid. And again she came back. This time she beckoned him over to the door.

"You really need to come. The guy has been waiting for a long time and I don't think I can make him wait any more. He's threatening to leave now."

"I have to go for five minutes. Don't go anywhere, I'll be right back, "Sid called to me from the doorway.

I watched him leave with Tracey and I glanced at my watch, thinking that if he didn't come back soon I would certainly go looking for him. I chatted to John and felt foolish. He told me how he felt the world in which we lived was false. He said he hated how people would respect a head of state or leader without questioning their actual abilities as leaders. He was bending my ear about how the Pistols were a symbol of people who could think for themselves and people who questioned the value of traditions. I got bored.

I had no strong opinions on the state of the world at the time. Norway was a great place to live. We weren't weighed down by unemployment, like the UK. Life was good and John's opinions fell on deaf ears. I had the feeling he was feeding me a script, something he'd rehearsed. It was the same feeling I'd had earlier, when they told me about the busking and the guy giving them a fiver to shut up. All I could think about was when Sid would come back. I looked at my watch again and saw that 10 minutes had passed since he left. I politely excused myself and went to look for him.

I'd looked everywhere except in Sid's room. I was afraid of what I would find in there, because not only could I not find him, but I couldn't find Tracey either. In those days, hotel rooms had ordinary, metal keys. I went to find a friend I could trust. I looked for Tore, but he had left.

I saw a guy in the corridor, who I knew vaguely from the Hawk Club, called Stein. He had been at the concert and turned up at the hotel after-party quite late. I believe he was a friend of the bouncer who guarded the stairs, and that was probably why he and his friend had been let in to the party. He was dark and stocky, and smiled at me as soon as I entered the corridor.

"Can you do me a huge favour?" I asked him sweetly, and he nodded. "Sid has disappeared with the English groupie and I need to find out what that is about. I've looked everywhere except his room and I'm afraid to look there on my own. Will you come with me for moral support?"

Stein agreed straight away. He'd been talking to his friend, but he came with me towards the door to the room Sid shared with Paul. I was very nervous now. Although I had a gut feeling that there wouldn't be anything going on between Sid and Tracey, I couldn't be completely sure. He had been gone for about 15 minutes now, and it was with dread that Stein and I opened his unlocked bedroom door, and peeked inside.

ROADENT: Back in the beginning, punk wasn't just about the bands. It was about the people around the bands as well that were important. It was about people like Debbie (Juvenile nee Wilson) and Tracey (O'Keefe) of the Bromley Contingent, and you can include me on that too. It was a scene, to use a hippy word, rather than just bands. There was some continuity. There was some cohesion to it, so it was more than just bands. All those years blur. There was an awful lot of amphetamine sulphate being taken. There was this guy who wrote for *Sounds***, Pete Silverton, that I met about 10 years ago and he was shocked to see me. He was convinced that if anybody was going to die through overindulgence, it was going to be me. He thought I was a ghost.**

A VICIOUS LOVE STORY

The room was dimly lit. I could see Tracey on the double bed and she looked like she was asleep. She was fully dressed and lay on the far end of the bed. Sid was sitting on the other side, closest to the door. He had his back against the headboard. He'd tied a scarf around the top half of his right arm and was trying to inject himself with something. He looked like he was having trouble finding a vein, or having trouble holding the needle in his left hand.

We quickly backed out of the room. We'd only peeked in for a second or two, and I was shocked. I didn't know much about drugs, but I knew enough to understand that injection was serious business. Stein was just as shocked as me.

"Teddie, we didn't see that and we tell no one," he said.

I agreed, and I never did, until recently.

Suddenly, I had a lot to consider. I thought maybe it was heroin because that was the only drug I'd ever heard of that you had to inject. I hadn't noticed any track marks on Sid's arm earlier, but then again I hadn't been looking for any. It was getting very late, and most people had already left.

I'd gotten into the habit of finding Roadent whenever stuff happened that I didn't understand or that shocked me. He just had this weird insight into all things and always took me seriously, whatever it was I wanted to ask. He never ridiculed me as being young and naïve. I made my way to Roadent and Boogie's room again. The door was closed, so I knocked carefully in case they had gone to sleep.

A VICIOUS LOVE STORY

I heard Boogie shout, "Come in."

I entered slowly as the room was dimly lit. I could only see Boogie, on the sofa with a beer, at first. Come to think of it, Boogie never really moved from that spot all night, and seemed happy to chat with whoever happened to turn up and join him.

"Is it a bad time?" I asked.

He motioned for me to come in, and that was when I noticed some activity on the bed, under the sheets. Debbie was naked under the thin sheet and somewhere under there was Roadent. They were making love and didn't stop just because I came in.

ROADENT: I do hope lurid tales of me shagging, then parading naked, are not included in this 'kiss and tell' or you may get a thrashing, Teddie.

"You're still here?" Boogie asked. "I thought Tore had sent you home a long time ago."

He was right. Tore had made me promise to go home several times already, and I had said I would, but I had no intention of leaving, until now perhaps. Roadent suddenly appeared from under the sheet and indicated that I should sit on the vacant half of the bed. He never actually stopped what he was doing though. I sat down with a cigarette and took a beer from the crate on the floor.

"You won't believe this," I said, "Well, you might, since you know Sid, but I just saw him putting a fucking needle in his arm!"

A VICIOUS LOVE STORY

I was drinking the beer faster now as I felt the need to get totally wasted, although I was probably pretty drunk already.

"A needle, Roadent! Injecting drugs is serious, Roadent," I said, as if he didn't have any experience with drugs or needles.

I could see Boogie smiling at my ranting. Roadent was moving rhythmically on top of Debbie, who was panting loudly like a donkey with asthma.

"Relax, Teddie, it's not uncommon for Sid to inject recreational grade A drugs at an after-party. It's what he likes to do and what a lot of people like to do, and you should just give him a minute and all will be well."

The last word was more of a groan, than a word. Talk about multi-tasking!

"Shut up, Ted!" Debbie shouted.

So I did. I waited for them to finish and after a couple of loud groans, Roadent detached himself from Debbie. He sat up with his back against the headboard, took a long sip of my beer bottle, and then handed it back to me. I immediately gave it straight back to him and got a new one from the crate on the floor. No way was I drinking from that bottle. He thought it hilarious.

"All yours mate," he said to Boogie.

Roadent walked around the room naked, looking for his clothes. I sneaked a peek and he had ginger, hairy legs that were tanned from the summer sun. I remember being surprised as I thought people with ginger hair didn't tan well.

A VICIOUS LOVE STORY

ROADENT: I thought you said you averted your eyes. You really are a slattern revealing all. Regarding the thrashing, it now depends on how generous the description.

"No thanks, I can't be bothered at the moment," Boogie answered lazily, and smiled at Debbie on the bed.

"Well, I suggest you make the most of it because I might not be bothered later," Debbie answered indignantly. Boogie didn't seem to care.

"Are you okay?" I asked Debbie.

"Yeah, I'm fine. Roadent tips us off about gigs and lets us stay in his room, so I let him have some. It's a mutual arrangement."

She smiled fondly at Roadent. I wasn't used to people blatantly making love in other people's company. I'd only had one boyfriend previously that I'd been intimate with, so I was shocked, but I didn't want them to think of me as prudish, so I pretended not to be affected.

Roadent put on a pair of shorts. "I love the name Algernon Aloysius St John. It has a certain ring to it, don't you think?"

He took the cigarette from my hand and inhaled a couple of times, looking at the glowing end and blowing on it, and then he slowly put the burning cigarette to his left arm. He held it there while it burned his flesh. I knocked it hard from his arm so it fell on to the floor, and I stood on it to stop it from burning a hole in the carpet.

"Oh well done, Ted." Boogie laughed and rolled his eyes. "You have solved the puzzle psychologists have

A VICIOUS LOVE STORY

been working on for decades about how to stop people from self-harming."

I knew he was being sarcastic, but I reacted instinctively. It was then that I noticed the crisscross of scars on Roadent's left arm. Long, deep scars, from where he'd cut himself.

"I like to burn myself – makes a change from cutting. It relieves tension and makes me actually feel something. It's a habit I've gotten into and I shall continue to do so for as long as I find it comforting," he said.

Roadent's earlier comment about my supposedly sheltered life had never rung more true. I seemed to have walked into a parallel universe where everything was taken to surreal excess. I wondered what had troubled Roadent so much that he found hurting himself to be comforting, or why Sid felt the need to put a needle in his arm. For me, the people I knew to do drugs were losers, the down-and-out addicts, and being a junkie was the very height of uncool.

Junkies were people who I never wanted to be associated with, and yet here I was totally besotted with a young guy who seemed so normal and intelligent, and yet had this dreadful vice that I couldn't get my head around. I had never tried any drug before. I'd barely started having a few beers at the weekend. I didn't enjoy the feeling of being drunk as I didn't like the loss of control, so I usually only had a little. I was shocked by what I had seen and at that moment I felt so young and naïve. I tried to look cool and unaffected by all this, but inside I was quite shaken.

A VICIOUS LOVE STORY

I didn't want to see Roadent hurt himself again or smell his burning flesh, so I went to John's suite. Sid was there and I noticed a shift in his personality. He didn't seem to mind that I had been away from him. A few minutes earlier he'd wanted nothing more than to sit close to me, talking and kissing, but now he couldn't sit still. He was hyper.

Sid suddenly thought it would be a great idea to throw the TV out of the window. He tried to get the electric cable out from the wall and I was afraid he would electrocute himself. Roadent was soon on hand to help. Sid couldn't lift the TV by himself so they both got hold of it together. Someone opened the window widely, which is when I started to panic. John thought it was all very funny and, as usual when Sid did something outrageous, he was there to egg him on.

I desperately tried to reason with them, saying they could kill someone on the street below.

"What are the chances anyone's standing out there at this time of night?" Roadent argued. It was about 4am.

"You can't be completely sure. I don't want to be a part of any murder," I said, dramatically, trying to make them see the gravity of what they were about to do.

"Great headline that would make – 'Band arrested for murder of innocent pedestrian, hit by flying TV'," I said to John.

He'd been giving advice on how to push the huge and heavy TV onto the windowsill, so he thought I was joking and chuckled. They finally managed to get it on to the sill, and John almost wet himself laughing when it turned out to be too big to go through the window. They put the TV back on the table.

The window was still open, and John turned and looked at me. I could see pure contempt in his eyes for daring to contradict him. Then he smiled at me, but the smile didn't reach his eyes. He turned and simply threw his empty beer bottle out of the window. We heard it crash to the ground in the market square below. Now that really pissed me off!

"You fucking wanker! You could just as easily kill someone with a flying bottle." I was virtually spitting out my words and to my knowledge that was the first time I'd ever used that expression before.

That's when John snapped. I've never seen anyone as angry before. He came towards me, hurling abuse. Who the hell did I think I was, telling him what he could or couldn't do? He was really close and in my face. Roadent nudged Sid, making him aware that we were having a serious argument, and it was getting out of hand. I wouldn't back down, as I was too angry and too drunk to be scared. Sid took hold of John and pulled him away from me. John then pushed Sid backwards, away from him.

"Back off her and leave her alone," Sid said, angrily.

"What the fuck do you care about her?" John barked back.

Sid didn't back down and stood his ground, but I could see him thinking carefully before he answered as he knew I was listening. "Just back off her, she's with me," he said, not looking at me.

A VICIOUS LOVE STORY

"We'll leave here and she will have forgotten you by Monday. She's a fucking idiot. Posh tart. It's my room. I do what I like in here. Nobody fucking tells me what to do. Not even you, Sid. You don't take her side against me. What the fuck do you care about her?" John spat out.

"She's with me, John. I care all right, so fucking leave it alone."

Sid avoided looking at me and seemed a little embarrassed that he had been forced into saying this in front of everyone. The room was silent and no one said or did anything. All their attention was on what was happening between John and Sid, and we all knew this was about as serious as it could get between them.

John was extremely angry, but when Sid said that last sentence it was like all the air went out of him and he thought better of it. He turned towards us and said, "Right, that's it. I can't be fucking bothered with idiots. Everyone get out. Go on, all of you, leave! The party is fucking over and you can thank her," he said, pointing at me.

"Fine, I'll leave. You all carry on with your stupid, childish party until you eventually hurt someone," I answered.

"John has a wicked temper, but he doesn't mean it. He'll be okay in a while," said Sid, as a way of getting me to change my mind and stay.

"Thank you for sticking up for me. I heard you say you cared," I said, teasing him a little.

"Yeah, well, I couldn't let you get hurt," he said, bashfully.

A VICIOUS LOVE STORY

"That's not what you meant," I said and prodded him in the stomach while I giggled. He laughed, took hold of me and kissed me again.

I was getting tired and I'd seen enough to last me a lifetime. Tore had almost forced me to promise I'd go home earlier, just before he left. Sid walked me down the corridor to the elevator. We waited and he went a little quiet.

"I saw you inject something," I said, as we stood close, waiting for the lift. "Was that why Tracey kept coming to talk to you, to tell you your drugs had arrived?"

He shrugged. "It's no big deal, Ted, it's just a party thing. It's not like I need it, just a little speed and it gives me a buzz."

I couldn't tell if he was still experiencing the buzz or not. I was suddenly very tired. It had been a long day. We kissed, and the lift came and went without us noticing it. After a while I felt it was time to end it.

"Goodbye. I hope you have a good trip back to Sweden."

I tried to open the elevator door, but Sid pushed it closed and kissed me again.

"Not going to Sweden tomorrow. I have a day off and we are staying here. Why don't you go home and get some sleep, and as soon as you wake up, come back to me and we can spend the day together?"

I was so pleased he wasn't leaving and wanted to see me again. "I'll come back on one condition – no drugs!"

"Okay, no drugs. I told you, I don't need them and I won't take anything," he promised.

CHAPTER 8 REVELATIONS

As I walked down to the lobby, I saw two journalists who were still there. One was clearly drunk and had a bottle of whiskey on the table in front of him. The other guy drank coffee from a thermos.

The night watchman, seated behind the reception, asked me, "What the hell is happening up there? We have had so many complaints. What are they throwing out of the window? Will you please tell them to turn the noise down?"

"I'm leaving. I've had enough. You can tell them yourself. I'm going home," I answered, and smiled at him wearily.

"There is no way I'm risking life and limb by going up there. The manager can sort it out in the morning," he said.

I saw some young boys waiting in reception and they asked me if I could get them into the party. They couldn't have been more than 13 or 14 years old. I told them to go home. I had to make a dash for it while leaving the hotel, as bottles were flying thick and fast on to the pavement, and I could hear ABBA's *Waterloo* blasting loudly from the open window on the top floor.

I started walking towards my home. It wasn't far and I was convinced my parents would be fast asleep, and that I could sneak in unnoticed. I started thinking about Sid and it made me smile. I was so happy he'd asked me to come back the following day, and I wanted to spend as much time with him as possible before he had to leave. I knew going to London to see him later would be very difficult. I couldn't imagine my mother allowing me go if she knew what I had in mind. I would have to go with a girlfriend and it would have to be a secret.

It was then, as *Waterloo* faded into a quiet whisper, that I came to the conclusion I was in so much trouble already that a little more wouldn't make much difference. I decided I should spend as much time with Sid as I could. I turned around and quickly headed back to the hotel.

When I walked in, the night watchman asked, "Are you back already? That was a short trip home.

"I've had a sudden, but dramatic change of heart," I replied, and he nodded, like he understood.

I went over to the lift and pressed the button, but nothing happened. The drunken journalist came over to me and stood swaying close to my face, between the stairs and myself. He put his hand on the elevator button so I couldn't press it. "I bet you've been out to get drugs for the boys. Why else would you go out and come back straight away?"

His stinking breath was in my face. I pulled away from him, but he grabbed my arm and then tried to grab my handbag. "Let's see what you've got in here then. I'm going to call the police unless you do us a favour," he said.

I pulled my handbag back and tried to get past him to the stairs. The sober journalist protested and asked him to calm down. He stumbled slightly.

"I'm sure the police will be very interested in what you've got in your handbag," he said again and followed me up the stairs. "I can help you though. I won't call them and get you all arrested if you get that idiot of a bulldog on the stairs to let us get into the party. It's late and there can't be many people there," he added.

His speech was slurred and he was panting as I ran faster up the stairs. I noticed the two young boys were following us, as well as the sober journalist. He didn't say anything, but held back like he was just there in case his drunken friend's strategy worked on me.

As I stepped on to the last flight of stairs, I saw the bouncer sitting in his chair, half asleep. He seemed surprised to see me and got up to stop us going any further.

"The elevator's broken," I said, as I walked past him.

"Nah, we had to turn it off, as Gunnar, who was guarding it, was tired and wanted to go home to his wife."

The bouncer let me pass, but stuck his large muscular arm out to stop the journalist from coming with me. "Is he with you?" he asked.

I shook my head. "Definitely not – none of them are," I answered, and walked the last four to five steps up to the top-floor corridor.

I was worried what I would see when I rejoined the party. There were plenty of girls there who'd jump at the chance of being with Sid, even though he said earlier that he wasn't interested. I didn't want to have the same relationship with Sid that Nancy had. If he chose to sleep with or even kiss someone else, I would be out of that hotel faster than a rat up a drainpipe. He only had one chance with me – if he blew it that was it. I would leave and he would never see me again, and I think I'd made that quite clear. I hadn't seen Anne for a few hours, so I didn't know whether she'd left.

At the top of the stairs I could see two groups of people. Closest to me were a couple of local boys, talking to Paul. One was Stein, the stocky guy with dark hair who'd helped me peek into Sid's room earlier, and he seemed a little drunk. His friend was a bit more athletic and slightly more sober looking. They were deep in conversation.

Further down the corridor, I could see Sid and Boogie talking to a pretty girl. She was flirting and showing Sid something on the back of her neck under her dark hair. Both Sid and Boogie looked at it and I could see them both laugh at something she said. I remember thinking that perhaps I should have just gone home after all, but as soon as Sid saw me, his face broke into a big smile. I smiled back.

As I made my way down the corridor, Paul stopped me and asked me to help him. Apparently, there was something he didn't understand, and he needed me to translate and explain it. I politely stopped to help out, which seemed to take forever, when all I wanted to do was go and talk to Sid.

Sid left Boogie and the girl. Passing me, he squeezed my hand before heading into the toilet at the end of the corridor. Shortly afterwards he reappeared, and went back to Boogie and the pretty girl. I could see her watching me intently while Sid was gone. I finally managed to get away from questions of Norwegian semantics and went over to

A VICIOUS LOVE STORY

Sid. I took hold of his left arm that was holding the beer and I simply wrapped it around my neck.

"Jeez I didn't think I would ever get away from there," I said.

He leaned towards me and kissed the top of my head, while talking to Boogie and the girl. As soon as he finished his sentence, he turned towards me and hugged me.

"You came back," he said, quietly into my ear.

"Yes, I came back, "I replied, "and I'm really tired. Can we go to bed?"

We kissed again and I remember thinking that we did seem to spend a lot of time locked together like this, and it was really nice.

The girl with whom Sid and Boogie had been talking said, "Damn!" in Norwegian. Sid laughed and asked me what she'd said. I told him she seemed upset that I'd come back, and it made him laugh again.

A little later, we entered the dimly lit room that Sid shared with Paul. A double bed took up most of the space, and there was a small night table on either side of it with little lamps on top. A small TV stood on a rickety table in the corner by the window, overlooking the shabby and dirty backyard, and there was a large chest of drawers beside it. Sid and Paul's luggage was there, one on top of the chest of drawers and the other on the floor.

A door led to the en-suite bathroom, and I could see a toilet and a shower with one of those plastic curtains. It was probably white at one time, but had now yellowed with time and use, and at the bottom I could see dark, mouldy stains. I made a mental note not to go anywhere near it. As in most of the rooms I had seen that night, this too had a worn and dirty carpet. The room smelled of wood polish and air freshener, mingled with something more sinister that I couldn't quite put my finger on.

I walked over to the window and looked outside while Sid busied himself with removing the worn bedspread from the bed, revealing white sheets with a grey blanket on top, tucked in tightly under the mattress. I could see the windows of the other rooms facing the backyard, but none of them were lit at this time of night, or was it morning? I looked down and saw several dustbins full of rubbish, some of which had fallen out on to the ground around them. There was a pile of cardboard boxes discarded in a corner.

I drew the dirty curtains, but left a tiny opening to let in some light. Sid had been right in his assessment of this hotel earlier that day. It was crap. We didn't need to turn any lamps on as the dim light from the window was sufficient. During the summer months, Trondheim barely gets dark at all.

There was nowhere to sit, so I kicked off my shoes and sat on one side of the bed. I was really tired and didn't know what to do. Sid kicked off his boots and sat down beside me. Apart from our brief walk together earlier, this was the first time we had been completely alone all day. I pulled my thin, white socks off and threw them on the floor. I've always hated socks. Sid laughed and did the same.

A VICIOUS LOVE STORY

We sat awkwardly beside each other on the bed with our backs against the wooden headboard. Sid put his feet towards mine and gently stoked my toes with his. We smiled warmly at each other. All of a sudden I felt shy, not knowing what to say. I took a cigarette out of the packet in my bag and we shared it while chatting about the girl I had seen him talking to a few minutes earlier.

"She came over to talk to me as soon as she saw you leave. She seemed very nice. When she saw you come back, she asked me directly if I'd like to go back to her place," he said, chuckling. "I told her I was with you and that you'd be so disappointed if I just took off."

"Bastard! Now she will tell anyone who cares to listen that you actually preferred her to me," I giggled.

"She gave me her telephone number and wants me to call her if we ever come back," he said.

"So are you planning to? Call her, I mean?"

"Yeah, I might do. She looked okay," he answered and then laughed.

"Don't you dare phone her!" I laughed. "What did you do with it?" I asked, feeling a little jealous suddenly and realising this was his intention.

Sid put out the cigarette in the ashtray and slid down so he was lying on his back with his head on the pillow. He gently pulled me down towards him and I placed my head on his chest.

"I binned it," he said and kissed the top of my head.

"I fucking hate people like her. Makes me feel like a piece of meat – like I'm the prize if she can win it. I'd barely talked to her all night. The only reason I did talk to her was because you got annoyed with me and I didn't know what else to do."

I stretched out and felt very tired. It had been a long day.

"Incredible," I said. "She must be desperate, offering herself to you like that after a two-minute chat. I actually think it is crude. I know she has a child at home. You would have been Uncle Sid tomorrow!"

We laughed and Sid ran his fingers through my hair. We kissed a little more intensely. Suddenly the door tore open and in the light from the corridor I saw Stein. He was very drunk and barged in, looking frantically around the room, his eyes not yet adjusted to the darkness. The light shone on Sid and me.

He barged over to us and pulled me off the bed by my arm, shouting, "Get out of here! I can't let you go through with this, Ted. He's a disease-infested junkie!"

"Calm down, I'm all right. I am tired and we are going to sleep," I lied, but he wouldn't let go of my arm and he was hurting me. "I'm perfectly safe, you idiot. This has nothing to do with you. What the hell do you think you are doing?" I almost started weeping.

Stein was seriously hurting my arm. I couldn't believe how easily he had managed to pull me out off the bed like a rag doll, and I was now standing in the middle of the room and he was pulling me towards the door. Sid reacted immediately and pulled at my other arm in the opposite direction, not realising he was only making matters worse.

"You fucking well let her go, you arsehole. Get out!" Sid shouted.

A VICIOUS LOVE STORY

He threatened to hit Stein if he didn't leave immediately, and he lunged forward towards him, trying to belt him and not me. I told Stein to leave too, but he was drunk and not listening to us. I managed to call out to his friend in the corridor, who came running in at once. It didn't take him more than a second or two to assess the situation and help me break free from his grip. He took a firm hold of Stein, forcing his arm behind his back, and frogmarched him out of the room, apologising for his friend's behaviour.

"Can you please keep him away from us or Sid will definitely have you both thrown out," I said angrily in Norwegian.

Stein's friend nodded and promised.

"This is a once-in-a-lifetime chance to party with the Sex Pistols and you are not going to spoil that for me, you fucking moron," he said to Stein in Norwegian, while pushing him ahead and out of the room.

"Who the hell was that?" Sid asked, after we'd shut the door firmly behind them. We suddenly realised that the key to the room was nowhere to be found, so we couldn't lock ourselves in.

"I actually have no idea. I don't really know him," I answered.

The top of my arm was smarting from where Stein had grabbed me. I knew him vaguely. The guy used to hang out with some people who frequented the Hawk Club, but I couldn't remember ever talking to him before that night. I thought his reaction to the situation was very strange.

A VICIOUS LOVE STORY

We could hear people in the corridor, talking. ABBA's *Bang-a-Boomerang* was blasting out loudly. Sid pulled off his jeans and T-shirt, and was sitting on the bed wearing only his underwear. I was rubbing the top of my arm, which was hurting, and Sid pulled me towards him so I was standing in front of him. He kissed my arm outside my shirt. Slowly, he unbuttoned my shirt, took it off and threw it on to the floor, before kissing my arm again, which was red and sore. Then we tugged off my jeans and I got into bed with him in just my underwear, and we huddled close under the sheet and blanket.

I thought it strange that the hotel used sheets and a blanket instead of the usual duvets I was used to. I felt cold, but that was more due to lack of sleep than the temperature. Sid pulled the blanket tightly around us and we started to kiss more passionately. Suddenly, we heard a thud, directly outside the bedroom door. It sounded like a fight. Stein was trying to get into the room again and his friend was clearly trying to stop him. I heard Stein cry out in pain and his friend telling him to calm down.

Sid and I chuckled, and then we kissed again even more intensely as the minutes passed. The bed was hard and looked drab. I could see cigarette burns on the blanket, and I remember hoping the blankets were washed and changed on a regular basis.

Suddenly, the door opened a few inches and then quickly shut. After a few seconds it opened again. It was Anne, wearing only a bed sheet.

"Ted, can I come in?" she asked in a drunken slur.

A VICIOUS LOVE STORY

Before I had time to answer, she half walked, half stumbled into the room, leaving the door wide open and letting in light from the corridor. Sid sighed irritably and we both sat up in bed. Anne helped herself to one of my cigarettes on the table without asking and lit it. She smoked in silence for a while.

"God, I'm so drunk," she said, as if we didn't already know that.

"I just woke up beside Steve. That was a waste of a good 15 seconds."

She blew smoke into the room, and Sid and I lit up yet another cigarette, which we shared. My throat felt dry from all the beer and smoking, and I was seriously getting sick of people coming into the room. I could see Stein hovering outside the door, looking in, and I am sure he noticed that I was not dressed any more, but he didn't try to enter.

"That's nice, Anne," Sid said, "but is there any point to this? Ted and I were having a private conversation. We're tired and we want to be alone."

"I just wanted to say I'm sorry for being such a cow earlier. I didn't know you were a couple. Steve just told me that you two had been together all day. Why didn't you say something? I would never have flirted with you had I known. Ted's a friend of mine and you don't do that to friends," she said, as a form of apology.

"But we are not a couple, Anne. Anyone can flirt as much as they like with him or me. It's not going to get them anywhere," I said.

Sid nodded and smiled in agreement.

A VICIOUS LOVE STORY

"We only just met this morning and we like each other. We're getting to know each other. It's complicated. You weren't to know, it's okay," I replied.

I must admit I was fed up with people coming and going, and it was getting really frustrating. I just wanted to accept her apology and get rid of her. It was all a load of lies anyway since she must have seen Sid with me at the Hawk Club earlier. I think, with hindsight, she was hoping I'd left and that Sid was on his own wanting company.

"Can you tell her to fuck off now, please?" Sid said after a while.

Anne made no move to leave, but continued to smoke her cigarette. I have no idea what she thought would happen, but both Sid and I were pretty frustrated by now. Sid told her to leave again and started to tickle me, which made us both laugh. We ignored her, so wrapped up in one another. Eventually, she reluctantly got up and left the room without another word, closing the door behind her. We laughed and kissed again, but the heavy padlock he wore around his neck hit me in the face.

"Can you take that off, please," I asked." It's hurting me."

He didn't want to, to begin with, so I asked him again, and he finally sat up in bed with a deep sigh. He got up and found his leather jacket on the bag on the floor. He took out a small key from his jacket pocket, reluctantly removed the heavy padlock and placed it in the palm of my hand. I couldn't believe how heavy it was and I put it on the bedside table.

A VICIOUS LOVE STORY

"I put that on the day I joined the band and I swore to myself I would never take it off again until I'd left the band. I know it sounds stupid and superstitious, but I don't know how long I'll be allowed to play with them. You better not have jinxed it and, just so you know, I wouldn't have taken that off for anyone," he said solemnly, stroking my face.

"I was born on Friday the 13th, so that zeros out any jinxes," I said. When he laughed, I added, "No, seriously."

I didn't believe in any superstitions, but I thought it very sweet though a bit childish that he told me about it, and even sweeter still that he actually took off the padlock for me.

We suddenly heard another loud noise from outside the door. It was pulled open and then sharply shut. Stein was trying to get in again. His friend was true to his word and tried desperately to stop him. He certainly seemed to have his hands full. They fought for several minutes, and then I heard his friend say, "You can't go in there. You'll get us both kicked out of here. What Teddie gets up to is none of your business. If she wants to be with Sid, she'll be with Sid."

I could hear Stein weeping and he quietly said, "But I love her."

He lay outside the door for a while, sobbing loudly, and I translated to Sid what he had said. He thought it was really funny, but I couldn't help feeling sorry for Stein. I had no idea he fancied me at all; I wasn't good at picking up on signals like that. I was tired, fed up and frustrated by all these people who wouldn't leave us alone.

A VICIOUS LOVE STORY

Sid suddenly jumped out of bed. He asked me to help him move the chest of drawers all the way across the room and put it in front of the door, to prevent anyone else from barging in. I couldn't believe how heavy it was. Sid threw the stuff that was on top of it on to the bed. We couldn't lift it and decided that shoving it along the carpet was the best way to go. As we pulled the chest away from where it stood against the wall, a cloud of dust emerged from the space behind it, making me sneeze, which made Sid laugh uncontrollably.

I told Sid to be quiet since I didn't want the sobbing guy to think we were laughing at him, and I certainly didn't want to provoke Stein into making a last attempt at getting me out of the room. I was pushing and Sid was pulling the chest towards the door, and we weren't making much headway. It was just too heavy for me. We decided we both needed to push from the same side and then we finally managed to get it standing in front of the door.

We could still hear Stein sobbing outside. I thought his behaviour very odd, as I hardly knew him. I presumed it was the alcohol talking. We jumped back under the sheets shivering, and laughed at finally being alone and not able to be disturbed.

"Thank God, finally," I said.

Sid kissed me again and pulled me closer.

"I am so glad we are alone and no one can get in. Don't you find it frustrating being stopped all the time?" I asked between kisses.

"No!" he said, sarcastically. "What the hell do you think?"

A VICIOUS LOVE STORY

He pulled me even closer and kissed me hotly.

"I swear if anyone else comes in, I am not even going to stop what I am doing because I don't think I can," Sid said breathlessly, and we finally made love.

Later in the night, the blanket had fallen to the floor. Sid pulled it back on to the bed and put it snugly around us both. We'd only slept for a couple of hours and I woke up when he pulled me closer to him. He lay on his back, relaxing and not saying a word. I felt exhausted. I had my head on his arm and snuggled close. I kissed the top of his arm, as it was the closest part of his body to me. I was warm and tired, and totally relaxed. He drew me closer still and kissed the top of my head.

"You know when I met you earlier this morning? No wait, I mean yesterday morning. I couldn't work out where I was to begin with and there you were, smiling at me," he said.

I didn't answer at first, as I had nothing to say. I was totally besotted with him, but it hadn't happened straight away. I thought he was nice, but it wasn't until later when I'd gotten to know him a little better that I noticed my feelings for him.

"Yeah, you looked a bit disorientated," I answered. "I'm glad I met you."

"I'm glad I met you too. I know I should have asked you this earlier, but do you have a boyfriend, Ted?"

"No, no boyfriend, not any more. I told you before, I have my relationships one at a time and I don't mess people around. I know you probably don't want to talk about this, but I really need to get a few things straight in my mind so I know what's what. I need to ask you some stuff straight out. Is that okay?"

"Yes, you can ask me anything you like, as long as I can ask you something back afterwards. And we both have to promise to be totally 100% honest. Go ahead," he giggled. "I'm ready."

"Are you comparing me to your girlfriend?"

He didn't answer to begin with. I knew that I shouldn't have mentioned Nancy as it only seemed to agitate him, but I felt so close to him at that moment and it was something we both needed to talk about.

He lay there quietly for a little while, as if thinking it over, and then answered me calmly, "Yeah, I suppose I am. When I first met her she looked okay, but then she put on a lot of weight very quickly. I couldn't believe how much she liked to eat," he said, laughing. "You know how sometimes at restaurants the portions are really big? Well, I'd eat as much as I felt I wanted and be really stuffed, and she would eat all hers and then finish off mine, and a couple of minutes later she'd be looking at the desert menu."

"So were you okay with the weight?" I asked.

"Yeah, it didn't really bother me," he replied.

"So what are saying? Do you prefer girls with a fuller figure?" I asked uncertainly, as I was slim.

My comment made him laugh. I didn't really want to talk about her, but I needed to find out exactly what he wanted from me, and whether he was serious about me or just saw me as an interlude before he went back to Nancy.

A VICIOUS LOVE STORY

"No, I don't. She's very different to you, Ted. She reacts to things differently, and she has fat thighs and no boobs, and it hasn't really bothered me until now." He laughed.

"Ha ha, you have to say you like me better since I'm here. Besides, you're just angry with her," I said, laughing.

"I don't have to say anything of the sort," he answered, and laughed too. "I never say anything I don't mean. What would be the fucking point of that? I had been with girls before I met her. I wasn't a virgin, only just, but she's very experienced."

"So I'm taking it you were not experienced when you met her?"

"I had sex for the first time when I was 19." He said quietly.

"Tell me about it. Who was she?" I asked.

"It wasn't a girlfriend, just with a girl I hung around with and we sort of agreed to have sex." He said. "She'd done it before, but I hadn't. She was called Mary and was Glen's girlfriend for a while. Mary told me that Glen was the first person she had sex with. He got tired of her and she used to come to talk to me about Glen. She was nice."

"How did Glen feel about you sleeping with his girlfriend?" I asked.

"I don't think he liked it much, but he never said anything. She wasn't his girlfriend at the time. Anyway Mary and I agreed to have sex and it was a totally embarrassing fuck-up. I felt useless and I didn't really know what to do. Well I knew what to do, but, anyway, Nancy is very experienced. It was good and I've learned a lot. So that part of it has been good, but she plays mind games. It's tiring, and my friends don't like her. We've had a sort of on-off relationship for a couple of months now. We've been free to see other people and to be honest I actually don't give a toss about who she fucks."

"Are you sure you're not just saying that to sound like you don't care about her?" I asked.

"No, I promised to be honest. She can fuck whoever she likes. I honestly don't care. But the fighting and the squabbling, and the whining are getting to me now, and I can't be arsed with it any more. I stupidly gave her a key to my new place, and the first thing she does is bring my worst enemy into my place and fuck him in my bed. Just goes to show what she thinks about me. She hasn't got that key any more." He started to get more agitated.

"Will you see her when you get back to London?" I asked quietly, dreading his answer.

"I don't know. I might phone her, or I might just leave it alone and not contact her. It's easier that way. I told you I'd make sure we can see each other. If not seeing her is what I have to do, then that's what I'll do, it's not a problem. Can we stop talking about her now because I get so fucking annoyed just thinking about her?"

"Yes, I noticed. I just had to ask. Sorry, we won't talk about her again if it upsets you," I answered and kissed him.

"Now it's my turn to ask a question. I only have one. I know you don't have a boyfriend, but are you seeing anyone casually or is there someone you wish you were seeing? What I want to know is, is there anyone I should be worrying about?"

"No, no one, not any more. I was seeing someone, but it didn't work out. I wouldn't be here with you if there was," I answered.

"Good," he said and kissed the top of my head.

"Is that it?" I asked, a little surprised that he didn't have anything else to ask me.

"Yeah, that's it. It's all I need to know."

"I am dreading tomorrow when you leave. I really don't want you to go," I whispered sadly.

"Me too, but we've got gigs planned in Sweden and I can't let the band down. I don't want to let them down, because I love playing with them. It's all I've ever wanted to do. But I don't want to leave you either. If I wasn't in the band I wouldn't leave. I'd stay here with you. I like Trondheim. You are right, it's nice here. People are nice."

"God, I am going to miss you so badly," I said.

"You know, you could always come with me?"

He left the question hanging.

I sat up in bed and looked him in the eyes. "What do you mean? Come with you where?"

"I want you to come with me. There's plenty of room in the van. I've been thinking about it ever since last night. I've already asked Bollocks-chops earlier and he said it was fine. I've been waiting for the right moment to ask you. We go to Sweden early tomorrow morning. I've got to go back to England for one day next week, for my court case, but it's just for one day. John will take care of you when I'm not there. You can stay with me at the hotels. Come with me, Ted."

I lay back down with my head on his chest while I thought about what he was asking me to do. There was nothing I wanted more than to spend time with him. Everything about him felt so right, but he was asking a great deal. I was a teenager, barely out of school. I still lived with my parents and I had to ask their permission for everything. I knew they would never agree to let me go to Sweden with Sid.

I was sure I could convince them that a week of shopping in London with my friend Grethe or Marith would be fine, as long as I didn't mention the drug-taking, punk rocker lover I would be staying with. But the idea of running off to Sweden with the Sex Pistols would definitely send them into a panic. Never before in my short life had I wanted to be older more desperately.

"I'd love to go with you," I answered finally. "I don't want this to end either."

"Okay, I want you to pack a bag and bring it here later. We leave early tomorrow."

I thought my heart was going to burst. I was thrilled he felt the same way I did. We connected so well on every level, but as soon as we started talking about the future my heart went cold. I'd just left school. My parents paid for everything and I hadn't bothered getting a job that summer. I'd done some modelling for various trendy shops in Trondheim, but it was more fun than work. Sometimes we didn't even get paid, but were allowed to keep some of the clothes we modelled. I hadn't applied for

A VICIOUS LOVE STORY

a place at college, as I was tired of school. I'd decided to enjoy the summer and make plans for the future when it was over.

I have to admit I was spoilt when it came to pocket money, and I knew that if I just took off for a week in Sweden with Sid I would be in serious trouble. He would go back to England, and I would have to go back to Trondheim and face my parents. There was no way they would ever let me go to England on my own after something like that.

"My parents will lay an egg if I take off. There is no way they are going to agree to it," I said. "Then you'll leave me next Saturday and I'll have to face them. It feels hopeless."

"We just need more time together and then you can come over to see me in London," he replied.

I was thinking hard. I didn't want him to leave, but I was dreading meeting the crazy, junkie girlfriend if I went to London. I was sure she wouldn't be too pleased about me being with Sid, however indifferent he thought she was.

"How would you feel about not going to London after Sweden, but coming back here with me?" I asked.

Sid was quiet for a while. I could see he was considering his options. "Where would I stay?" he asked.

"Well, to begin with, you could stay in my room at our flat. It's huge and we have plenty of room. You could make some cash at weekends, playing with other bands, until you have to go on gigs with the Pistols. Tore will fix you up, I'm sure."

A VICIOUS LOVE STORY

As soon as the words had left my mouth, I knew it would never work. My mother would never agree to have Sid in the house. I had only ever had one boyfriend and he'd never even been allowed to stay over, even though they knew him well. My family were very conservative. They wouldn't like Sid simply because of the way he looked and spoke. I was sure they'd love him if they'd only give him a chance. But there was no way they'd even let him stay the night, never mind live with us on a permanent basis.

We talked at length about our options. I think Sid was beginning to realise the complexity of the situation just as I did. If we stayed in Norway, he'd have to make enough money to get flights to the UK in order to attend gigs. Back then it was very expensive to fly. It was all looking a bit hopeless. All we wanted to do was spend some more time together and get to know each other better, but time and distance was working against us. We made love again and fell asleep, tightly wrapped together.

CHAPTER 9 FRIDAY – THE DAY OFF

    I woke up to the sound of laughter. I was alone. Sid had moved the heavy chest of drawers just enough to open the door and squeeze out. It was light, but I had no idea what time it was. I could hear voices speaking in English from outside the room, but I didn't recognise them. I dozed off again for a while and was woken up by Sid creeping back into bed, fully clothed. He was munching on something.
    "Where have you been?" I asked sleepily, as he got back in and hugged me.
    "Boogie's room. You were sleeping and I got hungry," he answered, still chewing something crunchy. "We keep some food in there in case we get hungry. It's cheaper than eating out all the time."
    We stayed in bed for a little while, just dozing and hugging, and then he seemed to get bored and sat up. On the table by the bed was a small toy, a metal motorbike, and Sid fiddled with it.
    "Nice toy, where's your teddy bear?" I asked, and he laughed.
    "Right here," he replied, indicating me.
    Then he started playing with the bike. He had two fingers on it and drove it around the little bedside table as if he were Evel Knievel on steroids, making childish "vroom" and screeching sounds to mimic the sound of the bike's engine and brakes. It made me laugh, but I realised that, although he was having fun, he was actually really playing with the bike like a big child.

A VICIOUS LOVE STORY

"A little kid just came up to me and gave this to me a few days ago."

"Why didn't you give it back? Small children don't usually give away their toys. They don't understand the concept and he probably just meant you could borrow it for a while to play with," I answered.

"He gave it to me and I kept it. It's a good toy. I like it." Sid laughed.

He kept playing with the bike on the table. I wanted him to stop and pay more attention to me, but it was like he was lost in his game.

"Put the toy away," I said and moved closer.

Sid ignored me. It was like he was waiting to see how far he could press this before I reacted. So I moved away a little, grabbed a pillow from the floor and threw it at him, making him jump and lose the toy on the dirty carpet. He laughed and took the other pillow, hitting me with it, square in the face and hard. I quickly picked up the toy from the floor and threw it into his open bag that was just by the bed so he couldn't get it any more, and flung the pillow at him again.

We laughed and had a pillow fight that he was determined to win. At one point he managed to pin me to the bed by sitting on top of me, and repeatedly walloped me with the pillow, saying I had to say I surrendered. I couldn't speak since I was laughing so much and trying to tickle him so he would stop hitting me.

One minute Sid was laughing and I was giggling, and then he suddenly became serious, threw the pillow away and started kissing me. He was wearing black jeans that were very tight and he threw his T-shirt on to the floor. I wasn't wearing anything but a sheet and we kissed again, and he took his jeans off. It was warm in the room so we'd opened a window to let in some air. A mild breeze blew in, making the curtains move a little while we started to make love again.

I suddenly heard Tore say "Hi" cheerfully to someone outside in the corridor. Then I heard my name. "Where is Teddie?" he shouted.

"We have not seen Teddie since she did a Cinderella on us last night and fled to her bed in the bosom of her family," Roadent replied happily.

I could hear someone laugh loudly at his comment and I am guessing it was Boogie.

"Well, her family haven't seen her and they are wondering if she is alive," Tore boomed.

Roadent's voice became louder as if to warn me somehow to take cover. "Well, alive or not, I have a feeling she'll turn up sooner or later. These teenagers usually do, I'm told."

Sid was still kissing me and wasn't paying much attention to what was going on outside, but I had a feeling I was in trouble with Tore and it wouldn't be long before he actually found me.

"Stop!" I whispered to Sid between kisses. "We have to stop."

I sensed Tore was getting impatient, so I pushed Sid away gently and quickly put on his T-shirt. I didn't want Tore to come in and see us in the middle of something. It wasn't because he would care at all, but I wasn't comfortable about something like that and felt making love was a private matter. First I thought Sid was just going to just sit there on the bed naked, but then he seemed to think better of it. I threw the black jeans he had only just removed a few minutes earlier towards him.

"Hurry up!" I said, and he pulled them on.

"Shit, I can hardly get the zip up," Sid said, indicating downwards towards his manhood.

We laughed and he kissed me some more.

"Damn, that's not helping either!"

He laughed again and we were both a bit breathless.

"Relax," Sid said, "he knows you are here and he knows you have stayed, so you might as well just come back to bed. Do you think he minds you being with me?"

"Why would he possibly mind?" I answered, not understanding the question.

So I slid down under the sheet again, wearing Sid's T-shirt, and lay there, waiting for Tore to find me and give me a piece of his mind.

"Now stop fucking me about, Roadent and tell me where she is," Tore said impatiently.

He didn't answer, and then I suddenly heard John's voice from the other end of the corridor. "Do we really need to answer that?"

The door to our room was suddenly flung open with force, crashing into the chest of drawers so hard that it swung back, hitting Tore in the face. He came into the room looking stern and angry, holding his hand to a sore spot on his right cheekbone.

A VICIOUS LOVE STORY

Sid sat down on the bed and I saw Tore notice his state of arousal. Sid didn't seem to care, quite the opposite; he seemed to take great pleasure in seeing how shocked and embarrassed Tore looked. It was like he became even more aroused by seeing Tore's reaction and he made no attempt to cover the bulge at the front of his jeans. Sid took a cigarette and lit it. It was as if he wanted Tore to see what we had been doing, not that there was any doubt, and I couldn't understand why.

I could see that Tore felt embarrassed. He looked at Sid with distaste when he realised what he had just barged in on, but he seemed to pull himself together and said "Hi" to him coldly, before sitting down on the bed beside me with his back to Sid. He was furious.

"I have had a not very nice phone call from Arthur, your stepfather," he said to me in Norwegian, as if I needed reminding who my stepfather was.

"He said to find you, and tell you that you are to come home and let everyone know you are alive and well. Then you can do what you like because your mother is so angry with you, you might like to give her a few hours to calm down before you meet her."

I squirmed at his heated words.

"I thought you left last night," he said. "You lied to me."

"No, I didn't lie. I did leave, and then I thought better of it and came back. And before you say anything, I'm so in love I want to puke," I answered bleakly, and it made Tore smile.

A VICIOUS LOVE STORY

I was looking towards Sid for support, but he just sat on the bed, smoking and staring straight ahead like this reprimand had nothing to do with him. Tore was talking to me in Norwegian, but I guessed Sid could work out he was very angry. Then Tore began to calm down a little. He looked around the dingy room and at Sid, who sat quietly smoking and not looking at him. We sat there like two kids who had misbehaved and were getting a telling off from a peer.

"I promised your parents I would make sure you went straight home after the concert. I'm sure they thought it was fine that you went to the after-party for a while. But this reflects really badly on me, and I want you to go home now and fix it," he said sternly.

"I promise I will go straight home, straight away in a little while, or sooner even," I said, and this made him smile again.

Tore got up, and looked at me as if I was five years old and just had a tantrum. He shook his head and sighed. As he left the room, he said to Sid, "I'll be back at fourish to take you all to the museum."

I thought I hadn't heard him correctly. What museum?

As soon as Tore left the room, Sid got up from where he was sitting and pushed the chest of drawers back towards the door. He turned towards me and asked, "Are you okay?"

I nodded.

"I am so fucking sick of people coming and going. Don't you think it's strange that they never come in here when we are talking or sleeping, but always when I really want you."

"Which is all the time, so chances are that's when it's going to be!" I said, laughing.

He removed his jeans again and got into bed with me, and we happily continued where we'd left off. It didn't take more than a couple of minutes before someone was at the door yet again.

"Sid, let me in. I need to get ready," Paul shouted.

"Go away," Sid answered breathlessly

"Come back in five minutes," I called to Paul, and Sid laughed.

"You better make that half an hour, mate," Sid called. We both laughed, but didn't stop what we were doing.

I had a shower and Sid let me use his stuff. I couldn't believe how many lotions and potions he had in his bathroom. Paul's stuff was in there too, but it was nothing in comparison. There was cleanser, moisturiser, and body lotions and haircare products that I had never heard of before. Sid had gone into the shower after me and I kept calling to ask him, "What is this for? Where do I apply this cream? Is this for the face or the body?" And he would shout instructions back to me.

Sid had skin that needed a lot of extra care. He told me he'd break out in spots if he didn't take care of it properly. McLaren had sent him to a salon to get a facial and he ended up buying all the products they recommended. He swore it worked, but I thought they saw him coming a mile off.

A VICIOUS LOVE STORY

"And having the facial is classified information, Ted. I felt like a poof, but it did the trick." Sid laughed again, but swore me to secrecy about it. I haven't shared this with anyone until now. I don't suppose it matters any more.

I giggled back. "Yeah, like I'll take out a whole page in the local rag to announce that!"

"Ah, my mouth feels like something has crawled in there and died," I called to him.

He turned off the shower and said, "You can use my toothbrush if you like. It's the blue one."

I had a look and there were two toothbrushes in the glass by the sink and they were both blue; different shades, but still blue. Sid had turned the water on again, so I put toothpaste on my finger and tried to clean my teeth as I didn't want to risk using the wrong brush. I had a feeling Paul wouldn't appreciate that and I didn't want to annoy him since I had slept in his bed. We got ready and when we left the bathroom, Paul knocked on the door again and Sid pushed the chest away so he could get in.

"Hi, Ted, we are going shopping," said Paul. "Give me a few minutes to get ready. I need to get some jeans."

The boys had been given some 501 jeans by Thor Greni, the guy who worked for Levi's in Oslo. However, he hadn't had any for Paul at the time, so he told him he could pick some up at a shop in Trondheim. Levi's 501 jeans were the thing to have and not readily available.

"I can't remember the name of the shop he told me to go to. I wrote it down and now I can't find it. Who has Levi's in Trondheim, Ted?" he asked me as he started getting fresh clothes out of his bag.

A VICIOUS LOVE STORY

"Several shops sell them. But this is a small town, so we'll find the right place. Try and remember what it sounded like," I answered.

"I've tried, but it was a Norwegian word, so I can't remember."

"Funnily enough, that actually narrows it down."

"I can't fucking believe this, but my drumsticks have gone missing again," Paul said, as he started to remove his T-shirt. "I told Roadent to keep an eye on them as the fucking fans keep stealing them, but he's managed to lose them again."

That made me laugh, and I told Sid about Roadent flogging the drumsticks the previous evening after Paul had gone into the bathroom, firmly closing and locking the door behind him.

Sid laughed. "Roadent probably has to do that with the pittance he gets paid. Honestly, Malcolm McLaren is a tight-fisted sod. I make more money poncing around in London than he pays us. He says we'll get more later, but it never happens."

I had no idea what Sid meant by that expression. I simply gathered that poncing meant he would stop people in the street and beg money from them. He had been living in a squat and needed money for food before he got the job as bassist for the Sex Pistols.

I later heard a rumour that Sid had worked as a male prostitute. I very much doubt that is true. Firstly, I didn't pick up any signals that he was bisexual. If he had any tendencies like that, I doubt Paul would have been keen to share a bed with him. I firmly believe it is just another story put out there by someone to make the caricature of Sid Vicious a little more shocking. I made love to Sid several times and he was too inexperienced in bed to have been a prostitute. Nancy had taught him to make love the way she liked and, other than that, he had no idea what he was doing. Well he did, but not like a pro. So I hope that puts that rumour to rest for good.

We were out of cigarettes again. Leaving the room, we shouted to Paul that we'd wait for him in the hotel lobby. It didn't take long before Boogie came down too, and we said "Hi" to Anne as she walked past us on her way out. She had obviously gone back to bed after we asked her to leave our room.

Paul joined us, and the four of us set off into the sunshine. There were two young boys waiting outside and I recognised them from the previous night as the ones who had begged me to get them into the party. They were called Åge and Ragnar. They hung behind us as we walked, with Ragnar taking pictures with a small camera. It didn't annoy us. We just thought they were sweet.

We crossed the market square and walked on until we came to Bruns bookshop. Some people called to us and Sid waved. Mostly, people would stop what they were doing and just stare at us. I felt uneasy about it. It was like they were scrutinising me from head to toe, wondering who I was. We entered the bookshop and looked around. I was talking to Sid one minute and the next he was gone. I couldn't see him anywhere. I called out a couple of times, but he didn't answer. Paul and Boogie were still there, so I asked them if they'd seen Sid and they said no. I looked outside and went back into the shop again.

There, behind a bookshelf, on the very lowest shelf was Sid. He was rummaging through a cardboard box full of single records. He seemed miles away, concentrating on what he was doing. Suddenly, he let out a cry of pleasure, "Finally, I've been looking for that everywhere. It's been sold out in the UK for weeks."

"Didn't you hear me calling you?" I asked. "I thought you'd left."

"No, I didn't hear you. Why would I leave without you? Did you call me Sid?"

I nodded.

"You know, I sometimes forget I'm Sid. People will be talking to me and calling me Sid, and I don't get that they mean me, because in my head I'm just John. If you had called out John, I would have reacted straight away."

ROADENT: Well, Teddie, I think you must have been drinking moonshine or something... as I remember (and remember that that probably excludes any trace of veracity), I knew him as Sid long before he joined the band. He was Sid at the 100 Club fest with Siouxsie, Sid with The Flowers of Romance (rehearsing at The Clash rehearsal rooms [with Viv Albertine (Slits) and Keith Levine (original Clash)] and Sid when we took drugs together in squats around town. If we were calling him John that would have only been a tease, and anyway my remuneration was so poor that I

would have already spent any sanction that might have been imposed.

The bookshop was filled with tourist paraphernalia; there were books on Norway and trolls, and T-shirts with 'I Love Norway' on them. There was a shelf containing badges that Sid found interesting. I told him they were for different marching bands. Every area had their own band and on May 17th every year, they marched through the town with their local school pupils to celebrate the Norwegian national day. The badges fascinated Sid and he decided he wanted a couple. They were quite expensive, but it didn't seem to put him off.

"These are great and no one else will have one," he said.

HONEST JOHN PLAIN (founding member of The Boys): I always called him Sid. Now I know why he didn't always answer me!

Sid tried to pay for the record and badges. We had a problem at the till because the girl working there suddenly became giggly and couldn't concentrate when she realised who was standing in front of her. She was obviously more in tune with the popular music scene than me. Sid asked her how much it was in UK pounds, but she couldn't work it out. I could virtually see her brain grind to a halt in her head, and Sid and I stood there, waiting for her to say something. The girl had a paper list of the conversion rates, but she couldn't concentrate enough to work out the

A VICIOUS LOVE STORY

price in pounds. She rummaged through draws, looking for a calculator, and Sid and I just watched her fall apart. Then she lost the change on the floor. I did the maths and Sid was a little shocked by the price, but he still wanted to buy them.

"Oh, get a grip!" I said to her sweetly, and she giggled again moronically and went bright red in the face.

The four of us went out into the sunshine again. Sid put his arm around me and we walked down the street.

"I haven't been Sid for that long and sometimes I forget, and Malcolm gets so pissed off with me about it," he said and laughed. "He's told everyone they aren't allowed to call me anything but Sid so that I get used to it, but it doesn't work. So if I'm not answering, just say John. I wouldn't ignore you on purpose."

VIV ALBERTINE: Hi Ted, he wasn't Sid until 1976-77. x

We walked for a while, and people would cry out to us and give Sid a thumb's up. He would wave when he felt like it, but mostly we just ignored the stares. It was getting a little warmer and I was not feeling too bright. I wasn't used to drinking and staying up all night.

We entered the music shop Chr Rian, and the boys split up and looked around. Åge Aleksandersen, a successful musician in Norway, was working there and, although I didn't know him very well, we knew of each other. He nodded to me, said "Hi" and seemed surprised at me being there with Sid Vicious, Boogie and Paul Cook. Sid bought

A VICIOUS LOVE STORY

a couple of plectrums, but Paul was taken aback by the extortionate price of a pair of drumsticks. Luckily, he still had a spare in the van and decided against buying anything in Norway.

It was mid-afternoon and we were getting hungry. We walked back up towards the hotel the same way we had come and found a restaurant halfway up towards the market square that had tables outside in the sunshine. All this time, those two young boys had followed us. We sat down at a table and ordered pizza, and Boogie had a beer. The youngsters took a table close to us, but didn't intrude.

There was a man sitting at another table who became quite excited when he saw us. He had long, wild hair and he seemed very pleased when we sat down. He got up and left, but soon came back with a large, professional camera with a long lens. First, he simply put it on the table in front of him and examined it, like it was a new toy. I kept a keen eye on this guy. By the size of the lense, I was pretty sure he was a professional photographer.

I was planning on going home, but I didn't think it would be good if there was a picture of Sid and me in the newspaper the next morning. I was in enough trouble at home already, and I was afraid of what my friends in Trondheim would make of all this. The people I hung out with were not punks, quite the opposite; they were people who liked the latest mainstream music at the disco.

Although I knew I was in love, I wondered whether pictures of me with Sid Vicious would be taken in the same way.

A VICIOUS LOVE STORY

Sid, Boogie and Paul Photo Ragnar Wold ©

A VICIOUS LOVE STORY

I was afraid I would be gossiped about and I would be perceived as being promiscuous instead of in love. I didn't want people in Trondheim to gossip about me, but I was pretty certain they were doing that already after seeing me with Sid the previous night.

As soon as the pizza arrived, I thought I was going to hurl when I smelt it. The cheese was stringy and it made me feel sick. The restaurant also had a bakery where they served soft ice cream. I bought one and took it back to the table where the boys had finished off the pizza, thankfully. Sid wanted a taste and we shared it. He liked ice cream, but it only made me feel worse. I wasn't used to partying so late and drinking so much. I was pretty green around the gills by now.

"Hey, you were popular with the babes last night," Boogie laughed. "I thought the one with the boiler suit was going to kidnap you when you kept running away from her. It was hilarious."

"Yeah, she was persistent. I was at my wits' end, wondering how I could politely get rid of her and not actually have to tell her to fuck off. Ted did fuck all to help me," Sid answered, smiling.

"You're a big boy, Sid, you can handle it yourself," I said, laughing too.

"I'm a good-looking guy, what can I say?" he replied, half-joking.

"If you can say so yourself, modest too," I laughed, thinking him a tad conceited.

A VICIOUS LOVE STORY

"What? You're saying I'm not good looking?" he asked indignantly, poking me in the ribs to get me to laugh. "I've seen girls' reaction to me. I know I look good."

His comment surprised me a bit because I had never considered him good looking. He was striking, and had a charm and presence that made you automatically look at him when he entered a room. He was extremely charismatic, but I didn't think he was handsome in the traditional way.

"Yeah, you are absolutely gorgeous in a pale and gangly, punky sort of way," I answered, laughing and not taking him seriously.

"Yeah, I am pale though. I can't understand it. I thought being tanned was something you built up in your skin. I spent some time in Ibiza when I was younger and would be nutty brown every summer. We never used any sun lotion. I didn't need to. But after we moved back to England, it doesn't work like that any more," Sid explained. "I just go pink and then I get burned – very strange."

"I think that's typical of English skin, except Roadent. I saw him in his birthday suit yesterday and he has surprisingly tanned legs," I said, and laughed until I saw Sid had a surprised expression on his face.

"What the fuck was Roadent doing around you with no clothes on?" he asked testily.

"She came in when he was in bed with Debbie," Boogie answered for me, and I smiled at him gratefully.

"Yeah, it was no big deal. He just walked around, looking for his clothes," I said sweetly, thinking I would have to be more careful what I told him since he didn't like the fact that Roadent had been naked.

"What the fuck were you doing in there? When was this?" he asked, a little irritably.

"When you took off with Tracey and left me. I went to find him because you scared me and I needed some advice. It wasn't a big deal, Boogie was there too," I answered, but regretted saying anything.

"He shouldn't have been walking around naked when you were there," Sid repeated, sounding pretty annoyed about it.

"Wow, Ibiza sounds nice. Did you enjoy living there? Are you fluent in Spanish too?" I asked, trying to change the subject.

"Yes, it was all right. I know a bit of Spanish, but we mainly hung out with the English people there. I lived with my mum. Then we moved back to England."

"Don't you have a dad either?" I asked. "I have a stepfather. He's all right, but it's not like having a real dad."

"My father works at Buckingham Palace as a guard and he's a jazz musician. When we moved back to England, he suddenly contacted us and said he wanted to see me. My mother took me to see him."

"So are you still in contact?" I asked.

"No I don't have any contact any more. I spent some hours with him, but he was a stranger and I didn't want to go again. She would send me there, and I would just take off and wait out the time. I'd walk around exploring London and then go home."

A VICIOUS LOVE STORY

"How old were you when you ran around in London on your own?" I asked.

Now, I really cannot remember exactly how old he told me he was. What I do remember is that I was shocked by the answer. It could have been anything between eight and ten years old, I think, and I was appalled at him being left to wander the streets of London unsupervised, but he just shrugged it off.

"I would go on adventures exploring London. It was great until I got found out. My father contacted my mother because he thought she was stopping me from seeing him. I got such a beating that day, it was unreal," he said, laughing.

"Wait! What are you saying? Did she hit you?" I asked, shocked.

He nodded very slightly, not wanting to go into details about it.

"Tore is taking us to a museum this afternoon, do you want to come?" he said, changing the subject.

That was the last thing I wanted to do. We had been forced to go to the local museums by our school and I found them very boring. I didn't fancy walking around some stuffy place, learning how a Cembalo was made, when I was so desperately hung-over. I am pretty sure it was the Ringve Music Museum they were going to.

I avoided answering the question by saying, "I'm not feeling too good. I'm not used to drinking or I must be having an allergic reaction to the sausages in condoms we ate at the restaurant." They all laughed at my joke.

A VICIOUS LOVE STORY

I was getting tired and thirsty, and just wanted to go home. I needed to eat something healthy and drink at least a gallon of cold milk. The chap with the camera took a couple of photos of us without asking.

"Hey!" I said, indicating that I thought him rude.

He apologised, but Boogie said, "Oh, to hell with it, Teddie, let him get his pictures and he'll leave us alone. It's when we say no that they become annoying."

The guy seemed very pleased, and said he was a freelance photographer and just having a coffee with a friend, so he hadn't followed us or anything. Luckily for him, another photographer at *Adressavisen*, Trondheim's largest newspaper, had lent him his camera, but it was different from his own and he had to get used to using it. I tried to stay out of the photos, but after a while he took so many that I just gave up.

"Why do you keep moving away when he takes a photo?" Sid asked me, sounding annoyed. "Don't you want to be seen with me or something?"

"It's not that," I answered, "they don't want pictures of me."

"No, you're wrong," the photographer said, "I really do want you in the picture. Snuggle up, please."

I didn't want to and protested, saying I looked like death warmed up and felt even worse, and definitely didn't want my picture taken. But Sid was beginning to react to the fact that I didn't like the photographer.

"I'm trying to keep out of the way so that your girlfriend doesn't have to see a picture of us before you have had time to talk to her properly," I answered, half-truthfully. With hindsight, I shouldn't have mentioned her as talking about her only made him angry, but it was the best excuse I could think of there and then.

Sid seemed to consider this for a while and then said, "It's not a problem. I don't give a toss if she sees us together or not. It's none of her fucking business anyway. It will take weeks before a picture like that comes to a UK paper. I doubt they would be interested even. And stop lying to me, there's something else. Who else don't you want to see that you're with me – one of your mates, maybe, a boyfriend, Tore?"

"Oh, for God's sake, Tore has just seen us in bed together. Why wouldn't I want him to see a picture of us? That's just silly," I snapped back.

"Yeah, but he didn't look like he was too thrilled about it, did he?" Sid almost spat out.

"I don't have a boyfriend. I told you that and besides you're the one with the girlfriend. I wouldn't even know about her if Steve hadn't kissed me," I threw back at him, angrily.

Sid looked like he was going to explode. "What the fuck were you kissing Steve for? When did that happen?" he asked, angrily.

"When you went to get his fags – I thought you knew." I regretted saying it now.

"No, I didn't know. He shouldn't have done that, the bastard. I'm going to have a word with him later."

"Oh, leave it alone. I told him to back off. Problem sorted, no big deal," I answered.

A VICIOUS LOVE STORY

"I'm beginning to wonder if we were at the same party. Is there anything else you want to tell me?" he snapped.

"He just leaned in and kissed me, and I told him to back off," I said angrily "It's not like I enjoyed it. I wasn't letting him get near me again. It took me by surprise."

I saw the people sitting on the tables close to us pick up on my comment about being in bed, and they were listening intently. I really didn't want to talk about this in front of Boogie, Paul, the two young chaps, the photographer and anyone else who was sitting around us, listening and watching.

For someone who kept a tough exterior and tried to make out he didn't give a shit about most things, Sid was certainly behaving a little obsessively. I didn't understand where it was all coming from. I leaned in and kissed him, and he let it happen for a few seconds before pulling back. He was angry. Everyone else kept quiet. I looked at Paul with an expression that said 'help!' No one said anything and the silence was getting embarrassing.

"So where do I go to get some trousers, Ted?" Paul asked me, changing the subject.

"If I could just remember the name of the shop, it's so annoying."

One of the young guys told Paul they could take them to the shop that sold the most jeans in Trondheim, called Haltvik. They started talking about where the shop was and the types of jeans it sold, and Sid and I didn't say anything. We just sat at the table, listening to their conversation and not looking at each other.

A VICIOUS LOVE STORY

I saw Sid gently kick Paul and Boogie under the table. Sid suddenly got up from where he was sitting and said he wanted another ice cream. He walked over to the counter and stood in line to buy one. Right on cue, Boogie said he needed to use the facilities, and Paul also got up and walked over to Sid, taking the plastic carrier bag containing the record with him.

A VICIOUS LOVE STORY

Photo Ragnar Wold ©

A VICIOUS LOVE STORY

I was left at the table with the photographer. The two young boys were still sitting at the adjacent table, and they looked worriedly at me and then at Sid, not knowing what to say or do. I'm sure they were anxious that the boys would just leave me there at the table.

"So how do you know Sid Vicious? Did you know him before he came to Norway?" the photographer asked me as soon as the boys were out of earshot.

I didn't answer him, but busied myself with my jacket and handbag. I was starting to feel insecure. Why on earth Sid thought I had something going on with Tore was beyond me. I regretted being so impulsive and telling him about Roadent and Steve. It was all very innocent. I couldn't understand why he seemed so angry. I hadn't done anything wrong. I started to worry that they would all just go off and leave me there at the table, without saying goodbye.

I was beginning to fear that maybe Sid had changed his mind about me going with him and I would soon be getting the brush-off. I decided that no matter what, I was going to keep my dignity in all of this. There was no way I was going to hang around Sid like a lapdog, hoping he wanted to be with me. I didn't give a toss about his celebrity status. If he wanted to see me, fine, if it was what I wanted too. If not, I would be gutted, but I wouldn't show him that. There was no way I was going to make the first move to go and join him, so I simply looked away and talked to the photographer.

He was fiddling with his camera and said, "If you give me your name and address, I can send you these pictures."

A VICIOUS LOVE STORY

"Do I look like I was born yesterday?" I snapped.

"Well, I was only being polite. I thought maybe you would like the pictures as a memory of your little encounter."

Now that snide remark was just rude and it was exactly the sort of thing I was afraid people in Trondheim would be thinking. I really couldn't be bothered with the hassle, so I gave him a false name and address, and could tell he didn't believe me. This was something I later regretted dearly. When the photographer left his film at the newspaper, they went missing. It wasn't until 2011, that the archives at Adresseavisen found the missing film negatives. They had simply been filed in the wrong place. The negatives were signed out of the archives by a local journalist and have not been seen again.

Sid had stayed by the door to the restaurant, eating his ice cream, and talking to Boogie and Paul. I stayed at the table, ignoring him, and talking to the photographer and the two young boys. It took a few minutes before Sid made his way back on his own, and I could see Paul and Boogie hovering by the door to the restaurant. Paul was still holding Sid's plastic bag. They both looked at us, but made no move to join us.

"Can you leave, please? I want a private word," Sid said to the photographer, who grudgingly moved back to where he had been sitting.

The two young boys politely got up from their table, and made their way over to Paul and Boogie. Sid sat down beside me, looking straight ahead and not directly at me. I found myself wondering whether I was about to be told to sod off now and that everything we had talked about earlier was just a joke.

"I'm going now to get jeans for Paul. Do you want to come with me?" he asked, quietly.

"You have no idea how rough I feel. I need to go home now," I answered.

"The museum trip is later. Do you want to come to that? I'm not sure when Tore is picking us up, but I think it's around 4pm."

I couldn't think of any museum in Trondheim I would want to see, so I said, "No, I think I'll pass on that too."

He was quiet now and still not looking at me. He was fiddling with the knee of his jeans and his face was fixed straight ahead, looking at Boogie and Paul.

"So, what are you saying? Are you saying you will pass' on me too then?" he asked quietly.

"No! You keep misunderstanding; I wasn't lying to you earlier. I'm just not used to all the attention you get and I feel rough. If I were certain my parents were not at home, I would ask you to come with me, but I'm not sure and it could get nasty. I can see you after the museum if you like," I said, smiling at his insecurity.

I took his hand in mine and squeezed it gently. He didn't object and I put my head on his shoulder. It seemed to cheer him up a little. The fact that he was insecure only endeared him to me even more. He tried to put on a tough, 'I don't care' front, but it shone through that it was just a false exterior and not the real Sid.

A VICIOUS LOVE STORY

"We're going out tonight for a couple of beers and then an early night since we have an early start tomorrow. Are you coming?" he asked.

"Is John coming tonight?"

"Yeah we all are. Why do you ask?"

"He's such a scary person. Last night I thought he was going to hit me. If he's still mad at me, he might not want me to be there," I said.

"Well, I want you to be there and I'll keep you close so you have nothing to worry about with John. He was drunk and he's probably forgotten all about it now. You are going to have to get on with him. We spend a lot of time together when we are on the road. He's a good guy. You just need to get to know him a little better," Sid answered reassuringly.

"I'm sure you're right. He seems to act like a big brother to you. But he is a bit quick tempered and I have a tendency to say things impulsively before I think. Things just pop out of my mouth before I can stop it. He seems like the type of person I have to be careful what I say around. My big mouth sometimes gets me into trouble."

"Relax, Ted, you'll be fine. You're with me. I'll take care of you."

"I need to go home now and face the music," I said. "I'll try to square things with my mother. I don't stay out all night normally and she's really angry. I'll pack a bag. What on earth should I pack?"

"Okay, I'll see you at the hotel in a couple of hours. Pack what you like really. You just need some clothes and toiletries because there is no way you are using my stuff every day. I can't get it here and your skin doesn't need it, young lady!" He chuckled.

I loved the sound of his laughter. It didn't come often, but when it did it was nice. I got a peck on the lips and it was a much happier Sid who set off with Paul, Boogie and those two boys to get Paul's trousers. The boys knew exactly where they had to go and promised to take the guys to the right shop. They were excited to be allowed to hang out with them.

A VICIOUS LOVE STORY

CHAPTER 10 THE LAST EVENING IN TRONDHEIM

    I knew my parents wouldn't be at home by the time I entered our flat; I hadn't been completely truthful to Sid about that fact. I just needed some time alone to think and my room looked like it had been bombed. Not that I thought it would worry Sid in the least, but I didn't want him to see how messy I was. It was quiet and I got something to eat in the kitchen while I wrote a little letter to my mum, saying I was sorry I'd stayed out all night, but I'd fallen in love and it was serious, and I would tell her all about it later.
    I tried to sleep, but couldn't. I had another shower, washed my hair and got ready for an evening out. I had found a large bag and begun to pack some things when my sister suddenly stood in the doorway to my bedroom. She was two years younger and very different to me in every sense.
    "You are in so much trouble, you won't believe it!" she said smugly. "Mum and dad have had a flaming row over you this morning."
    She came into my room and watched as I packed some clothes into my bag. I found myself getting a little irritated with her and the fact that my mother hadn't emptied my laundry basket, so some of the clothes I wanted to take had not been washed. I stuffed them into the bag anyway, thinking I might find a coin laundry in Sweden. I opened

A VICIOUS LOVE STORY

the drawer where I kept my documents and money. I was surprised to find my passport was missing and so was the wad of cash I'd put in there.

"Where are you going?" my sister asked, as she sat on my bed, fiddling with my half-packed bag.

"None of your business," I answered, as anything I told her would go straight to my parents and thereafter to all her mates.

"Mum said that if you don't come home today, she is going to lock you in the coal cellar until you are thirty when you finally do."

"We don't have a coal cellar," I said and started looking for my passport again.

"Oh, you know what she means. Can I have your room when you're gone?"

I looked everywhere, but I couldn't find my passport or my money.

My sister finally said, "If it's your passport you are looking for, it has been hidden."

I was surprised how fast my parents had anticipated what I was going to do. It was strange as I was acting totally out of character and would never have dared run away. I was too cowardly, and besides I liked my family and my mother made the best food ever.

I searched high and low, and all the time my sister followed me, wearing a smug grin on her face and singing, "You will never find it, you will never find it."

I went back to my room and closed the door, so I didn't have to listen to my sister, and sat down on my bed. The bag I'd half-heartedly packed was on the floor. I looked at it and sighed once again, realising how serious the idea of running away really was.

Our flat was above a cinema. There are several of them in Trondheim and I was lucky that on that particular Friday afternoon my stepfather was working at the one downstairs. I entered the building and saw him straight away. My stepfather was a soft touch. I knew my mother would be furious, but he seemed to understand I wanted some freedom and didn't judge. He smiled at me when he saw me and shook his head like I was a lost cause.

"You better keep away from your mother," was the first thing he said to me.

He sighed. "Teddie, what are you thinking of, going off with some scruffy pop star? He will only end up breaking your heart, or worse. I thought you of all people would have your head screwed on."

"He won't hurt me," I tried, but my stepfather simply waved me aside.

"He flaming well better not or he'll have me to deal with. But your mother is frantic and she's hidden your passport as she thinks you might run away over this, silly woman. Do please tell me they have left and you are not going to do that."

He only had to look at me to see my mother was spot on.

"Oh, Teddie, you silly girl! If you are planning anything stupid, I want you to know this – if you run away, your mother and I will contact the police straight away. We will get Sid arrested. You are not 18 yet and therefore still our responsibility. Tore has told me they are

A VICIOUS LOVE STORY

going to Sweden, so you will be found and brought back to us within a few hours. There is absolutely no point to any of this."

"How on earth did she find out about this so quickly?" I asked, surprised. "Honestly, the jungle telegraph in this town is amazing."

"Your mother knew last night. She got a call at work from someone she knows at the Hawk Club. Someone at the Hawk restaurant said the person you were seen with got into a fight and you all got thrown out of there. What I want to know is who the hell let you in there in the first place? You're barely 16 and too young, end of story."

"You don't know him. He's not like that. He's not what you think. He's a guy who has had a shit life and still turned into a decent, fantastic human being. I know you will like him and so will mum when she meets him. He's kind and nice, and smart, and really wants me to come with him. We don't want this to end. I've finally met someone I really like, and you and mum are not going to ruin it," I said stubbornly.

Even as the words left my mouth, I could hear how childish they sounded. I was behaving like a spoilt child, and sounded naive and stupid. My stepfather stood there, looking at me for a few minutes. Everything was hopeless. I knew Sid had his court case and he didn't need any more hassle with the police. He had told me earlier that he had been afraid he wouldn't be able to come on the Scandinavian tour because of the case. He had to be back in the UK in person. If he was arrested or even delayed in Sweden because of my parents calling the police, it might have huge consequences for him. Money was beginning to be a worry too.

"Can I borrow some money from you?" I asked sweetly.

I had calculated the cost of the flight to London from Sweden and enough money to survive on for a few weeks, and it was a staggering amount.

"How much money are we talking about?" he answered, and laughed when I told him.

"I can't give you that amount of money. I can't help you run away. You will only be brought back, Ted, so it would be money wasted."

I knew there was absolutely no point in asking my mother.

My stepfather then went on to ask me about Sid. Where did he come from in England? Where did he live? Was his family still there? I tried to answer as best I could, and it certainly made me realise how little I did know about him, even though we had told each other as much as we could about our backgrounds and lives. With hindsight, I think that might have been my stepfather's plan. He looked disdainful when I told him how Sid had lived in a squat, but now lived in a flat in London, and I had no idea where. He shook his head and laughed.

"Teddie, love, can you really see yourself living in a grotty squat? How will you make a living? Does Sid make a lot of money from this band? Enough to keep you with the things you are used to? You will be totally dependent on Sid in London since you can't work. Can you see yourself being happy like that?"

A VICIOUS LOVE STORY

He made a fair point. I would never have been happy living like that, but it wasn't going to be forever – we weren't thinking more than a couple of weeks ahead. It wasn't like I was planning on moving to London permanently. I just wanted to see where this led. I simply wanted to spend more time with him.

"Listen, love, I can let you have a little money. Go and find this Sid, and explain what I've told you and that you can't possibly go with him anywhere. Let him down gently. Go out tonight and have a good time, and then come home and try to forget him. And don't tell your mother I've let you have any money or she will have my guts for garters. She has taken what was in the drawer in your room to stop you from running away."

My stepfather pulled some bills out of his wallet and gave them to me. It was more than twice the amount I usually got for a week's pocket money, so I could see he felt sorry for me. I sat for a little while, thinking about what he'd said. I turned over in my mind what Sid's reaction might be when I told him I couldn't go with him after all. I was pretty sure he would be hurt. I remember thinking how strange it was that I would be the one hurting him and not the other way around since he was the big pop star.

I was beginning to realise how difficult all this was. If I took off to Sweden, I would only have to come back the following week when Sid went back to London. I'd be in deep trouble and my mother would never let me go to London. If I let Sid go to Sweden without me, I could possibly persuade my mother to let me go to London on my own from time to time, which was a better idea.

I left my half-heartedly packed bag at home and walked the short distance to the Phoenix hotel. No one questioned why I was there or where I was going. I took the lift to the top floor, and Sid and Paul's bedroom door was open.

Sid's smile froze as I entered the room. "Hi, no bag I see," he said.

Paul took a pair of jeans from a pile on a chair into the bathroom, like he knew we needed to talk.

"We have a huge problem," I said, kissing his cheek and sitting beside him on the corner of the bed.

"How did you get on with your parents? Don't tell me, mummy and daddy don't want you to go," he said mockingly.

I sighed deeply, and he said, "Fuck them, Teddie, they have lived their lives. It's our turn now. You have to do what's right for you, not them."

My mother was 35 years old. I explained how my parents would contact the police straight away, and then come and get me, and how I couldn't leave just now.

Sid argued, "It's not a problem. I haven't done anything wrong. You are over 16. They can't lock me up for you running away. Besides it probably takes ages for the police to react. They will be telling your parents to wait for a day or two and you'll come home. By that time we'll be long gone."

He was right, of course, but I was sure my parents had more tricks up their sleeves to prevent their wayward daughter running away with a drug-taking punk rocker.

A VICIOUS LOVE STORY

My stepfather had hinted that, barring the police doing anything, they would simply drive to Sweden and bring me back.

Paul reappeared from the bathroom wearing a stiff pair of Levi's 501s. They were much too tight and Sid said, "No mate, you need the larger one", pointing to the pile of jeans on the floor.

Paul agreed, picked up another pair, and took them back into the bathroom.

I asked, "Are you shy Paul? I have seen a man in his underpants before, you know."

He laughed and said, "Yeah, but you haven't seen me in my underpants before, and I don't want to spoil you for Sid."

We laughed and Sid showed me the jeans.

"Where did these come from?" I asked.

"The shop gave them to us for free. You can have a pair if you like."

I looked absentmindedly at them. I already had a pair. Sid loved them.

"What do you mean you got them for free? Did you let them take your picture as PR for the shop or something in exchange?"

Sid shook his head and Paul re-emerged from the bathroom in another, better fitting pair of jeans that were a little too long.

"No. They just gave them to us. Was ace! I couldn't believe it. It was only supposed to be a pair for Paul, but they kept giving us more pairs in different sizes," Sid laughed.

A VICIOUS LOVE STORY

"Can you sew these up for me?" Paul asked. "They're too long."

"Well, if you can get me a needle and thread, I'll do it," I answered. "Barring that, we can ask reception to borrow their stapler and I'll staple them up, but you have to be careful and make sure you take the staples out before you wash them. They'll shrink if you use warm water. Mine were too long too, so I put them on and sat in the bathtub in hot water. They fitted perfectly, like a second skin, when they dried. But now I have to use pliers to get the zip up! Oh, and lie on my back on the floor. So I don't wear them that often as it gets difficult when I use the bathroom at the disco."

"What? Do you walk around with a pair of pliers in your handbag?" Sid asked.

I nodded and we laughed.

"How was the museum," I asked, "and who did you go with?"

"We all went. There wasn't enough room in Tore's car, so I took the tram with Debbie, Tracey and Boogie."

I laughed. "I can't believe it – Sid Vicious on public transport. Were people a bit shocked?"

He shook his head. "No, there was only this one old man on there. He must have been about 50. He did stare to begin with, but no one bothered us. And the museum was good. You should have come with us. I used to take the bus and the underground all the time in London. Well, I have to take the bus because I can't afford a taxi. It's gotten a bit more difficult now because there are some idiots that don't like what we stand for and want to start fights – Teddy Boys – so I have to be careful. But it's great being able to move around here in Norway and everyone is so nice. We don't get much hassle and I like it."

"So, you not coming to Sweden then?" he added casually.

"I don't know, Sid. I want to, but I don't want to get you into any trouble," I answered. "I know they can't arrest you, but what if they make it difficult? What if the police turn up at gigs or they want to question you about me disappearing? Or stop me from coming into the gigs at all since I'm underage. What if it means you can't get to your court case in time because they make trouble?"

I could see him thinking about it. The fact that I most certainly would be sent home from Sweden made going there hardly worth the trouble it would cause.

ROADENT: For Trondheim, a rich fan from Stockholm offered to fly us up in his toy aeroplane. Steve was always averse to flying, particularly in a toy machine with no spare propeller, so I took his place. Steve and Bollocks-chops were in the white van.

They would be flying back with a friend of Bollocks-chops, and therefore I could travel in the van with Bollocks-chops and Steve. They would go straight to the airport and then over to the Swedish border. It was only a two-hour drive from Trondheim to the border, and I would be out of the country before my parents had even woken up the next morning. It was then a long drive to Växjö, I was told, but we'd be there by late afternoon. They had a gig in the evening and Sid said I could stay with him at the hotel.

Sid said he needed a shower. Paul busied himself by folding up the jeans into a neat pile. I sat on the bed, watching and was bored. I could hear the water cascading in the bathroom.

Paul fiddled with something and then he said, "I don't know how to say this. Promise you won't take this the wrong way, Ted," he said seriously. I nodded.

"Can you leave for a few minutes whilst I get ready?" he asked.

It made me laugh that Paul was obviously very shy.

"Of course, I'll go and find Roadent and the girls whilst you get ready. Tell Sid he can come and find me when he's finished making himself gorgeous," I replied cheerfully, as I left the room.

"Yeah, but he might find himself struggling with the gorgeous bit," Paul called after me.

I laughed, and made my way to Roadent and Boogie's room across the corridor. I knocked on the door and heard Roadent shout, "Enter!"

Roadent, Boogie, Debbie and Tracey were hanging out, relaxing. The maid had cleaned the room, and the beer crates and empty bottles had been taken back to the shop. The room looked rather bare without them.

"How did you get on at home?" Boogie asked me, as I went to sit on the nearest sofa with Debbie.

"Not too good. My mother has confiscated what little cash I had, hidden my passport and is threatening to call

A VICIOUS LOVE STORY

the police if I leave Trondheim. They can make a lot of trouble for Sid. I think I might have to give Sweden a miss," I said unhappily.

"But you don't have to have a passport to go to Sweden," Boogie said, looking confused. "Has Sid asked you to come to London with us as well?"

"Yes and no. He asked me to visit him in London, but hasn't said anything about going straight from Sweden," I explained. "The thing with my passport is difficult to explain. If I just take off, I will never get it back. I'll be able to be with you for another week, but then that's the end of it. When I come back to Trondheim I will be grounded, forever, or at least until I'm 18. They don't make empty threats."

"You can get a passport when you are in Sweden," Debbie suggested.

"She's 16. She'll need her mother's signature. Oh, and your birth certificate," Boogie added.

My birth certificate! Of course, I hadn't thought of that. Plan B would have to be to get that.

"I'll play mummy if you like," Roadent said in a silly voice, indicating that he would forge her signature if I wished.

"But it will take a couple of weeks for you to get it. So you need to decide whether you want to stay for two weeks in Sweden alone and wait for a passport, or take some time to get your parents to realise you are serious and just come after us in a couple of days," Roadent said. He always made a lot of sense.

A VICIOUS LOVE STORY

"It was fun watching you and Sid last night," he said, laughing.

"Fun? Why?" I didn't understand.

"Well, back in England the girls sometimes fight over the boys. If one girl feels someone else is getting more attention, they will get some mates together and pick a fight. It's hilarious sometimes. It's good your friends had so much respect for you, they actually left you and Sid alone last night," Roadent said.

"God, that's dreadful. I mean about the girls fighting. Actually, it's quite funny when you think of it. We are not like that here. It's got nothing to do with respect for me. We're just not a scrappy kind of nation. So what does Sid do when a gang of girls try to beat up the girl he's flirting with?" I asked, amazed.

"Nothing, I don't think he gives a toss really," he replied, shrugging.

"What's funny is that you do the complete opposite and just sod off when someone else tries to chat him up. He's not used to that. I think you confuse Sid" Boogie said.

"I sometimes don't understand him at all. He seems to keep this tough exterior, like he doesn't care about anything. Then he'll be so sweet towards me and then pull back a little, like he thinks he's said too much. I get confused. It's the same with him asking me to come to Sweden. One minute he is really into me coming – he'd asked Bollocks-chops already before he even asked me – and a little later I feel like he isn't really bothered either way, like I can come if I like or not come, doesn't really matter. Am I making any sense?"

A VICIOUS LOVE STORY

"Yeah, well, the fact that he's asked you to come to Sweden should tell you something," Boogie added.

His comment surprised me, as it made me realise that asking someone to go on the next part of the tour with him wasn't something Sid normally did.

It was soon time to go down to the bar and meet the others. Debbie, Roadent, Boogie and I trooped out of the room and into the corridor, so Tracey could get ready. I knocked on Sid's door and we all waited, but didn't enter. Sid was sitting on the bed, wearing a thinly worn towel around his waist. I could hear the water cascading in the bathroom and I assumed Paul was in there, taking a shower.

Roadent and Boogie just peeked in, said "Hi", and started to make their way towards the elevator.

I noticed a subtle change in Sid's mood and he seemed to be avoiding looking directly at me when he said, "I'm not ready yet. Paul has locked the door again, so I can't get in to brush my teeth until he's finished. You just go on down and I'll come when I'm ready."

Debbie and I closed the door. I didn't say anything, but I found his behaviour a bit off. I had expected Sid to ask me to come in and wait while he got ready. He knew I was anxious about meeting John again and he had promised to be there with me. Everything had been fine when I came to his room earlier, but now he seemed distant, and I couldn't understand what had happened between then and now. Debbie and I walked together down the corridor towards the elevator where Roadent and Boogie were waiting.

A VICIOUS LOVE STORY

I was a little anxious when I entered the hotel bar. Set towards the front of the hotel and to the side of the reception area, the bar was shaped like a semi-circle and surrounded by tall bar stools. The furniture was covered in plush, red velvet, and the table's dark wood was stained with time and wet beer glasses. The windows looked out on to the market square and the large statue of Olav Tryggvason in the centre.

We had run out of booze and Bollocks-chops said we could just put our drinks on the hotel tab for Tore to pick up later. I thought that was a little cheeky, but maybe it had been agreed. John, Steve and Bollocks-chops sat together at a table and Boogie went to join them. Roadent positioned himself on a bar stool; he and Debbie seemed to be very fond of each other. As we entered, I looked at John carefully to try to work out what sort of mood he was in, thinking I would just ignore him and keep out of his way.

But, as soon as John saw me he smiled and said, "Oi, Blondie, sorry!"

I smiled back and made a non-committal grunt in answer. It was strange for him to call me Blondie. I was fair, but it was certainly not as blonde as some of my friends' hair, so I guessed he'd just forgotten my name.

I sat down on a bar stool beside Roadent. It wasn't that I preferred to sit with him; it was just that I preferred not to sit with John as he made me nervous. The bar was just opening up and we had to wait a few minutes before we could order our drinks. The bartender was a young man with a cheeky smile, and made a great show of polishing

A VICIOUS LOVE STORY

the brass beer tabs and the counter while he whistled an unmusical tune. He looked at us with interest. He must have known the Sex Pistols were staying at the hotel and he didn't seem surprised to see us there. We were the only guests.

When we ordered our drinks, he took the time to try to make small talk with us in bad English. I ordered a beer and paid for it. The barman questioned my age, but Roadent and Debbie quickly backed up my story of just having turned 18. As I got my beer, I started a conversation with Debbie while I anxiously waited for Sid to arrive and hopefully explain to me what was wrong.

Debbie told me they had enjoyed the museum that afternoon and that it was very good. "It was much better than the one we saw in Germany earlier this spring, wasn't it, John?"

He nodded.

"Did you follow the band on tour to Germany?" I asked.

She laughed. "No, we went on holiday," she said.

"What do you mean, on holiday?" I asked.

Debbie laughed some more when she saw how surprised I was by her remark, and she suddenly seemed to realise I still thought that she and Tracey were groupies.

"Well, the boys were getting a lot of hassle in the UK and they really needed a holiday, so we went to Germany. Was okay," she repeated, gesturing again to John. "I'm just telling Teddie about our holiday in Germany, John. It was nice, wasn't it?"

Once again, he agreed.

A VICIOUS LOVE STORY

Everything on that Friday was totally different to the night before. Everyone seemed much more at ease, and Debbie and Tracey were much friendlier towards me than they had been previously, when I only talked to them briefly. They seemed to stay in Roadent and Boogie's room, and didn't go into John's suite.

It was quite some time before Sid entered the bar. I'd caught a glimpse of him earlier, standing behind the doors. He hovered there like he didn't want us to see him, and looked at us when he thought we weren't looking. I found this behaviour totally confusing and started to wonder whether, perhaps, he was regretting inviting me in the first place. He kept running hot and cold, and I was getting more and more confused.

Paul suddenly appeared at the door and stopped to talk to Sid for a few minutes. They stood chatting for a little while and Sid kept looking over at us in the bar, so I had a feeling I was the topic of conversation. Then Tracey arrived, and she too stood there for a couple of minutes before she came and sat down on a bar stool next to Debbie, Roadent and myself. Paul came in as Sid left the hotel, and he stood beside me as he ordered a beer.

"Where is Sid off to?" I asked casually.

"I dunno. I think he went to get some fags. They are cheaper at the kiosk next door," replied Paul, and he went to sit with the other guys at the table.

Some time later, Sid came into the bar. He'd been gone for almost 20 minutes and I was pretty sure it didn't take that long to buy some fags in the corner shop. He didn't acknowledge me, but went to sit down with John at the table, not looking in my direction. Debbie could see I was beginning to worry. She poked Roadent in the arm and sort of raised her eyebrows, suggesting she couldn't understand what was going on either. Roadent, noticing my concern, put his arm around my shoulder and gave me a little hug. Out of the corner of my eye, I saw Sid flinch and look angry. I couldn't understand his behaviour.

"Relax, Ted, it will be okay," Roadent whispered in my ear.

"What the fuck is this about? If he ignores me any longer, I am going home. Why the hell invite me to come if he doesn't want to know, for God's sake," I whispered back, swearing again as I'd started mimicking the rest of them.

Tracey leaned in to listen to what we were saying. I hadn't really spoken to her much, but now she seemed to empathise. She smiled at me warmly and whispered, "I shouldn't be telling you this, but I just heard Sid say to Paul that he wondered what the hell Roadent wants with you, Teddie, as he always seems to be hanging around you. He sounded like he didn't like it much."

"God, he is so difficult. I don't know where I am with him. One minute he's all over me and wants me to come with him, and to come to Sweden and England, and the next he totally ignores me. I think I'll just leave."

"I think you should just go over there and talk to him. I don't think he wants you to leave, Ted," Tracey answered.

"Can I ask you something, Tracey?" I asked and she nodded.

A VICIOUS LOVE STORY

"Why do you follow the band? I don't get it. Is it the music that's the attraction or do you like one of them?"

She hesitated before answering. Debbie and Tracey looked at one another as if they were trying to agree on whether to confide in me or not.

"It's definitely the music, but, yes, I like Steve," she finally answered, quietly.

I was rather surprised by her answer because, as far as I could see, Steve hadn't talked to her at all since she arrived. I saw Tracey looking at him, but she kept her distance and he ignored her. I don't think he acknowledged her presence at all during that weekend. At least I have no memory of it.

"So why don't you go over there and talk to him?" I asked.

She shook her head. "No, I can't do that, he doesn't want me to."

"You don't know that until you've tried. So you are happy to just hang around on the off chance he wants to talk to you?" I asked, smiling at her, warmly.

She nodded.

"He'll let me know when he wants to see me," Tracey answered, a little sadly. "Until then, I just hang around and wait for the signal. There is no point trying to get him to be with me."

I didn't understand the girls' friendships with the boys at all. We were all whispering together when Sid got up from where he was sitting and came over to the bar. He didn't say anything to me and Roadent sat in between us. Sid ordered a beer and took a lot of time discussing with

A VICIOUS LOVE STORY

the bartender which one he wanted. He made a big deal out of choosing and the barman was explaining in great detail the finer qualities of the various varieties of local Dahl's beer.

I felt Sid was making a point of ignoring me. He seemed sullen. He finally chose the type of beer he wanted and stood quietly beside Roadent, waiting for it. I didn't say anything and neither did he. There was definitely something wrong, but I couldn't work out what exactly. I didn't understand and I decided that if he went on ignoring me, I would simply leave when they went to a club.

Sid paid for his beer, walked passed Roadent and me, and started talking to Debbie and Tracey. This was strange since none of the band had spoken to the girls the previous night, as far as I could see. The girls seemed to stick with Roadent and Boogie mostly.

Sid and the girls seemed to be remembering something, talking about someone, and they giggled about it. I was sitting on the bar stool beside Sid, but he had his back towards me, like he wanted to make a point of excluding me. I found his behaviour very strange indeed, and I turned slightly so that I could listen in on what they were saying.

Tracey made a point of trying to include me in the conversation. Sid moved closer to my chair, and I touched his shoulder so I could see Tracey's face while I asked her about the story she was telling. I really just wanted him to move slightly to the side, but he misunderstood the gesture and placed his hand on top of mine, keeping it there. He still had his back towards me, but he leaned closer. They were laughing at something that had happened with a person called Siouxsie, but I had never heard of her.

I turned my chair a little more and pulled Sid towards me, so he was standing between my legs but with his back towards me. I hugged him from behind. I listened to what he and the girls were talking about, and it was now obvious that Debbie and Tracey were not groupies but friends of the boys. Yet it was a strange friendship that I didn't quite understand. Tracey and Debbie seemed to keep their distance to the guys. Debbie was the chatty one of the two, and she seemed to keep close to Roadent.

When Sid had finished what he was saying, he turned around to face me. He took both hands and put them around my neck, and put his forehead against mine like he had done the previous night. Then he moved closer, so he was standing between my legs, and kissed me.

"What the fuck are you doing, sitting here with Roadent and not over there with me?" He asked, pointing to the table he had shared with John and the others.

It suddenly struck me: he was jealous! He didn't know how to react to that emotion. The things he had said earlier about Tore and boyfriends suddenly made sense. The thought of him actually being jealous and possessive had never crossed my mind until now. The way he talked about Nancy implied he didn't really attach too much importance to relationships. He had also been closely observing us all while standing at the door earlier, probably wanting to see what was going on without me noticing he was there. Perhaps Sid thought he would catch me flirting with someone. It was all rather ridiculous in

A VICIOUS LOVE STORY

my mind, but this sudden realisation also brought confirmation that maybe he did feel he was getting too close, and he needed this tough exterior so he wouldn't be seen to care should I not be interested after all.

"You haven't been listening to what I have told you at all, have you?" I said. "You come in here and simply ignore me."

"I wasn't ignoring you, I was talking to John. I expected you to come over and sit with me, but you just stayed here. You were ignoring me and I was worried you preferred someone else's company to mine." Sid looked in Roadent's direction.

"Of course I don't," I said, "but you seemed annoyed, and I couldn't work out why because I haven't done anything wrong. When I am as close as I feel I am to you, I don't go off with someone else. I'm not interested in anyone else, but I'm not going to push myself on somebody who isn't interested back. It's called dignity, Sid."

"It's called being fucking stupid. You did it last night too. You keep waiting for me to take the initiative with everything and I expect you to just fucking grab me. When you don't then I'm wondering what's wrong and I don't crawl for anyone. We keep getting our signals crossed, Ted. I thought I had made it very clear how I felt yesterday. I spent fucking hours trying to get close to you. I was struggling with trying to work it out. You keep fucking off to find Roadent. It is actually really annoying. Don't go off and find him for advice. Ask me!" he said, but he was smiling now.

A VICIOUS LOVE STORY

I thought it a little strange that Sid would openly have this conversation with me and not care that sitting next to me was Roadent, who didn't comment.

"I will, I promise," I answered and hugged him.

Tracey was standing behind him, and she smiled and nodded to me in approval when I hugged Sid. I suddenly understood why he had been annoyed and sullen earlier. Paul had probably told Sid I'd gone to find Roadent, but neglected to say that it was he who had asked me to leave for a little while; it wasn't a case of me running to Roadent as soon as Sid got in the shower.

I did seem to go off and find Roadent a lot, but it was simply because he was nice and supportive, and had some absolutely brilliant insights into all things, and I really liked the girls and Boogie too. I didn't presume too much with Sid and needed constant reassurance that he wanted to be with me. It was my way of testing that he still liked me, and it was getting in the way of us being together. He pulled me off the bar stool and we walked over to where John was sitting.

"Have you..?" Sid asked John.

"Yeah, I've said I'm sorry, haven't I, Ted?" replied John, seriously. "Not many people dare stand up to me when I get really angry and I never apologise, so you are in a very small and very exclusive club, young lady."

I was pleased Sid had taken the time to ask John to apologise to me. One thing was for sure: I did not want to experience John Lydons anger first hand ever again. He could be a really scary guy.

A VICIOUS LOVE STORY

Roadent got up from his chair at the bar and made his way to the men's room.

"I was asked for an autograph today at the shop around the corner and I suddenly saw Roadent had also signed the paper. What the fuck is Roadent doing, going around and signing autographs? He's not in the fucking band!" John said, indignantly.

"Well, I heard some of the roadies talking at the Student Union yesterday and for them, Roadent is almost as famous as you are," I replied,

I was trying to be helpful and explain the reason why someone might want his autograph, but Sid kicked me gently under the table.

"He's not fucking famous! And he has no fucking right going around writing autographs. These kids probably think he's in the band," John said, and I could hear him getting agitated, so I followed Sid's advice and shut up.

It had been decided that we would go out for a few beers and then have an early night since we had an early start the next day. Bollocks-chops was rambling on about going to a club he'd been told about called Beduinen. It had an over 21s door policy and I was pretty sure they would never let me in. I tried to suggest the Hawk Club again, but they were put off by the previous evening's events and didn't fancy going again.

"They won't let Sid in there," John said.

I tried to argue in favour of it, as it was one of the few places I knew I might stand a chance of getting into.

"It's okay," I said. "It's the weekend and Wally won't be there. The bouncer is called Roger and he is my aunt's neighbour. I'm sure I can persuade him to let Sid come in."

But Bollocks-chops was adamant that we go to Beduinen. I soon realised that as Sid's Norwegian girlfriend, I was lowest in the pecking order and what I said would be ignored if anyone else thought differently. Bollocks-chops always got his way and it wasn't long before we all set off to the nightclub I knew I wouldn't get into.

As we walked, Debbie told me about how she would help out with backing vocals for a band in London when they went into the studio to record, and I was impressed. They all seemed so different now that I'd gotten to know them better, and there were no fans hanging around. We were just like any group of friends out on a Friday night, apart from the fact that these guys stood out with their outlandish looks and clothes.

We trooped into the entrance of the Beduinen club. The bouncer, seated at a table in the entrance hall, shook his head when he saw us. "You lot are not coming in here. I have already heard about yesterday at the Hawk Club, as Rune is a good friend of mine," he said sternly.

"We don't want any hassle, mate," Bollocks-chops answered in Swedish. "We are leaving early tomorrow and we just want a quiet beer before we have an early night."

The bouncer didn't want to listen and kept letting people pass us. Bollocks-chops started making arguments for letting us in, but it only seemed to irritate the bouncer even more. I felt John's hand on my arm and he pushed me forward, indicating with his eyes for me to do

A VICIOUS LOVE STORY

something before we had to spend the night in front of the TV with a cup of tea. Actually, I would have preferred that, but I came forward and tried to get Bollocks-chops to shut up.

"What happened yesterday was a misunderstanding. It wasn't Sid's fault, he was provoked. Look, phone the Hawk Club and talk to Roger, he knows me well. We don't want any trouble," I tried.

The bouncer lifted the receiver of the telephone on the desk next to him and made a call. He was still letting people in before us. The music in the disco was pretty loud and I couldn't hear much of what he said. He had a short talk and then said, "Right, you can come in, but if there is any trouble I am calling the police and you will be barred from here for life," he added, pointing at me.

Everyone was pleased, paid their entrance fee at the counter and walked straight into the club, not looking back. But then the bouncer suddenly said, "Not you and you," pointing to Debbie and me. We had been the last in the queue.

We stood there for a while in silence. Everyone had happily traipsed into the club without realising we were left at the door. We tried to plead our way in, but the bouncer seemed sure the band would cause trouble and the police might get involved, and they would shut down the club if they saw me in there. It was hopeless.

"Shit," I said under my breath. "I'm going to go to the Hawk Club. We can go together if you like."

Debbie nodded, but said nothing.

Tracey suddenly appeared at the door. "I was told to find out what's taking so long" she said.

"He won't let us in," I answered, and pointed to the bouncer who was stopping other people from entering.

"Okay, I'll see you back at the hotel," Tracey said, and turned to go back into the club.

I remember being surprised by her actions. If it was one of my close friends, they would never just leave me at the door, but go with me. Debbie and Tracey obviously didn't have that kind of loyalty towards each other. Or it was a matter of Debbie not getting in the way of Tracey hanging out with the guys, and maybe she would get lucky and hook up with Steve if he didn't find anyone else he preferred that night.

"Actually, Debbie is 21," I told the bouncer." I saw her passport earlier at the hotel. We can go and get it if you like."

The bouncer seemed to consider this for a while, and then nodded and let Debbie go into the club.

"Nice one, Ted," Debbie said, as she stalked off with Tracey, smiling.

"Can you tell Sid I'm going home?" I asked her, and she nodded.

It took a few minutes until Sid arrived at the door, just as I was beginning to wonder whether Debbie had actually said anything to him at all.

"I wondered where you were," he said, "I thought you were in the loo or something. We sent Tracey out. Whats happening?"

A VICIOUS LOVE STORY

We tried to argue with the bouncer to let me in if I promised to just drink Coke, but he was adamant.

"It's fine. I'm tired anyway and I'll just go home," I said.

"No, don't do that," replied Sid. "Listen, Ted, go and get your stuff, and meet me at the hotel. I'm just going to have a couple of beers and I'll be straight back. One hour tops. We leave early tomorrow."

I walked out into the summer evening and sat down on a nearby bench. The night was warm and humid. It never gets really dark in this area during the summer, so although it was getting on for 9pm, it was still as light as an English afternoon. Some people passed me, coming and going between the discos in the area. I saw a couple of them look at me as if wondering what on earth I was doing sitting there, when the night was still young, and there were parties to be going to and fun to be had.

I wasn't feeling in a party mood at all now – I kept turning things over in my mind. I remember thinking, what the hell are you doing, Ted? I was in trouble with my feelings and I knew nothing good could come of this. There was nothing I wanted more than to go with Sid, but I knew, deep down in my heart, that I couldn't do it. I was sure he wanted to be with me, but I also understood now that I would have to fend for myself.

I desperately wished I was older. I started thinking how embarrassing it would be if they were to play a gig in Sweden and I wasn't allowed in. I was sure my mother would make sure every venue at which the Sex Pistols were scheduled to gig would know about the underage girl travelling with them, while she drove there to get me. It was hopeless.

I wished I could trust Sid, but I wasn't sure I could. There were the drugs and the girlfriend. I kept wondering whether he would have told me about Nancy himself if Steve hadn't mentioned it. I knew he was angry with Nancy now, but what would happen when they met again? They had been seeing each other for a few months, and he knew her a lot better than me. He said he wanted to end it, that it was a crap relationship and that he was angry with her, but anger was an emotion and, from my point of view, indifference would have been a lot better. Another aspect was that I didn't really know how he felt about me. I knew he liked me, a lot, but how much exactly? More than he liked Nancy?

If I left Trondheim, I would be running away from home, and since my mother had my passport, I would have to make my way back to Trondheim when Sid and the band left Sweden the following weekend. I would be in an awful lot of trouble when I got back. I would most certainly be grounded for a long time and wouldn't be allowed on any trips to London alone. I would be giving up a lot for a guy I'd only known for two days. I knew that if I did go with him I would get even more attached, and it would be even more difficult to handle the separation that would inevitably come at some point.

There were so many thoughts running through my mind that it was giving me a headache. I got up and walked away from the club; not in the direction of my flat, but towards the Hawk Club. My shoes were new and uncomfortable, and my feet were killing me by the time I got there. It turned out I was right about the bouncer. Wally wasn't there and Roger, the weekend bouncer, said "Hi" to me as I went in. I took a seat by the bar and noticed a few people look at me. There was some whispering and pointing going on. I ignored it and ordered a beer.

Roger came over and kept me company, and wondered what on earth I was doing at the Hawk Club when he had been told our group was at Beduinen. It was a slow night and he wanted to know everything that had happened the previous evening. He'd heard about it from Rune, but wanted to know more. I wasn't really in the mood for talking, but I gave him the big picture. Roger assured me that had we come to the Hawk Club that evening, he most certainly would have let us all in. It was good for business and he would have made sure there wasn't any more trouble. He was really nice.

I sat at the bar for a while longer and then decided to go home. I was chickening out, and thought if I just went home and went to sleep, Sid would just leave the next day without me and I wouldn't have to go through all the emotional turmoil.

I walked slowly back towards my parents' flat. I had to pass the Phoenix hotel on my way and I considered making a detour to avoid meeting them, but the blisters on my feet stopped me. I walked on in the summer evening, and just as I passed the hotel I realised I couldn't go through with it. Sid had a right to know how I felt and maybe that would make it easier.

A VICIOUS LOVE STORY

I entered the hotel lobby and the old night watchman was once again seated behind the reception desk. He greeted me cheerfully. I asked him if the English people had returned yet, and he said no. I sat down on the red sofa that Sid had been sleeping on the very first time I saw him. It felt like it had all happened weeks ago, not a mere day and a half earlier. The watchman came out from behind his desk with two cups and a thermos, and poured us each a cup of steaming coffee. We sat quietly for a while.

Then he said, "I've been at this job for a long time, and there are a lot of stories I could tell you that would make your hair stand on end. The things I've seen would amaze you and make you lose faith in human nature."

I hoped he wasn't going to go into a long monologue because I really wasn't interested, but he was a kind, old chap and I smiled at him, after thanking him for the coffee.

"You're a bit young to be hanging out here, young lady. Don't misunderstand; I know you are only here for that young fellow. Where is he, by the way?"

Just then, Roadent, Tracey and Debbie entered the hotel. They smiled at me, not at all surprised to see me there. When I asked where Sid was, they said he was just behind them, and then they piled into the lift. I was just wondering whether my first plan of simply going home, and not seeing Sid before he left, had been the best one after all when he suddenly walked into the lobby with John and Steve. He broke into a bright smile as soon as he saw me and put his arm around my shoulders. We went into the lift together.

A VICIOUS LOVE STORY

"Did you have a good night?" I asked.

He turned me towards him and looked at me closely, like he heard something in my voice and could sense that something was wrong. "Yeah, was okay, bit boring. You?"

"I was at the Hawk Club for an hour," I said meekly, as we entered his room. "Where is Paul?"

I had spent the night in the place where Paul was supposed to sleep. He had slept on John's sofa in the suite and I doubted he would want to stay there again.

"He stayed at the club with Boogie. We got talking to some girls and one seemed to like Paul. He and Boogie decided to stay, and make the most of it. He doesn't have much luck with the ladies. It's not that he doesn't want to. It's just that he doesn't really know how to go about it and he's really shy," Sid said, laughing. "Seriously, he could fall into a barrel full of boobs and come out sucking his thumb," he added, and we laughed.

I sat on the bed after kicking my shoes off. Sid looked around, as if suddenly noticing that the bag I was supposed to have brought with me wasn't there. He sat down heavily on the bed.

"Still no bag, I see. What's going on, Teddie?" he asked in a serious tone. "If you don't want to come with me then just tell me. Stop stringing me along and making excuses."

I took a deep breath and told him everything I'd been thinking, and all of the problems I foresaw if I went with him. I said I thought he should go and do his 'pop star' stuff for as long as he was able, that he should enjoy it, and if he was one day told he wouldn't be allowed to continue in the band then he could come back and find me. My words hung heavily in the air in the dimly lit room.

Sid didn't say anything. He just sat there in silence for what seemed a long time. Slowly, he got up from the bed and took all his clothes off. He got under the sheets and turned his back towards me. I didn't know what to do. Did he want me to leave or join him? I put my hand on his back and when he didn't remove it or move away, I slid under the sheets with him. We didn't talk, but I cried after we made love and he held on to me.

A little later, I snuggled close to Sid. I could feel him stir and he stroked the top of my head.

"Your hair smells so nice. It's like fruit," he said quietly. "Reminds me of apples."

"God, I am going to miss you so badly," I answered

"You don't have to miss me if you come with me," he said and sighed.

"I'm going to do what I can to get over to London as soon as you get back, but remember to make sure you are free to see me," I said. Thinking about Nancy made me extremely jealous and insecure, and I think he knew it.

"I've told you I will. What more can I say?"

I leaned in and started to kiss him hotly, and then I moved down on to his neck and bit him carefully, at first.

"Okay, so this is what I'm going to do. I'm going to mark you so you are mine and not hers," I said, a little childishly, between kisses and bites.

He laughed. "Ouch, you can bite me all you want. I told you, it's none of her fucking business."

A VICIOUS LOVE STORY

Sid laughed again when I bit him a little harder. "Go ahead and make your mark. Make as many as you want if that proves to you that I'm serious."

I made two big love bites on his neck. He said, with a laugh, that it was painful and then it was my turn. He leaned in and started to bite me, but I was too ticklish and kept giggling. Sid finally managed to make a big bluish-red mark on my neck. We made love again, having made a pact to be together as soon as I could get over to London, and then we fell asleep.

At some point, Paul came back and simply took a place in the bed. I was woken up when Paul started moving around and I said there wasn't enough room. I whispered to Sid that I would leave, but he said, "No!", and simply pulled me closer to give Paul a little more room. It wasn't long before Paul was complaining again.

I could hear Sid snoring peacefully and I poked him gently, but he didn't wake up. I slithered carefully out of the bed and put my clothes on.

Paul sat up and looked at me with a sleepy face. "Is it morning already," he asked quietly.

"No, Paul, go back to sleep."

"Where are you going, Ted? I'll make more room," he whispered.

"No, it's okay, I'm going home. Please tell Sid I'll come back before he leaves," I whispered back, but Paul had already put his head back down on the pillow and was breathing quietly.

I sneaked out of the hotel, waving at the night watchman as I passed.

A VICIOUS LOVE STORY

"Out for another short trip?" he asked, cheekily.

"Yeah, you know me, keep turning up like a bad penny," I answered.

I hurried back to my parents' flat. I knew I only had a few short hours of sleep if I was to make it back to the hotel in time to say goodbye to Sid. Being back home felt good, because once I had decided I wouldn't go with Sid, it was just a question of getting through saying goodbye to him. I set the alarm and went to sleep, vowing to myself that I would never, ever let anyone get that close to me again.

A VICIOUS LOVE STORY

CHAPTER 11 THE LAST GOODBYE

I was very tired and nervous when I re-entered the Phoenix hotel on Saturday, July 23rd. I had made sure I looked my best. When I walked past reception, the girl at the desk called out to me, "Morning, Teddie, they are in the restaurant having breakfast."

I smiled and thanked her. It was strange, but everyone at the hotel knew us all by now. I stood at the door to the restaurant and I could see that everyone had gathered for breakfast; even Debbie and Tracey were there. Tore was talking to John and waved when he saw me at the door. I waved back, but didn't enter the room. I couldn't see Sid to begin with.

"Sid!" Debbie called and pointed to him, standing by the cereal at the buffet. He was concentrating on what he was doing and didn't react. Both Debbie and Roadent called to him, and still he didn't look up.

"John, Ted's here," Roadent shouted, using his other name.

"We are not allowed to do that," Paul said.

"He's not answering to Sid. What the fuck am I supposed to do? I don't give a toss if Malcolm has said we can't use it. Fucking stupid," Roadent answered angrily.

Sid reacted with surprise and looked up at Roadent, who, along with Debbie, was pointing towards where I was standing at the door. Sid's whole face broke into a wide smile. He came over to me straight away and pulled me towards him. People in the hotel lobby were staring at us, so he moved me aside so that we stood under the stairs, and he kissed me for a long time.

"God, I'm so glad you came," he said when he finally let go of me.

"I wouldn't just let you go without saying goodbye," I said, struggling to control the tears that were threatening to well out of my eyes.

"I was gutted when I woke up and found you'd gone. I didn't think I would ever see you again," he said, kissing me again. "Damn!"

"What?" I asked, thinking it was something important he'd forgotten.

"Now I really want you!"

We both laughed.

"What? Again?" I asked, teasingly "I don't think I can handle any more sex for a little while." I answered with a giggle, but I did actually mean it.

"Damn! I have checked out of the room," he said, but then became serious. "I hate this. I don't want to go."

"And I don't want you to go," I answered.

We stood together, kissing for a while. When the others had finished their breakfast, we all went outside into the morning sunshine and watched as Roadent and Boogie put the last of the stuff into the van. All the luggage and instruments would be driven to Sweden. The van was packed solid. Sid had his favourite T-shirt on again and I could see it was speckled with blood.

"I look a mess," he said, pointing to the bloodstains. "I was in such a hurry this morning and really tired since someone kept me up half the night!"

A VICIOUS LOVE STORY

He laughed and nudged my shoulder, indicating that I was that someone.

"Roadent kept nagging me to give him my bags, as they were packing the van, and I just grabbed what I thought was a clean T-shirt. I didn't notice until it was too late that this is the one I wore when I got into the fight at the after-party. Roadent has packed my luggage furthest in, in the van and I can't get at it."

We laughed as we looked at the dried stains.

Debbie and Tracey sat to one side on a wall, watching us. They had to hitchhike back to Oslo and time was running out for them, as they couldn't be late for their boat. I remember thinking how strange it was that they spent so much time and expense to see the band for just a couple of days. Tore and the hotel manager had locked themselves in the manager's office to discuss the fee for the damage we'd done to the rooms, and compensation for all the trouble we had caused. It was getting late and I could see Bollocks-chops getting edgy, as his friend with the aeroplane had filed a flight plan and couldn't wait indefinitely to leave.

"Come with me," Sid said as we stood together beside the van.

"I can't. You know why," I answered. "I'll get into so much trouble. They will cause trouble for you and I'll have to make my way back to Trondheim on my own since I can't go with you any further. It's hopeless."

I was beginning to wish I had brought my packed bag and whatever money I could find, and just got in to the van with him. Debbie and Tracey were looking at us, and I could see them talking. Debbie got up from where she was sitting and marched towards us, just as Bollocks-chops came out of the hotel and made his way towards the van.

"Get in the van, Ted," she said, annoyed. "You make me so fucking angry!"

Sid and I clung to each other, and I couldn't keep the tears at bay when it was finally time to get into the van. It was getting late. Bollocks-chops said they had to leave now and that an English journalist would also be travelling on the plane. I didn't catch his name and thought it strange as I hadn't seen any English journalists around us after the concert, or on Friday. I couldn't imagine what he would be doing in Trondheim. The fact that a journalist was flying with them made John furious.

"I don't fucking believe this," he said angrily. "That journalist is a total wanker. I won't speak to him."

"Wow, what's that all about?" I asked Sid, as we stood clinging to each other by the van.

"John doesn't like him. He wrote very positively about us to begin with. He's actually a mate of mine," Sid replied, and was smiling at John's temper.

"He wrote that our concert was totally crap. He fucking stabbed us in the back," John spat.

"We played fucking crap, John," Steve said, from where he was standing by the van, smoking a cigarette. "He just wrote his opinion and he was right. You can't say we played well at that gig."

"I know we played crap, but he doesn't have to write it, does he?" John answered. "I won't fucking talk to him."

A VICIOUS LOVE STORY

"It wasn't all that bad," Sid told me, "but John tends to take everything personally."

John got into the van.

"It's still not too late to change your mind," said Sid.

"You really want me to come with you?" I asked.

Sid nodded and said "Yes."

"Room for one more?" he asked Bollocks-chops, who responded with a nod.

"Come on, Teddie, you can keep Steve and me company back to Växjö. The rest are flying. No room on the plane, I'm afraid."

"I'll come with you in the van, if you want," Sid said.

"Listen to me, I want to, I really do, but I can't. I'll try and come after you. I'll get myself sorted here and come to London as soon as I can," I replied.

"Get into the van, you total fucking idiot!" Debbie called to me, from where she was sitting on the steps of the main entrance to the Phoenix hotel.

I turned and smiled at her, but didn't respond.

Tore had finished talking to the manager and he was red in the face when he finally emerged from the office

Everyone except Sid was in the van and they were ready to leave. Tore gave Bollocks-chops instructions on how to get out of Trondheim and get the right road to the airport, and on to the Swedish border.

Sid and I kissed again, and this time it lasted for a long time as neither of us wanted to let go. Once again, we agreed I would do what I could to get to Sweden or London. I cried and the tears were running down my cheeks when they called for him to get into the van.

A VICIOUS LOVE STORY

"I'll be there before you miss me," I said, "and you never know, you might meet ABBA in Sweden."

"Probably not. The places we play are crap and I doubt I'll ever meet ABBA there, but get to me as soon as you can. Promise," he said, taking a step away from me, as the others were now getting a little anxious to be on the road.

I ran my hand over his face. I could see he was tired. "I promise. You never know, Sid, ABBA may come and watch you play. Stranger things have happened."

Sid let go of me and walked away. I saw him sit down in the van, and his face was sad and bore a serious expression. I heard John say something, and Sid responded by throwing himself at him. They started fighting. Sid pinned John to the back seat where he was sitting, and I noticed he was gurgling as if Sid was throttling him, but then John started to laugh. Sid pulled away when Bollocks-chops shouted for them to settle down. I could see he was red in the face and serious, with anger in his eyes, so I am guessing John's remark was probably something to do with me.

I waved as the van pulled away from the curb. I had such a dreadful feeling in the pit of my stomach. It felt like I'd turned him away and sent him out into the world alone. I know it sounds strange, but with hindsight I felt that I'd let him down somehow. I had a feeling he was used to people bailing out and letting him down, and that he was used to being disappointed. He just accepted it and tried not to show it bothered him too much, but I knew it did, and I made a promise to myself that I would get to him one way or another.

A VICIOUS LOVE STORY

Debbie and Tracey waited anxiously as Tore went to make a phone call, since he had a band that would be driving to Oslo for gigs and the girls could get a lift with them. It would be quicker than hitchhiking. I went to sit with them on the wall by the steps to the hotel. I was weeping and snotty.

"You make me so angry, Ted!" Debbie almost spat the words out. "Do you know that any girl in England would kill to be Sid's girlfriend? He's like this needy puppy around you. I've never seen him like that with anyone before. You have Sid Vicious fall in love with you and you let him go. It makes me so mad. Are you insane?" she asked.

"She feels bad enough already," Tracey argued in my defence.

"I feel gutted. If I went to Sweden I'd only have to come back. My parents have seen to that and they have threatened to cause a lot of trouble, and they don't make empty threats," I said sadly.

"Yes, but at least you would have been able to spend some more time with him," Tracey said.

"You are right, but if I take off there is no way I will ever be allowed to go to London, ever! So it's better for me to do what Roadent said and square things at home, and then go to London in a week or two. I need to be sneakier about this. Will you see Sid in London?" I asked, and they both nodded.

"Can you tell him I really miss him already, and I'll do anything and everything I can to get over as soon as I can?"

A VICIOUS LOVE STORY

They nodded again, but I could see Debbie was shaking her head as if she didn't really believe me.

"You are totally mad, Teddie," Debbie said again. "You have Sid fall in love with you and I can't believe you just let him go!"

"What would you do, Tracey, if Steve had asked you to go to Sweden with him now?" I asked, hoping she would support my decision.

"I would be in that van faster than a rat up a drain pipe, Teddie. I wouldn't care about anything else."

"Then you're braver than me," I answered.

Debbie just shook her head at me like I was the village idiot who didn't understand a thing.

"You would have been okay. He would have taken care of you. Jesus Christ, you really are so fucking stupid."

She was almost fuming with anger. I was beginning to think that maybe she was right, and that I was the most stupid person alive. I just felt so cheated. Tore stood quietly beside us for a few minutes, listening to what we said.

"Oh, leave her alone, you two," he said and gave me a hug, but we both knew that the girls weren't being vindictive.

"Right, I have a band driving to Oslo now, and they will come here in a few minutes and there is plenty of room, so you can get a lift with them and get there in time for your boat," he told the girls.

I remember thinking how dedicated Debbie and Tracey were to the band. They had taken a boat that took more time getting back and forth to England than they had spent

A VICIOUS LOVE STORY

in Trondheim. We said our goodbyes and hugged each other. The two English groupies, who turned out not to be groupies, had become my friends, however weird the circumstances of our friendship had been. Tore drove me home, and I went up into my room and cried for the rest of the day.

CHAPTER 12 DESPERATION

The day after Sid left me in Trondheim, I felt so empty. I had spent the entire previous day in my room and refused to talk to anyone. My mother had knocked at my door with food, but I didn't touch it. There was absolutely nothing I could do about my situation and I felt so cheated. I was angry with everyone and my parents in particular. I felt it was their fault I was so unhappy for hiding my passport and taking my money. As soon as they left for work later that afternoon, I started the search for my passport once again, with no luck.

On Sunday afternoon there was a knock on my door and Grethe arrived. She was my closest friend and I poured my heart out to her, and she listened for hours to all the details. "I'm so in love Grethe, I feel sick," I told her. "I have never felt like this about anyone before and it scares me."

We decided to lie to my parents and say I was staying with Grethe for a few days, since I was so upset with them, and then we would hitchhike to Sweden together. It was the best plan we could come up with to actually go after Sid, and not have to deal with all the aggravation from my parents. This way there would be no trouble. I was annoyed with myself for not being more devious from the start.

When Sid had said he was staying in a small place in Sweden, I had thought it was just across the border. I found a road map of Scandinavia and sat down to study it, looking intently for the town of Växjö, but I couldn't find it. I traced the road starting in Trondheim and over the closest border, by Östersund. I had heard which motorways Bollocks-chops would be driving and we spent hours looking for the town.

ROADENT: We flew from Trondheim to Arlanda, Stockholm airport. As we passed through the airport towards Customs we saw Anni-Frid and Agnetha of that other band, ABBA. Sid and I walked straight up to them, and Sid said, "Oi, are you ABBA?" When they said yes, he said, "We are the Sex Pistols, we like your music." Anni-Frid and Agnetha told us that they were on their way to London with British Airways, and Sid told them that we had just arrived in our private jet from gigs in Norway.

We spent the rest of the day in my room, taking turns to study the map of Sweden. Things weren't working out the way I wanted them to. Grethe and I didn't have any money. We decided we would have to get some cash first and it was proving difficult. On the day I knew Sid had his court case I was jittery. It was either Monday, 25th or Tuesday, 26th of July. I was afraid things wouldn't go the way he wanted them to, and that he would be found guilty and thrown into prison. I was also afraid he would meet Nancy while in London, even though he had said he wouldn't. He said that there wouldn't be time, even if he wanted to, which he didn't.

A VICIOUS LOVE STORY

Grethe finally found the town we were searching for and I couldn't believe how far away it was – right on the other side of Sweden, outside Stockholm. It was Wednesday now and Växjö might as well have been on the other side of the world. The Sex Pistols were due back in England on Saturday, July 30th. Time was running out. As the weekend drew closer, we decided we needed a plan B. It was now clear that there was no way I could get to Sweden in time.

We agreed that I would have to find my birth certificate and apply for a new passport. Grethe and I would get jobs, save all our cash and optimistically get a flight to London in a week or two. Every day I checked the newspapers for the pictures that the photographer had taken when we were out shopping, but they never surfaced. I regretted not giving him my real name, but at the time I was so sure I would be with Sid in Sweden.

I recently learnt that the photos were archived in the wrong place for over 30 years and had been found, only to disappear again. There was a small thing about us in *NÅ*, a gossip magazine. It included the picture of me with Steve Jones at the after-party at the Hawk Club. Most of the things that were written about the band were exaggerated. One article explained how Sid had been frothing at the mouth with spit at the club. Another said he had burped loudly too. There was one article that stated he was too drugged up to be coherent, and yet another said the band was so high when they walked on stage at the Student Union that John had to be helped out.

A VICIOUS LOVE STORY

> Under: For søte jenters oppmerksomhet smelter selv en steinhard punker. Det er nå så rart med det.

Facsimile from NÅ magazine

A VICIOUS LOVE STORY

Most of what they wrote was lies and I found myself getting angry on their behalf, but there was nothing I could do. There were even people gossiping in Trondheim about how we got thrown out of the music shop for spitting.

> **Bassisten Sid Viscous (i midten) ser litt forpjusket ut etter slagsmålet. Den svenske turnélederen til venstre må nærmest sette seg på ham for at han skal holde fred.**

Facsimile from NÅ magazine

A VICIOUS LOVE STORY

Totally ridiculous stories with no truth to them at all, made up because people wanted them to have been outrageous.

Neon leon (left) and Eileen Polk (right). Photo Eileen Polk ©

The weeks passed without either Grethe or I gaining employment. We had a pact to go to London, but we were getting nowhere fast. I was pining away in Trondheim and becoming very thin. I knew my parents were worried about me. I refused to speak to my mother for several weeks. I told my stepfather that I wanted my passport and then we could talk. I'd stopped going to the Hawk Club and I avoided the Phoenix hotel. I threatened to run away

A VICIOUS LOVE STORY

on several occasions and argued myself blue in the face, asking for my passport and the money to go to London.

EILEEN POLK : I know it must be difficult to read all the lies, and I can tell you and Sid were in love. I know what that feels like. Many people have never loved anyone and only think about the negative sex and drugs aspect.

My parents were so worried that they sent me to Tromsø, to spend a couple of weeks with my grandmother at our summer house by Kattfjord. It didn't help at all. I was pining away, taking long walks by the fjord and planning my escape. One morning in mid-August I woke up to the news that Elvis Presley had passed away and I broke into tears. I wasn't a fan of Elvis, but it was just so sad and I was feeling so emotional that I couldn't cope with it. My grandmother arranged for me to go home two days later.

I was having lunch with a few friends at a local café in Trondheim when the first message arrived from London. We ate there almost every day, so it wasn't difficult to find me. It was the end of August and over a month since Sid had left. I was beginning to get used to the idea that I would never see him again.

A mutual friend of Casino Steel had been to London for a visit. I didn't know him well, but he came to find me at the café. He was beaming at me and obviously knew I would be happy about the news he would give when he came to talk to us.

A VICIOUS LOVE STORY

"I have a message to you from Sid Vicious," he said, smiling, and I felt my heart leap into my throat.

"I met him in London when I went to visit Cas. He said to tell you he met ABBA at Stockholm airport right after he left you, and you were right and stranger things could actually happen. He asked me to tell you that he hopes you will come to London and look him up. He said remember what you promised. Oh, and he said can you get a move on because he's waiting."

I remember how thrilled I was to finally hear from him, and the fact that he still wanted to see me.

"Was he with anyone when you met him?" I asked anxiously "A girl?"

"Not that I could see. There was a group of people sitting together and I think there were a few girls there, but he didn't look like he was with any of them in particular. And he didn't try to hide that he was asking about you from anyone of them as far as I could see. So I didn't see a girlfriend, if that's what you are asking," he said, and smiled reassuringly at me. "Funnily enough, he asked me the same about you. He wanted to know if you were seeing anyone that I knew of. I said I didn't think you were seeing anyone."

I was relieved and happy. I still had no idea where my passport was and I still had no job or money, but the message he sent motivated me all the more to get myself sorted out. I left the cafe early and went to the office where birth records were stored. They wouldn't just give me my birth certificate. I had to apply for a copy to be sent to my house in the post. And the application form had to have the signature of my legal guardian; my mother, in other words.

It angered me that as a 16 year old, you have absolutely no rights at all. I took the form home with me and secretly filled it in. I forged my mother's signature and posted it the following day. I contacted a travel agent and was told the price of a week in London, which didn't sound too expensive.

Mates of Casino Steel visited him on a regular basis. These guys were older than me and, although I knew them well, they didn't see me on a daily basis, and most of them never thought to tell me they were going to London so that I could send a message back to Sid. There was one guy who had heard I wanted to get a message to him who actually looked me up a week before he left. I was so excited. I wrote Sid a long letter, telling him about everything I was doing to get to London. I told him I'd come soon. I included the telephone number to the cinema, if he wished to phone. We didn't have a telephone at the flat yet.

I walked around in a daze all week, imagining how Sid would feel when he got the letter, and wondering what he would write back to me. It was with great disappointment that I learned that my friend hadn't met him. He had been told the Sex Pistols were away on a tour. I was devastated when I was handed back my letter, unopened.

ROADENT: Look at Sid on the Holland tour. It was Malcolm's bright idea to send us on a Holland tour to get Sid off smack. That was a great idea. Send Sid to

A VICIOUS LOVE STORY

Holland to get off smack, where smack is an everyday occurrence. Good idea... not. Sid would be playing the wrong tune and things like that, or he would be playing a bar behind. It was dreadful. But you could do that. You didn't actually have to be good musically. Punk was a movement. It was music and fashion, and attitude.

It took a couple of weeks for my birth certificate to arrive and by this time I was feeling a little desperate, as I couldn't get a job. I wasn't qualified to do anything. It was late that autumn when I managed to get a job at a menswear shop. I worked six days a week for a pittance, but at least I was finally earning some money. I would never have done this type of job on a full-time basis had it not been for the fact that I so desperately wanted to go to London.

After a few weeks though, I found myself thinking less and less about going to London, and more about what I wanted to do in future. Selling Y-Fronts was not something I was going to do for the rest of my life. I knew if I went to London it would only be for a week or so. I knew deep down that anything between me and Sid was hopeless, and I started to resign myself to that fact. The feelings I had for him gradually became a cherished memory.

It was in late November that a second message arrived from Sid. Another friend of Casino Steel had been to London to visit him. Once again, I was having coffee with friends at our usual place and again a guy came up to me to tell me he had a message, but asked for a private word. The guy asked that we sit alone, as he didn't want the others to hear what he had to say.

"Right, Ted, I promised to talk to you as soon as I got back. He was so insistent. It was actually a bit annoying, but I promised, so here I am," he said seriously. "Okay, so there are several points he wanted me to be sure I told you. Firstly, he said that you were right about stranger things happening and he actually met ABBA at Arlanda airport after he left you."

"I know. He sent a message about that earlier," I said and smiled.

"Then he said to tell you that he hasn't forgotten about you and that he would be very happy if you came to see him in London. He said you promised him something, but he wouldn't tell me what it was. Just said, remember what you promised. He said try to get over as soon as possible because it was very important he see you before he goes on a tour of the US next year. He said he misses you and to get yourself over to London as soon as possible because he has some good news. There is going to be another tour of Scandinavia and he said tell her I'm coming back! He said you can meet up with him in Stockholm before the start of the tour and don't let him down this time."

"Wow, that's great. How did he look? Was he well?" I asked. I was smiling so broadly that if I didn't have ears, it would have gone all the way around my head.

"I don't want you to take this the wrong way, but I don't think it's a good idea for you to go and see him," he said seriously. "You certainly shouldn't stay with him. If you go, stay with Casino instead, then at least I'll know you are taken care of properly."

"Why? Was he drunk when you talked to him?" I asked.

"I have no idea what it was he was on, but it was definitely not just alcohol. He latched on to me as soon as Casino introduced me. He kept asking after you and was so insistent it got a little too much. He asked me what you were doing and if I knew whether you were seeing anyone."

"What did you tell him?" I asked.

He smiled. "Don't worry. I told him that as far as I knew you were not seeing anyone in particular since he left. He would nag me about what I was to tell you, and made sure I repeated it back to him so I didn't forget anything, and made me promise. I actually almost regretted saying I knew you, Ted."

It was strange of Sid to say he wanted to meet up in Stockholm since I later learned that the tour would start in Finland, but that's what he said. I gather they would be going to Finland via Stockholm. It's the only explanation I have.

ROADENT: I was meant to be on the US tour, but I got my visa refused. Everyone got their visas refused to begin with, but they managed to get the band visas. Malcolm (McLaren) and Boogie had already got visas, so they could travel on ahead on tourist visas. I got mine refused so I stayed behind to try to sort out the next tour, which was again a Scandinavian tour that

was to start in Finland. Of course that was all cancelled.

I got home one night to the Pistols' rehearsal rooms at about three in the morning, from the Speakeasy, and *The Sun* phoned up, saying, "Is it true you have all been banned from Finland?" *The Sun* always knew before us what was happening. So I phoned up the Finnish Ambassador's residence, thinking I'd get a sort of low-ranked assistant, but the Finnish Ambassador answered the phone. I said, "What's this about us being banned from your country?" and he said, "I don't know anything about this".

Anyway, we had all been made 'persona non grata' in Finland, based on reputation alone. Well it was a quasi-communist country, wasn't it? I then heard that the band had split up anyway. Malcolm didn't want people to know to begin with because he thought he could persuade them to continue. I had booked an English PA (sound system) and Lighting System to go over to Stockholm, and all of the crew had actually got on the plane, and they were paged off and had to give back their Duty Free. For which they haven't forgiven me to this day.

I didn't want to hear about Sid's drug problem. Everyone just assumed he was drugged up all the time and I thought this to be untrue. I thought it was an image they had made for Sid, and the lies and the rumours were often exaggerated to the extent of ridiculousness. The fact that he had been coherent enough to get another message to me made me believe that he was probably just on a little speed, which he said gave him a buzz. The fact that he had been insistent and sounded a little hyper tallied well with what I had seen when he used speed in Trondheim. I think I was in denial when it came to Sid and drugs. I had no experience of drugs and neither had my friends, as far as I knew, so there was no one I could ask about it.

EILEEN POLK: I think Sid had a really sweet and caring nature. I think he would just snap in to another mode or alternate personality when he was really drunk. Nancy was always buying him drinks. I am sorry that your mother kept you from seeing Sid again, but I'm sure she was just trying to protect you from drug addiction. I don't know why some of the people in the punk scene become addicts and others don't. I was always careful never to use any drug more than a couple of times. My drug use was only experimental, but because of the friends I had, many people assumed I was using a lot of drugs too. (When you lie down with dogs, don't be surprised to wake up with fleas, they say). So I have a much worse reputation than I really deserve!
    But other people like Richard Hell, for example, were really smart – so why did they become addicts? I think it's part of the 'down and out bohemian culture – like Tom Verlaine of Television having the fantasy that he was some late 19th-century poet (like Verlaine or Rimbaud) A 'derangement of the senses' was considered a cool way to be inspired (Jim Morrison

A VICIOUS LOVE STORY

thought this too). Other people like Johnny Thunders were not that smart or literate, but just liked getting fucked up! DeeDee Ramone was smart in his own weird way, but he could be a real idiot sometimes.

"Was he with anyone else when you spoke to him?" I asked, finally.

"Yes, he had a couple of mates there. I didn't see anyone else. He basically latched on to me that first evening and wouldn't leave me alone," he answered.

"No, I mean, did he have a girlfriend with him?" I asked, anxiously.

"If there was one, I didn't see her. There wasn't any girlfriend there whilst I was there, and I met him several times during the two weeks I was there. I actually asked Cas if we could avoid him towards the end as I got a bit sick of him."

I was pleased to hear he hadn't had Nancy in tow. There was sometimes stuff in the newspaper and in magazines about the Sex Pistols, and I had seen a couple of photos of Sid with Nancy. But he had told me earlier that they used old photographs when articles were written and I decided I would just avoid reading anything about them. It infuriated me when they wrote lies. My friends would try to show me articles if there was anything in a newspaper, but soon stopped when they saw I refused to read it.

A VICIOUS LOVE STORY

Photo Peter Gravelle ©

A VICIOUS LOVE STORY

I was so happy when I walked back to our flat. My birth certificate had arrived earlier, but I'd still done nothing to get a passport. I assumed Sid had gone back to Nancy and forgotten all about me, and that I was exaggerating his feelings for me in my mind to coincide with the feelings I had. The messages from him made me adamant to go to London and see for myself.

ROADENT: Nancy was a complete nightmare. We tried to kidnap her once. We sent Sid to the dentist. We had a one-way ticket to New York for her. We were all outside the band's HQ in Marble Arch, right by the Holiday Inn Marble Arch. It was me, Boogie, Jamie Reid and Sophie, The Glitterbest (Pistols' management company) secretary. Sophie was great and held everything together.

We were all wearing these bluish gabardine coats that Malcolm was selling at the time. It was like this strange sort of gangster thing. All these blue gabardine coats trying to hustle Nancy into the taxi. And she was shouting, "You can't do this. This is kidnapping. You can't do this," in a loud American accent. And then she ran off to the Holiday Inn and we'd all follow her. We dragged her out and said, "Look Nancy, you know it's for the best." And she'd be saying, "You can't do this. Does Sid know you are doing this?" It was complete nonsense, but quite fun. We failed miserably unfortunately.

A VICIOUS LOVE STORY

I contacted Tore and he gave me Casino Steel's phone number. I thought Cas could help me get a message to Sid and we could arrange a time for me to call. I phoned Cas several times too, with no answer. In mid-December, I let the phone ring a lot longer than I usually did and to my surprise a girl answered it, who told me it was a pay phone in the hall at the flats where Casino lived. She went off to knock on his door, but came back to tell me he was probably at work since it was the middle of the day. I decided I would leave things alone over the holidays. It was important I co-ordinated my trip to London with Sid. In the late 70s, getting on a plane to London was a very expensive thing to do. I didn't want to risk going to London at a time when he was on tour.

ROADENT: I was on the SPOTS tour (Sex Pistols On Tour Secretly). Wolverhampton Lafayette was the first gig. Then we went somewhere down in the West Country where Julien Temple managed to fall through the ceiling. Great hilarity and right in front of the stage. He was trying to get a moody camera angle. He was crawling over this false ceiling to see if he could get a better shot. Of course, false ceilings aren't very strong and he came falling down on to the dance floor in front of the stage. I remember the last two gigs with the SPOTS. One was the Cromer Pavilion on the East Anglia coast on Christmas Eve and the last one was Ivanhoe's in Huddersfield on Christmas Day. We did two gigs. One for the kids and one for the grown-ups. It was probably the best Christmas day I ever had.

A VICIOUS LOVE STORY

I tried to phone Cas again during the first days of January, but still no answer. I met Tore at a disco one night during the first days of January 1978. He was sitting with a group of mates. There was a guy with him that I'd never seen before. He had short, spiky dark hair and looked like a musician. You know the type, with the leather jacket and the studded belt, etcetera. "Hey, Ted, come over here. There's someone I want you to meet," Tore called. "This is Casino Steel," he said, pointing to the dark-haired guy.

Casino smiled at me and motioned me to sit next to him. I introduced myself and sat down.

"I have been calling you for weeks," I said, laughing. "No wonder you are not answering."

He told me about life in London and about playing in the band, and a little about what Sid was up to. He couldn't help me though as he was going to be in Trondheim for a few more weeks. In fact, he said he was so disillusioned with what he was doing in London that he didn't know if he would go back for some time. I instantly liked Cas. He seemed so level-headed and honest. That day marked the start of a friendship that has lasted ever since.

"I think you should be very glad you didn't get into that van, Ted, and you should seriously reconsider seeing him. He's into some heavy stuff and I don't think it's a good idea for you to get involved with him. But that's just my personal opinion. He's a mate, but he's in deep shit," he said.

A VICIOUS LOVE STORY

Looking back, I can see how Cas was warning me not to get involved with Sid for my own sake, but at the time I really wasn't listening. I wanted to see for myself. I was getting desperate, so I asked Tore for advice. He gave me the telephone number for Virgin records, which was the one he had used to contact the Pistols before their tour. I was so nervous I could hardly breathe when I phoned the number.

A woman picked up. I explained I wasn't a fan, but knew Sid, and was trying to get in contact with him since I would be visiting London soon and just needed to let him know I was coming. The lady was very nice and told me that the Sex Pistols had already left the country to go on a tour of the USA. She wasn't exactly sure when they would be back, but thought it would be in several weeks. I was dreadfully disappointed. I hadn't anticipated that they would leave England straight after New Year.

It didn't take long for me to learn that the Sex Pistols had split up during their US tour. I remember it well as it was the day after my 17th birthday. I was worried about Sid. There were quite a few articles in newspapers about his addiction to heroin and how it was part of the reason for the split. I couldn't ignore it any more, and started to read as much as I could about what was happening to him. There were lots of stories I knew in my heart to be untrue. The most disturbing one was Sid having sex with a transvestite, not that there is anything wrong with having sex with a transvestite, if that is what you prefer. I have later seen a photograph of the transvestite and she was absolutely gorgeous. What was disturbing was the fact that people would say just about anything about him if they thought it shocked enough.

I knew it to be a lie as soon as I read it and it made me angry again that the media seemed to want Sid to be this caricature. I knew Sid was heterosexual and I doubted he would let another man fiddle with his bits just because he was drugged up, quite the opposite.

DEN BROWN (let Sid and Nancy live with him in London): Nancy told Jannie & I that Sid was "practically a virgin" when they'd met, & she'd taught him everything he knew about sex. By then though their sex-life was practically non-existent (much to her annoyance) as he was usually too out of it on heroin; it tends to have a 'disabling' effect on guys until you're used to it.

EILEEN POLK: About the story of the transvestite, I think that is made up too. When Sid was on the final Sex Pistols tour, a lot of people were getting paranoid because of the negative publicity, and the tour was attracting a lot of crazy and violent people. There were rumours that the CIA was following the tour (which may be true); however, many of the people who were accused of being CIA were just people that other people didn't like. So there were a lot of rumours and lies being spread around on that tour.

I was not on that tour, but some people who were on the tour with the band say that they don't remember that story being talked about on the tour. They only

heard it after the tour. This indicates it is made up, because if it really happened, everyone would have heard about it, and talked about it the next day!.

I was angry with Sid for being with Nancy and I blamed her for his addiction. I was told she was using heroin long before Sid, and I had a theory that she used this to keep him close to her. That was the hold she had on him. I felt useless in Trondheim and decided Sid's relationship with Nancy was obviously what he wanted, and I tried to put him out of my mind.

GLEN MATLOCK : We all used to live in the same area in London in Maida Vale. When Sid went off to the states we did a one off gig, me and him. We called ourselves The Vicious White Kids. It was me and Steve New and Rat Scabies. It was to show we were not enemies, more than anything else. We did the gig and a day later he was going to the States. We had a lunchtime pint in my local pub.

Later, during 1978, I read that Sid was living in New York and had formed another band, and Nancy was now his manager. My heart ached with jealousy. It felt strange seeing pictures of them together. Usually, they would look totally out of their skulls on drugs and I didn't like seeing them. I went back to avoiding such reports at all costs.

DEN BROWNE: In early '78, Sid started to change – mainly due to doing too many drugs, but also starting

A VICIOUS LOVE STORY

to believe in the image constructed for him by people like McLaren, & so losing touch with his positive side. By the time they left, I didn't like being around him that much. He could still be good company & generous, but then suddenly become violent & aggressive (usually towards Nancy) without warning.

A VICIOUS LOVE STORY

CHAPTER 13 NEW YORK

The weeks turned in to months and I had, by autumn 1978, given up all my plans to find Sid again. He became a fond memory of love lost. He was in New York with Nancy, making a name for himself.

Neon Leon Photo Aigars Lapsa ©

NEON LEON : I remember we saw Nancy on the day she came back to New York. Honi O'Rourke and I

were coming through the lobby at the Chelsea and we saw a blonde woman from the back standing there looking a little wobbly in the legs, with money all over the lobby floor, by the front desk. I tapped the woman in the shoulder and said 'Excuse me...' but all of a sudden she turns around and she's this wild person shouting 'Neon Leon wow !'. It was Nancy with her mascara running down like Alice Cooper and her hair all a disarray and dollar bills and pound notes all around her and I said 'Hey Nancy, what's wrong with you ? Pick your money up'. We helped her pick her money up. She asked if we wanted to meet Sid as he was upstairs so I said 'Is that the John that used to play with Siouxsie ?' and she said 'Yeah, yeah, yeah !' Both Honi and I thought she looked a wreck. So we went to their room and Sid was sitting there, Mr Vicious, with a little kitten. He was stroking this little kitten like a little boy. I didn't see anything vicious about Vicious. He became Vicious when he left the room and had to do his act. He looked at me and said 'I've got some baked beans I'm making. Do you want some ?'

    KENNY 'STINKER' GORDON (Played with Sid at Max's Kansas City, New York) : The Pistols were designed to be the voice of the extreme rebelliousness of youth living under a monarchy long past its due date. I've been describing my affiliation with the same influences that sparked the movement, so I understood where Sid and Nancy were coming from when Nancy

A VICIOUS LOVE STORY

brought Sid to New York after the band dispersed. The unbridled ride that was the Sex Pistols, had flung them in scattered and tattered directions. Nancy encouraged Sid over here (New York) on his reputation alone. Both of them were too young, now that I look back, to measure necessary discipline. I would have helped them along if I could, and if that tragedy hadn't happened mere weeks after we had met. We, my band Pure Hell and I, were off on a European tour.

I have no idea what took place between them as we weren't in New York the week after we played Max's with Sid, Steve Dior, Jerry Nolan etc. I just know Nancy had a very cocky attitude (mimicking Sid perhaps ?). Heroin and personal declination breeds the nastiest situations.

I remember watching Sid and Nancy get out of the taxi at the Chelsea Hotel. I was on a balcony looking down at them. Sid was wearing his black leather motorcycle jacket, black jeans and black engineering boots. He teamed it with a white T-shirt with the word 'DESTROY' in red lettering. It was from Malcolm McLaren and Vivienne Westwoods shop Seditionaries, in London. I don't remember what Nancy was wearing. I remember it was something black and that she had racoon mascara on.

Pure Hell with Sid at Max's. Kenny 'Stinker' Gordon second from right. Photo Curtis Knight ©

Nancy's hair was yellow-blonde with black roots and she wore it in a big, curly hairstyle. I could feel Sid's aura, as he emerged from the taxi, even though I was standing on a balcony on the first floor. He was ragging his hair. They staggered and strolled out of sight under the awning into the entrance of the building.

Peter Crowley had booked us, Pure Hell, for one of Sid's Max's Kansas City appearances. The people who played with him were our people too. Jerry Nolan and Arthur 'Killer' Kane of the New York Dolls; same circle on both shores, with Malcolm and Vivienne.

A VICIOUS LOVE STORY

Kenny 'Stinker' Gordon, Pure Hell. Photo Curtis Knight ©

Whilst we were all at the Chelsea that Thursday evening, the night we were set to play Max's, I remember what one of the girls that caravanned along with us told me. She was up from Philadelphia and barged in to our room and said; "Guess what ? I was just in the elevator with Sid and Nancy, and riding up Nancy says to me 'Do you know who this is ?' I said back to her 'I don't give a fuck who it is!" I'm quite sure Nancy wished her dead on the spot, either because she couldn't lure her into feeding the habit, or just because Nancy felt she was Queen Bitch Pistol, because of being with Sid.

Later Bard, the manager at the Chelsea Hotel, had to switch rooms for Sid and Nancy. They moved from their third floor room, to room 100, as apparently a

A VICIOUS LOVE STORY

mattress had caught fire. That's how they had the room that we'd had a week earlier when the tragic event took place there (ref. Nancy's death).

The sound check at Max's Kansas City had a positive and fun atmosphere among the collection of musicians from various backgrounds, who were there. The weight of combined status was heavy and attractive to anyone present. We, Pure Hell, knew we were on our way on tour for the first time, to England and Holland. Here we were on stage at Max's with legendary British star Sid Vicious, and original Max's legend friends from the New York Dolls; Jerry Nolan and Arthur Kane. Everyone was upbeat and graceful. We were asked if some of our rigs (amplifiers – equipment) could be shared, and of course, whatever, no problem !

We took individual and together photo shoots between Sid Vicious and Jerry Nolan for British press promotion mainly. Sid groped on a joint I was smoking and I said something hilarious about on-lookers, mingling around off stage, that made us both crack up with laughter. He'd been informed about who we were either by Jerry Nolan, Peter Crowley, Stiv Bators or Neon Leon and that we were about to go on tour in Europe.

Spider, my drummer, mentioned to me that he'd once attended middle or high school with Nancy Spungen in Philadelphia. Whatever kind of signals they may have had between them, I only experienced what I saw in Nancy. I know the type. We'd go

A VICIOUS LOVE STORY

'through' girls like her at some of the hotels and places in NYC. But it wasn't new or surprising to see her cocky and bitchy mood, even aimed at Sid. I watched how she compromised with people, like some lewd wench. Mind you, don't get me wrong, she would have been anything else if she wasn't so young and in the position of being with British punk star, Sid Vicious. Sid didn't know, at that point, any other tactic than keeping his hand on the throttle of an image he had no control over or a conformed ending to.

As the guys were all making adjustments and equipment settlements for the performances to be carried through, kick arse, she hastily complained over percentage amounts to be divvied out at the end of the night. You know like; 'three bags wont work, man. It takes six or I ain't feeling anything'. We were definitely on our game and psyched during our sound check, and she witnessed that stark contrast of excitement with envy perhaps ? The attitude I could tell, right off the bat from experience was; Nancy's concern was getting high, along with all the prestige she thought she had because she was with Sid Vicious. Whenever she was involved with anything she injected thickness in to the atmosphere that you could cut with a knife (no pun intended).

There was no reason for Sid to be enthused about her, making it appear that she cracked the whip at will, no matter what his situation was. I'm sure this kind of relationship situation was the reason that when we next saw Sid arrive upstairs on the floor with the dressing rooms, he was furious. He kicked a door off its hinges with his engineer boots on the way, storming in to the office at the end of the hall. No telling what transpired in between them leaving sound check earlier and returning for show time. I seem to remember that Nancy was thrown out of Max's, and not allowed in, when she herself kicked and broke the glass entrance door.

I felt very bad when I heard that Nancy had been killed in the Chelsea hotel in New York and that the police were questioning Sid about it. There was no doubt in my mind that the Sid I knew would never have been capable of doing anything like that. But it was argued by friends that the stories we were reading in the press told of him being a hardened junkie, ravaged by heroin.

He wasn't the Sid I'd met any more, I was told, but I refused to listen. I had seen, first hand, how the media twists events to make them look like something they are not. I felt an urgent need to go to New York and help him, but I no longer thought that I could make any difference in his life.

NEON LEON : Sid and Nancy had their last dinner before Nancy died, with me and Honi O'Rourke. Sid brought his jacket by and said I could borrow it. Nancy had the portfolio with her and they were a bit depressed. She was looking at old photos of them and saying 'Look how gorgeous we used to be. Look at Sid in this photo and look at us now.' I could see two worn out people.

After Nancy died, people tried to make me the pawn, the scapegoat, thinking that I did it. 'Yeah it was the black heroin guy'. Firstly I don't do heroin, but they just assumed it. Everything I said happened at the Chelsea, was confirmed and the police said I wasn't a suspect any more. But the newspaper tried to drag me through the mud. I had to leave the Chelsea Hotel because there were so many death threats. Some people were leaving black prints on our door saying DIE NIGGER and YOU'RE NEXT. PAY. Stan Bard said I'd been a great artist, but they just couldn't have this and I had to leave. It changed everything for me. I was in shock. I was pretty much having a nervous breakdown.

I wrote Sid a long letter, but never posted it. I wasn't sure he would want to see me if I turned up on his doorstep. Too much time had elapsed and we were not the same people any more. The story was that Sid had been taking Quaaludes and drinking alcohol, and had gotten very drowsy and fallen asleep – I am told it can have this effect on people – the day after Nancy was found stabbed in the stomach and had bled to death on the bathroom floor.

PETER GRAVELLE: When I bumped into Sid afterwards, it's too hard to go to someone you've known for a while and say, "Did you kill her?" But why did he go to the methadone clinic? That's the one thing that holds against him. Maybe he didn't realize how badly she was messed up. You had to go to the clinic at a certain time, and they gave it to you in a little cup and you had to drink some water afterwards. So him going to the clinic is strange. Then there are too many other questions that are unanswered. Like what happened to all the money that was there? What happened to their belongings? Too many things went missing. The door was open. I think something had happened that night.

    They got themselves involved in the low-level junkie scene in New York. Sid would go down and play Max's (Max's Kansas City Bar), which wasn't very far away. He put together a couple of messed-up musicians to back him up. He would walk away with a lot of money. I forget the figures, but it was a lot of money and it was all cash. And all that money would then go into Nancy's bag. They were terrible. They would be walking around with money falling out of their pockets. Then they'd go to the hotel room where the doors are open half the time. People were walking in and out. It was too easy for someone to come in, maybe to steal from them.

    I imagine Nancy wakes up in the middle of the night and shouts, "What the hell are you doing?" Pulls out the knife Sid bought the day before, and ends up getting stabbed herself. As much as Nancy was a complete pain in the arse as an individual and as a human being, and virtually in every regard, Sid sort of loved her in a strange way. You don't live with someone without liking them with all their faults and everything. I don't think he wanted to kill her. But if he did, she would have driven him to it. I think it's more likely that somebody else came in and it was death by misadventure.

The police stated Sid had said, "I did it because I'm a dirty dog." But that is a typical Sid expression if someone had been pestering him saying, "I know you killed her." It was a typical English sense of humour when doomed. Sid would have been mocking them in a sense. "Yeah okay I did it because I'm a dirty filthy pig." And the police are saying, "Yes, great you admit it!"

EILEEN POLK: I am sure Nancy was a terrible influence on Sid, and he was probably in much worse shape psychologically in 1978 than when you were with him in '77. It is too bad that the record company didn't do more to help Sid. I always wondered why they kept sending Sid and Anne, his mother, cash, instead of just putting them in a better hotel and just paying the bill by credit card. As you recall, I had to lend Sid and Anne money to keep them from getting evicted from the Deauville Hotel in November of '78.

I helped Anne and Sid because I felt sorry for them, but wondered the whole time where are their good friends? I think John Lydon cared about Sid, but he was pissed off at him, and with good reason to be pissed off. Unfortunately many of Sid's New York friends were junkies. I think Joe Stevens was probably Sid's good friend (and not a junkie), but Sid didn't seem to have many friends in New York who weren't trying to get something out of him. Sid would probably have been better off if they had just kept him in Bellevue hospital.

I have no doubt that he had a serious mental health problem after Nancy died. And I don't think Sid remembered the night Nancy died, so you can imagine how guilty he felt. This may be why he got Anne to promise he would be buried next to her, because he was so terribly depressed, wondering what happened when he was totally out of it that night,

Furthermore, Nancy's knife wound would not have killed her if someone had called an ambulance sooner. And it is interesting that not many people have discussed the fact that whoever stabbed Nancy was probably not trying to kill her, they were probably just trying to harm or hurt her. If the murderer wanted Nancy dead, they would have stabbed her in a place that would have caused her death, not in the stomache. I don't even think the knife wound was that deep. She just bled to death without medical care.

After Nancy died, I secretly hoped this was what was needed for Sid to get himself sorted out, get off the drugs and come back to the world of the living again. I always thought I would see him again when I was a little older; that I would come into a club in London one day and we would just pick up where we had left off in July 1977. Sid was arrested and sent to prison, but quickly got out on bail.

PETER GRAVELLE: I wasn't actually in New York when Nancy got killed. I arrived about a week later. I can't remember how long he was in prison for after Nancy's death, but I bumped into him at Max's Kansas City. We were all sitting at a table. People were saying, "Hey Sid's out!", and they were coming up to him and slapping him on the back. Then this huge biker-type guy came in. He was 6ft 4 tall and about 6ft 4 wide. He came over to the table and he said, "So you're Sid Vicious? You don't look so vicious to me." We all just ignored him. There were probably 6 or 8 of us at the table. So Sid gets up and we are saying, "Sid, what are you doing?" He stands up and says, "Fuck you!" and the guy says, "Fuck you too!"

So anyway, we all get up. I think there were pills around that evening. Probably Quaaludes. You mix them with drink and you can go a bit doolally. So we left and went up to Hurrah's, which is a club on the upper west side and quite large. It was myself, Sid, I think maybe Barry Jones might have been there too, but I'm not sure. And there was Dave Burkman, who was my assistant. We went up there and the place was empty, but there was a band playing, loud as anything. We got a drink and had a look around to see if there were any cute girls around.

Sid was standing quite close by, certainly not very far away, and the next thing I know Sid smashed a glass in a guy's face. We just grabbed him and dragged him along to the elevator, and took him off in a cab, but of course he was highly visible. People didn't know who I was, but everyone knew who Sid was. So, of course, the next day he gets arrested. I gave a statement that there was an altercation between the two, as I didn't want to see him go back to prison. I basically lied and perjured myself. I didn't really see it. I mean Sid was tall and thin, and Patti Smith's brother was a little guy. I asked Sid, "What could he have said that bothered you so much?" But he would have this crazy bit where he just saw red and lashed out.

I was reading what was happening to Sid in English newspapers since the Norwegian ones took weeks to pick up on any stories. I was shocked to learn of his arrest, but even more shocked to read that when he had got out of prison, he got into a fight with Todd Smith, the singer Patti Smith's brother.

EILEEN POLK: Now about Michelle (Sid's girlfriend after Nancy died) and Nancy, and about how Anne felt about them. Anne didn't really like either one of these girls. She thought Nancy was a bad influence on Sid, but he knew that there was nothing to say to keep Sid from being with Nancy. In fact it seemed as if Anne was being a smart mother and saying very little, because knowing how rebellious her son was, he would probably date a girl she hated just to stir the shit. So Anne knew that Sid was with Nancy

A VICIOUS LOVE STORY

just to upset people. Anne used to tell me that she thought Nancy was 'fat' (Anne was very thin and strong, she was a tomboy and rode a big motorcycle) and that she didn't understand why Sid had an attraction for her. But apparently he did, as all junkies do for their prostitute drug supplier.

I think Anne didn't like Michelle because Anne was sick of Sid's whiney, attention getting girlfriends, and since Sid had been with Nancy for so long, and no one could seem to stop him from being with her, everyone just accepted Nancy as a 'necessary evil' in Sid's life. But Anne knew that Michelle didn't have the hold on Sid that Nancy had, and I think Anne was not going to let Michelle use the spot as 'Sid's new girlfriend' to get a lot of attention – because that is what Nancy did and Anne was very sick of it.

I think Sid was with Michelle because she had money. I'm sure he liked her, but he had no place to live. Plus, she told him all of her exploits with rock bands like the NY Dolls and other glitter bands. I think she made a lot of that stuff up – that's why the tabloid writers sometimes call her a 'supergroupie', because she was bragging about her exploits. But she was not a supergroupie; she just enjoyed dating a few guys in bands, like most young girls!

I couldn't understand it. Sid was an intelligent person. His lawyers must have warned him what would happen if he violated the terms of his parole, yet the first thing he did was to get into a fight. I honestly didn't get what he was thinking, and I was afraid he was reckless and had met a point where he didn't give a damn about himself any more. It scared me.

EILEEN POLK: The truth is that both Anne and Sid sometimes bullshitted people. That was just their way. It was a bit of mischievousness. That's probably why Sid was impressed with Malcolm in the beginning, because Malcolm was full of it. For example, when Sid got in the fight with Todd Smith (Patti Smith's brother) at Hurrah and had his bail revoked (which is why he was in Riker's Island prison from early December '78 till Feb 1st) Sid told his mother that the cuts he had on his hand were from "falling down", I always wondered why he didn't just say "I got into a fight" it seemed strange that he would try to hide the truth from his mother. Of course she found out when he was arrested, and would have found out anyway.
So he did have the drug addict's tendency to tell "lies" or just be in "denial" about what was going on. But Sid liked to mislead people, I think he had had alot of fun doing that with the press, just like all the Sex Pistols, he liked to stir the shit, just for a laugh. Plus, Sid admired Johny Thunders and Dee Dee Ramone, who were both consummate troublemakers because of all the bullshit they told people and the dramas that this created. But they enjoyed the chaos. They liked the attention.

A VICIOUS LOVE STORY

PETER GRAVELLE: I'd met Sid earlier that day on February 1st. I'd gone down to the courthouse with Terry Ork, from Ork records, who had gotten busted buying quaaludes from an undercover cop and he wanted me to come with him. This guy walks up to me and said, "Your friend's going to be let out in a few minutes." It was someone from Sid's legal team who had recognised me from making the statement earlier. He told me they were letting Sid out and that he should be downstairs within the next hour. So I told Terry I had to leave him as I had something else to take care of, and I went downstairs.

Sid was released from prison on February 1, 1979. I had turned 18 that January and was keeping my eye on the stories in the press. I wasn't planning on meeting him again and had no plans to go to London if he went back there; nor was I thinking of going to New York. I had an interest in what was happening to Sid because I still cared deeply about him and I was very worried. He seemed to be spiralling out of control and didn't seem to have the people around him to help.

PETER GRAVELLE: I saw Sid's mother, Anne Beverley, sitting there. Now his mother was a 'no go' area. A lot of people maintain that Sid had this wonderful, close relationship with his mother. Not that I saw. Any time that I was with him and he saw his mother come into a place, he would say, "Let's hide, Peter." He didn't want to see her. His mother couldn't

A VICIOUS LOVE STORY

take care of herself, let alone take care of Sid. Malcolm McLaren should have done a much better job on that one. It was like 'send one reject over to take care of another reject'. Get a grip, Malcolm! But as long as he could wash his hands of it, and as long as he didn't need to pay too much for it, then it was perfect. It led to the guy's death, maybe.

It was only about 5 minutes and Sid came down. We left the court together. Sid's mother had picked up some "stuff" for him. It turned out she had been ripped off totally by Jerry Nolan, and had bought basically rubbish. He started asking me if I could get him something. He had things to do that day. I had things to do that day. So we agreed to meet up in the evening. He gave me his telephone number. I didn't even know Michelle, or whatever her name was. He said he was staying over at this girl's house. I said I'd see what I could do and I'd give him a call either way. Sid had to go and pick up some new clothes. When he came out of the courthouse he had black jeans, black T-shirt and black jacket. It was February and freezing cold.

What was happening to Sid in America was all over the English newspapers. I had to wait a couple of days before they arrived in the Norwegian shops, which was frustrating.

EILEEN POLK: : Sid was wearing a white button-down shirt, like every other criminal who goes to court

A VICIOUS LOVE STORY

in New York and has a lawyer with common sense. I remember clearly that Sid was dressed clean and neat, and in a pressed white button-down shirt and black pants for court on Feb 1st. The other people who were at the courthouse that day were: Anne, Michelle, myself and later outside the courthouse, I remember Peter Kodick (Gravelle) was there too. I had only met Peter once before and didn't know him, or even know his last name. The photographer, and friend of Sid and Anne, Joe Stevens was there, and took some pictures of Sid and his lawyer.

The mixed up story that has become myth, is that Anne showed up at the courthouse with heroin in her pocket and that she was the one who caused Sid's death intentionally. But I know that it was a complete suprise to us (Anne, Michelle, and me) that Sid was realeased on Feb 1st) We thought we were just going to be there to show support, and that Sid would be taken back to prison right after the hearing. His lawyer must have been pretty convincing.

So, if it is true that Sid was suicidal, he would have had to decide to kill himself AFTER he found out how strong the heroin was, which would have been after midnight (after Pete arrived with the drugs) Since Sid really didn't have anything to kill himself with until he overdosed and found out how strong the drugs were right?

So, Sid was talking positively about his case, and his next record album which he said he had written songs for, and even introduced Pete and his friend as the

"Guys who will be photographing my new ablum cover".

So Pete and his friend were getting a job out of it, they didn't want Sid dead, and if Sid and Anne conspired to kill Sid, in some "assisted suicide" pact, then they either decided secretly to do it after midnight (when they had the drugs) or they were planning the suicide all along and Sid was lying to us about his "future" all day just to put us off guard (and was really trying to kill himself all along).

Can you see why this doesn't make alot of sense? If Michelle had pills (and I am sure she did because she was a mental patient) I think Sid would have tried to get some, but I never saw Michelle hand Sid any pills, and even if she had a pill or two, it was nothing compared to the strength of that heroin. I didn't take any myself - but I saw how it affected Sid and I knew he had been given a dose of something very powerful.

Sid, Anne, Michelle, Jerry Nolan, Ester (Jerrys girlfriend), Howie Pyro, Jerry Only and myself were there when Pete and his friend arrived. Peter arrived at Michelle's apartment at about midnight. As soon as they arrived, a party that was supposed to be a 'no drug party' (according to Anne) was ruined! Sid's behaviour changed and he became a junkie with one thing on his mind.

Howie Pyro, Jerry Only (of the Misfits) and I decided to leave. I knew that I didn't want to be a part of Sid's misbehaviour. Just as we gathered our coats to go, Sid overdosed. I did not see him shoot up; in fact I saw no drugs at all at the party, but it was obvious by Sid's overdose exactly what had happened.

Then Howie, Jerry Only and I stayed, and helped Anne and Jerry Nolan revive Sid. It only took a few minutes for Sid to regain consciousness. Anne has been quoted as saying that Sid was 'out for 45 minutes and had a pink aura around him'. He was only unconscious for a few minutes. When he came out of it he said, "Oh, I'm sorry I scared you all." Not the words of a guy trying to kill himself, more like a recently detoxed junkie who wasn't expecting the drug would hit him so hard. (I saw no aura, but Sid's skin was blue while he was out. It was only about 5 minutes at the very most. If he had been out for 45 minutes I would have called an ambulance).

When I finally left the apartment at about 2 am, Sid was walking around the kitchen, drinking a cup of tea; apparently fully recovered. That's when Howie Pyro, Jerry Only and I finally got to leave Michelle's apartment. I would not be surprised if Sid took more drugs after that, but since I was not there, I can't be a witness to that.

Howie, Jerry and I shared a taxi to the club Hurrah's, but it was almost closing. Sid was also talking positively about his next album and the songs he wrote in prison, and mentioned that he wanted Peter to photograph the album cover.

PETER GRAVELLE: I went over to the house, I would say, probably about 8 o'clock. There was

A VICIOUS LOVE STORY

nobody in the house apart from Michelle, Sid and Sid's mother. I arrived on my own. Everywhere I see it portrayed like there was this huge party at Michelle's house the night before Sid died. There are even people who claim they were there. Well maybe they were, but it must have been a 6 o'clock in the afternoon kids' party. There were two people who Sid knew from London that say they came over and "arrived". Rubbish! It was only me.

Some people just want to be associated with him and it's pretty hard for me to comprehend. Michelle actually won't say anything about that evening. A lot of people gain kudos by saying they were there the night before Sid died. I never said anything.

The day after, when I learned Sid had died, I felt it was time to lay low and stay out of it. The police never interviewed me. I was never asked anything. As far as the police were concerned the case was closed. Junkie died; death by misadventure. Who killed Nancy? Well, probably Sid killed Nancy, so we won't really reopen that case. I got to Michelle's house, as I told you, at 8pm and I left at 2am. And during that time, there were no phone calls, and nobody else arrived. I had to leave as I was going to see, I think it was, The Only Ones, play their first gig of their US tour at Hurrah's. I arrived so late they had finished. So I ended up just taking a taxi and going home.

I was woken up the next afternoon by somebody telling me this story about Sid. I was more in shock than anything else because he wasn't suicidal. We spent most of the evening talking about the songs that McLaren wanted him to do. One of the amusing ones being YMCA. And Sid was saying, "There is no way I'm doing this song!"

I didn't ask him face to face – Did you kill Nancy? But we did get on to it a bit. I think his answer was more that he couldn't really remember, but he thinks he didn't. The more that it goes on the more he thinks he didn't, and the more he wants to clear his name of it. I don't think he would have killed her. They had been together for some time. I mean, did he not see any other way out of it? He could just have gotten on a plane to London, leaving her behind.

EILEEN POLK: I think Peter just wants to blame someone else for Sid's death. And in the end, the only person to blame has to be Sid for being so reckless, even though he was probably mentally ill at the time and should have gotten more help from the US Mental 'Health' 'Care' system, and the record company too. If Michelle had pills and Sid knew about it, you betcha Sid would be asking her for pills! But the drugs Peter supplied Sid with were very potent, and that is what killed Sid – it was the purity and potency of the drug. It was not a 'Hot Shot' (implying poison) – it was pure heroin.

I heard, after Sid died, that if you overdose you should not go to sleep afterwards, because your heart can just stop in your sleep – the body slows down too much. That is probably why Sid died. The next

A VICIOUS LOVE STORY

morning Anne told me she went in to Michelle's room with a cup of tea to wake him, and he was dead. I don't know if that is the truth (or if Sid shot up more than once that night) but that is what Anne told me on Febuary 2nd, 1979.

PETER GRAVELLE: Nobody knew about my involvement for a long time. I only told about my involvement years later when the Sex Pistols reformed. I did something for the Italian edition of *Rolling Stone Magazine* and it came out on *Uncut* in Japan, just to clear the story about who killed Sid, and who killed Nancy and what actually happened on the night of Sid's death.

If you look at the Gary Oldman movie, they didn't really know how to end it because nobody said anything. Michelle never said anything and I never said anything. I was never interviewed. It's quite annoying that people know more about that about me lately than the photography work I've done. But it doesn't bother me now.

There is more to this story, but I can't really go into that because it involves the possibility of a set-up. If it was a set-up, then it was backed by somebody and it came from government sources. It's a tricky road to go down. There are certain things I can't be absolutely sure about, but I could have been used as well.

It was on a cold, but sunny day in February 1979, that I entered my usual cafe for lunch. We had frequented this

A VICIOUS LOVE STORY

cafe for years, and I knew I would always find someone there I knew to have lunch and a gossip with. It was the same cafe where I had received my messages from Sid. This day looked to be like any other. I had started studying at the local college and I was moving on with my life.

I had ordered lunch, and it had been brought over to the table I shared with a couple of friends, when another girl I knew vaguely came rushing in. She looked around and when she saw me she came straight over. I didn't know this girl really well, so it surprised me that she came straight over to our table. She said "Hi" and I could see she was excited.

Suddenly she asked, "How are you coping, Teddie? I'm guessing you've heard?"

I didn't know what she was talking about, so I just looked at her blankly. I was very surprised when she asked my other friends to leave the table as she had something she needed to talk to me about. They left reluctantly. There was something in her voice that scared me.

She sat down, held my hand across the table and said, "I'm so sorry, Teddie, but Sid is dead."

I couldn't move. I couldn't breathe. I just looked at her like she was making a cruel joke. I sat like that for what seemed like a long time, but I'm sure it was only a few seconds. I got up, took my coat from the back of my chair and simply walked out of the restaurant. I hadn't paid my bill and I didn't care. It didn't even cross my mind. My other friends called to me as I left, but I could see the other girl hold them back and let me leave.

A VICIOUS LOVE STORY

I was in shock. I tried to hold it together as I walked home, but the tears were streaming down my face and people looked at me in shock as I passed them. I walked faster and let myself into the flat. As usual at this time of day, there was no one at home. I kicked my shoes off in the hall and barely made it into my room before I wailed in pain. I cried for several days, only coming out of the room to go to the bathroom. I didn't know how Sid died. I didn't care. All I knew was that I had lost him forever. It hit me really badly. I suddenly realised I would never see him again and I was so angry with him for that.

At the same time I also realised that although a lot of time had elapsed since we were together in Norway, I really hadn't processed my feelings for him at all. I'd just put them away in a place in my heart, and there they would have stayed and faded with time. They might have blossomed up again should I have met him, but when the person dies that's a totally different matter.

Sid's death knocked me over and it took a long time before I could put him away, back into that place again. I made a place for him in my heart and put all my memories of him there, because to think about him and process his death was too difficult.

EILEEN POLK: On February 2nd, I was left alone in Michelle's apartment with Sid's body for several hours while Anne and Michelle were questioned by the police. I was the one who let the coroner's people into her apartment to take his body - so it was really horrible. Michelle has accused me of making this up;

she also said that I made up the story about Jerry Nolan being there. I am absolutely sure that Michelle has very little memory of the details of Sid's last night alive. Everyone has been waiting all these years for her to tell her story, and I don't think she remembers what really happened.

I think Michelle was on a lot of prescription medication at the time, she had just been released from the mental hospital. I don't talk about this too much, because I think that Sid, Anne, Nancy and Michelle were all having psychological problems and it makes me really angry that people who are in crisis and need help were treated so badly.

I may have upset you saying what happened to Sid's body. But you must know the truth. I think that Michelle, didn't remember that I was with Sid's body in her apartment, because she was so upset, the cops asked me to watch the apartment, answer the phone, and wait for the coroner's office to come for his body. She has said on some message boards that I lied about all of that and said "why would they let her stay in a "crime scene".. but it was not considered a "crime scene" there was no attempt by the police to control the environment in that apartment, like they would have done if they suspected murder or foul play.

They questioned me extensively about everything, and since they knew that I had known Malcolm the longest (since 1974) I might give them some essential information. But I didn't know who Peter Kodick was at the time, I didn't even know his last name (real or made up) And I don't think Malcolm wanted Sid dead. I think he had tried to help Sid (Just as he had helped Arthur Kane of the New York Dolls - who was my former boyfriend; when he became alcoholic) I think Malcolm was just too busy (he was being sued by John Lydon) and didn't really know what to do - so he left Sid's care to the Doctors, and his mother.

The police officer who investigated has a TV show called "Autopsy" and one of the detectives was in that "final 24" TV program. They are now saying that they should have suspected Anne. I wonder if this is just hindsight and lies. I can't stand it that over 30 years later so many people have said "they saw someone at the Chelsea who might have killed Nancy - a drug dealer - they even have a sketch of what he looked like I heard (This may be in Alan Parker's film Who Killed Nancy - which I have not seen) Where were these people in 1979? If their testimony could have helped prove Sid's innocence, why didn't they help Sid??? So it seems to be a bunch of people just shooting their mouths off to get publicity.

The time after Sid died was really difficult for me. I read a theory in the newspaper that Sid's death was suicide and that he had a death pact with Nancy. I didn't believe that for a moment. I read that they found a note in his jeans pocket about wishing to be buried beside Nancy. There was a photo of the note in a newspaper some time later, and I looked at it closely and saw that it was not Sid's handwriting, as I knew it.

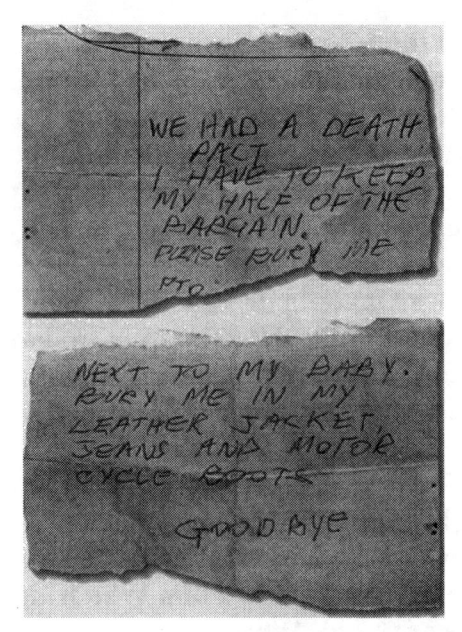

A VICIOUS LOVE STORY

> WE HAD A DEATH PACT I HAVE TO KEEP MY HALF OF THE BARGAIN. PLEASE BURY ME
> PTO

> NEXT TO MY BABY. BURY ME IN MY LEATHER JACKET, JEANS AND MOTOR CYCLE BOOTS.
> GOODBYE

> SEX PISTOLS
> Sid Vicious
> John Rotten
> (A TRUE STAR)

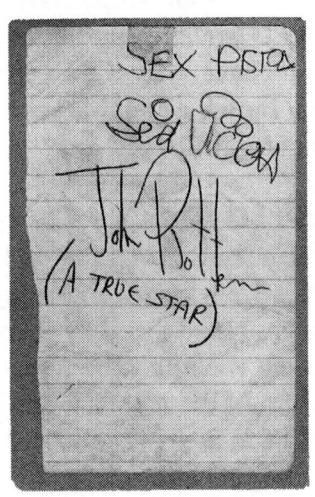

A VICIOUS LOVE STORY

This 'suicide' note was in capital letters, which were edgy and sharp. I'd seen Sid sign autographs and sign for things at the hotel in Trondheim, and his writing was curly whirly and he used a circle instead of a dot above his 'i'. Another thing is that the note said he had a suicide pact with Nancy and he had to keep his part of the bargain, but she didn't committed suicide as far as I know.

For the sake of argument; if the note is Sid's handwriting, then I'm guessing it could have been written earlier, at the time Nancy was still alive. They might have made a suicide pact and put it in writing, not really believing they would actually do it. I can imagine Nancy pressuring him to write something like that as a confirmation of his love for her. I found it strange that his mother should tell the world this story, which, so obviously to me, was untrue. It wasn't logical. I tried to think it through, even though it was painful, but I think maybe I was looking for confirmation to the fact that Sid did not love Nancy.

If he had decided to kill himself that night, why put the suicide note in the pocket of his jeans? Surely a suicide note would be found much more quickly beside him in bed or on the table by the bed? I doubt he would take the risk of being buried before anyone found this note with his last wishes. It just didn't ring true to me.

EILEEN POLK: Something happened during the time I was in Michelle's apartment when Michelle and Anne were taken down town for questioning by the police. When they left the apartment at about 5 pm,

A VICIOUS LOVE STORY

they were getting along OK, and Anne was just very sad and irritable. By the time they arrived back at Michelle's place, after a long questioning by the police (around 11pm), Michelle and Anne hated each other. Anne didn't even stay in Michelle's apartment that night. Anne came back from the questioning very angry and grabbed all her belongings from Michelle's place, and just left me there to watch over Michelle and chase the reporters away. So after that, Anne would not speak to Michelle. I don't know why.

After Sid died Anne had no tolerance for Michelle's hysterical behaviour, and she had the power to cut her off. In a way, Anne may have projected some of her anger against Nancy on to Michelle. Anne had just had enough.

Something obviously happened between Michelle and Anne at the police station: something so serious it made them hate each other. I can imagine how hurt Michelle must have felt when Anne found the 'suicide' note. It told Michelle, in no uncertain terms, that her boyfriend still loved his old girlfriend and he couldn't live with himself: that Michelle obviously meant so little to him, that he took his own life to be with Nancy. It must have made her feel very sad and hurt indeed. Or was that Annes intention? Imagine if Anne wanted to hurt Michelle, then this was a perfect way of doing it, and at the same time makes what happened that night in Michelles apartment even more confusing.

A VICIOUS LOVE STORY

The media could say anything they liked and Sid couldn't argue, and no one seemed to be fighting his corner. I didn't watch any of the documentaries about Sid and Nancy, and about his death after that. I avoided anything about him in the media and it is only now, as I write down my memories of my encounter with him, that I am learning more about what happened to him from the people who were there.

EILEEN POLK: Teddie, you have to know the truth about Sid's funeral. Anne planned the funeral secretly so that no one would know what was happening until the last minute. This was good for me because you understand that Anne was staying at my mother's home and the last thing I wanted was to harm my mother by having the press camped outside her door. My mother was a professional woman and had her own business and her own office and to jeopardize her privacy would have been unacceptable to me. So Anne was really good about not being seen outside my door, if she was spotted in the neighbourhood she made sure she lost them before coming to my mother's house.

The phone was ringing constantly - it was Sid's lawyer, the record company Malcolm the funeral parlor and relentless calls from Michelle trying to find out about the funeral. But I didn't have any information to give her, because Anne kept it all secret. Anne told me that at one time she had promised Sid that he would be buried next to Nancy. I dont know

A VICIOUS LOVE STORY

when Anne made this promise, but she was the kind of person who would keep a promise.

When Anne called Mrs Spungen, I was in the room with her so I heard Anne ask Mrs Spungen if Sid could be buried next to Nancy. Nancy's mother told her "No, because it is a Jewish Cemetery." That is when Anne decided to have Sid's body cremated, because burial in the USA didn't make sense unless it was with Nancy.

The expense of burial or shipping Sid's body back to England could only be afforded if Malcolm (or the record company) would pay. Malcolm wanted Sid to be buried next to Karl Marx! in London. So Anne was just really depressed that she could not do what Sid wanted, and she didn't want to be part of Malcolm's publicity circus anymore. That is when Anne decided to have Sid's body cremated.

The myth that has been spread about, is that Anne asked Mrs Spungen if Sid's ashes could be put on Nancy's grave. This is not true. Anne only asked if Sid could be buried next to Nancy, she never asked Mrs. Spungen if Sid's ashes could be put on Nancy's grave.

As Sid's funeral loomed ahead, the press were writing more and more lies, and twisting and turning the truth. I had learned to be very critical to what I read. I heard Sid's mother had asked that Sid be buried with Nancy, but was refused. Malcolm McLaren wanted to turn it all in to a circus. I later read that Sid had been cremated and that his mother had brought the ashes back to London with her.

A VICIOUS LOVE STORY

That she had spilled the ashes at Heathrow airport and a janitor had swept them up with the rest of the rubbish.

It infuriated me and I was back to not reading the newspapers again. I found myself getting really angry with people making a joke out of Sid's death and disrespecting the person he had been. I couldn't handle talking about him and I couldn't go anywhere near the Phoenix hotel. I was grieving and I put Sid Vicious, who was really John, into a place in my heart and mind, and left him there so that I would remember what he was really like.

The media could say anything they liked and Sid couldn't argue, and no one seemed to be fighting his corner. I didn't watch any of the documentaries about Sid and Nancy, and about his death after that. I avoided anything about him in the media and it is only now, as I write down my memories of my encounter with him, that I am learning more about what happened to him from the people who were there.

EILEEN POLK: After Anne decided on cremation, we were able to choose a place where it could be done. Anne decided on a crematory New Jersey, and the date was set for Feb. 7th. Anne instructed the limousine to come to my mother's house on the morning of the funeral, and all the people who were invited were told to meet at my house. The location of the funeral was still secret. These are the people who were invited: Anne, Eileen Polk, Howie Pyro, Jerry Only, Jerry Nolan and his girlfriend Esther, and Sid's friend Danielle Boothe. I'm sure that some of Sid's friends

could have come too like Johnny Thunders, or the people in his back up band (Arthur Kane, or Steve Dior, etc.) But Michelle was not invited.

There was some sort of rift between Anne and Michelle that I cannot explain. All I know is that Anne did not want her there. With all of Michelle's calls coming in I finally snapped and told her "Stop Calling!" (I had to answer all of the calls because it was my mother's house - so I was like the phone secretary!) Michelle said to me "At least tell me which funeral home is handling it" So I told her "Walter B. Cooke" and somehow she found out from them where the funeral was to be held and showed up there with a girlfriend.

On the way to the funeral, I asked Anne "Are you sure you don't want to pick Michelle up?" and Anne said "No!", Jerry Nolan didn't want her there either (I think Michelle had gone out with Jerry once before and he know she was crazy - so he said "There is no reason why Anne should have to put up with that"). And I dropped the subject. Michelle was very rude to Anne and me at the funeral, but she was not as rude to the other people (mostly punk rock stars!).

After the funeral, Anne told me that she wanted to put Sid's ashes on Nancy's grave because this would be as close as she could come to fulfilling the promise she made to Sid. So Jerry Only of the Misfits drove Anne, her sister Renee (who had flown in from London and was also staying at my mother's home) Howie Pyro, and myself to Philadelphia and we visited Nancy's grave. It was daytime and there were guards there so we just said some prayers and left some flowers on Nancy's grave. It started snowing lightly while we were there. We did some things in the area, like lunch at the mall and a visit to a rock club where the owner had been a friend of Sid's - stuff like that.

At the mall, Anne Renee and I went into the ladle's room to open the can of ashes because we had planned to do that at the gravesite but Anne had decided against it. Anne wanted to see what the ashes looked like and see if she could pry the container open. We waited till dark, and drove back to the cemetery where Nancy was buried and Anne and I walked to the edge of the woods. By this time it was snowing hard. Anne left me at the edge of the woods, and ran off to climb the wall of the cemetery and do what she had promised for Sid, sprinkle Sid's ashes on Nancy's grave.

I first told this story to Legs McNeil when he interviewed me for the book "Please Kill Me" because I was sick of hearing that terrible lie about Anne spilling Sid's ashes at Heathrow Airport and then his ashes being swept up by the janitors. I don't know who made up that story, but it is not true.

Sid's life was too short and I cherish the time I got to spend with him. I will never forget him. Let there be no doubt, I sincerely regret not running away and getting into that van in July 1977, if only to have been able to spend a little more time with him. I don't know whether I would have been able to split Sid and Nancy up had I come to

A VICIOUS LOVE STORY

London that autumn, nor whether it would have made any difference to what happened to him later. I was too young and I guess we will never know.

But I hope this book helps you catch a little glimpse of the real man behind the name Sid Vicious, the guy called John. There have been so many lies told about him, and he has been ridiculed and made to look like a fool and a self-destructive caricature of popular myth. I hope my story has somehow helped to bring some insight into the real Sid Vicious, not the cartoon. He was just a really great guy called John.

ABOUT THE AUTHOR

Teddie Dahlin is a freelance music journalist and author who lives in Oslo, Norway. She writes in English and mainly for UK publications.

Teddie Photo JBD ©

Lightning Source UK Ltd.
Milton Keynes UK
UKOW05f1506100515

251227UK00002B/70/P